Orkney and Shetland Sea Kayaking

Second Edition

Tom Smith, Chris Jex & Rachel Shucksmith

Pesda Press

WWW.PESDAPRESS.COM

Second edition re-titled *Orkney and Shetland Sea Kayaking* 2025

First edition titled *The Northern Isles*

First published in Great Britain 2007 by Pesda Press

Tan y Coed Canol, Ceunant,
Caernarfon, Gwynedd
LL55 4RN
Wales

Copyright © 2007, 2025 Tom Smith, Chris Jex and Rachel Shucksmith
ISBN   978-1-917182-02-7

The Authors assert the moral right to be identified as the authors of this work.

All rights reserved. No part of this publication may be reproduced or transmitted, in any form or by any means, electronic or mechanical, including photocopying, recording or otherwise, without the prior written permission of the Publisher.

Maps - Bute Cartographic

Foreword

When I first visited the Northern Isles over thirty years ago, I realized I had stumbled upon a sea kayaking paradise. Today, decades later, I'm still uncovering new facets of these incredible islands. Orkney and Shetland, two archipelagos lying far to the north of Scotland, are world-class destinations that truly stand out – even in a country known for its stunning landscapes. These islands are more than just scenic – they're unique.

Both Orkney and Shetland offer a profound sense of remoteness, home to an array of wildlife that thrives along their coastlines. Their rugged shores have been shaped by centuries of swells, winds, and tides, resulting in towering cliffs, dramatic caves, and sea stacks – some of the tallest and most impressive in the world. Yet alongside these wild outer coastlines, you'll also find sheltered waters, perfect for quieter exploration, and a haven for both wildlife and paddlers seeking refuge.

The islands' inhabitants, including a vibrant paddling community, share a culture that is as welcoming as it is distinctive. Whether it's the passionate kayakers who live and paddle here, or the people who call these islands home, their warmth ensures that visitors feel like they've found a home away from home.

Though Orkney and Shetland share many similarities, such as their rich history, unique wildlife, and dramatic coastlines, they also have distinct differences. Orkney is steeped in ancient history, from its prehistoric ruins to wartime relics, and boasts a patchwork of diverse landscapes across its islands. In contrast, Shetland, with its harsher and more remote environment, has been shaped by modern industries like oil, renewable energy, and even space travel, all set against a coastline filled with some of the most dramatic caves and cliffs in the world.

For me, these islands, and the people who live there, hold a special place in my heart. I know I'll continue exploring them by kayak for many years to come. I firmly believe they are a world class destination and offer something truly unique for any sea kayaker. Visit the Northern Isles, and decide for yourself whether they live up to this bold statement – you won't be disappointed.

Doug Cooper

Contents

Foreword 3
Scottish Outdoor Access Code 6
Important Notice 7
Acknowledgements 7
How to Use the Guide 8
About the Authors 10

ORKNEY 13

1 Pentland Skerries 15
2 Swona 21
3 South Ronaldsay 25
4 Hoy 31
5 Flotta 39
6 Burray & Hunda 45
7 Lamb & Glimps Holm 51
8 Copinsay 57
9 Cava & the Barrel of Butter 61
10 Holm & Rose Ness 65
11 Deerness 71
12 The String & Tankerness 75
13 Scapa Flow 79
14 Lochs of Stenness & Harray 85
15 Stromness to Skaill 91
16 Evie to Marwick 97
17 Auskerry 103
18 Shapinsay 107
19 Gairsay 113
20 Stronsay 117
21 Rousay & Egilsay 123
22 Eday & Faray 129
23 Sanday 135
24 Westray & Papa Westray 139
25 North Ronaldsay 145

SHETLAND ... 149

- 26 Burra & South Havra ... 151
- 27 Skeld to Scalloway ... 157
- 28 Reawick to Walls, & Vaila ... 161
- 29 Foula ... 165
- 30 Papa Stour ... 169
- 31 Vementry ... 175
- 32 Muckle Roe ... 179
- 33 Hillswick Ness ... 183
- 34 Eshaness ... 187
- 35 Ronas Voe & Uyea ... 191
- 36 Fethaland & the Ramna Stacks ... 197
- 37 South Yell ... 201
- 38 North Yell ... 205
- 39 Fetlar ... 209
- 40 Unst ... 213
- 41 Out Skerries ... 221
- 42 Nesting ... 225
- 43 Whalsay ... 229
- 44 Bressay & Noss ... 233
- 45 Lerwwick to Cunningsburgh ... 237
- 46 Mousa ... 241
- 47 Grutness to Levenwick ... 245
- 48 Sumburgh Head & Fitful Head ... 249
- 49 Fair Isle ... 253
- 50 St Ninian's Isle ... 259

APPENDICES ... 264

- A Planning ... 264
- B Coastguard & Emergency Services ... 264
- C Weather Information ... 265
- D Glossary ... 266
- E Bibliography ... 267
- F Index ... 268

Scottish Outdoor Access Code

Access to the outdoors in Scotland is encouraged; visitors and locals have a right of responsible access. NatureScot is responsible for promoting and publicising the Scottish Outdoor Access Code (SOAC).

Where you have access rights to is not shown on Ordnance Survey maps, or any other map in Scotland. The Scottish Outdoor Access Code deals with the land and freshwater access which is pertinent to the sea kayaker as you have to gain access to the sea over land or down a river and then again land to camp, walk or rest.

You are completely free to kayak on the sea; there is no limit how far offshore you can travel. However, for safety rather than access reasons, the further you travel offshore, during a crossing to an island for example, the more reason there is to contact the Coastguard and let them know your plans.

THE SCOTTISH OUTDOOR ACCESS CODE IS BASED ON THREE KEY PRINCIPLES AND THESE APPLY EQUALLY TO THE PUBLIC AND TO LAND MANAGERS.

RESPECT THE INTERESTS OF OTHER PEOPLE

Acting with courtesy, consideration and awareness is very important. If you are exercising access rights, make sure that you respect the privacy, safety and livelihoods of those living or working in the outdoors, and the needs of other people enjoying the outdoors. If you are a land manager, respect people's use of the outdoors and their need for a safe and enjoyable visit.

CARE FOR THE ENVIRONMENT

If you are exercising access rights, look after the places you visit and enjoy, and leave the land as you find it. If you are a land manager, help maintain the natural and cultural features which make the outdoors attractive to visit and enjoy.

TAKE RESPONSIBILITY FOR YOUR OWN ACTIONS

If you are exercising access rights, remember that the outdoors cannot be made risk-free and act with care at all times for your own safety and that of others.

Getting more advice and information

The Scottish Outdoor Access Code cannot cover every possible situation, setting or activity. Free information and advice on access rights and responsibilities, and on who to contact in your local authority, is available online at:

outdooraccess-scotland.scot

Important Notice

As with many outdoor activities that take place in remote and potentially hostile environments, technical ability, understanding of the environment and good planning are essential. The sea is one of the most committing environments of all, and with this considered it should be treated with the constant respect that it deserves. This guide is designed to provide information that will inspire the sea kayaker to venture into this amazing environment, however it cannot provide the essential ingredients of ability, environmental awareness and good planning. Before venturing out on any of the trips described in this book ensure that your knowledge and ability are appropriate to the seriousness of the trip. If you are unsure, then look for appropriate advice before embarking on the trips described. The book is purely a guide to provide information about the sea kayaking trips. For the additional essential knowledge of safety at sea, personal paddling, environmental considerations and tidal planning the authors recommend gaining the appropriate training from experienced and qualified individuals.

WARNING

Sea kayaking is inherently a potentially dangerous sport, and with this considered, users of this guide should take the appropriate precautions before undertaking any of the trips. The information supplied in this book has been well researched, however the authors can take no responsibility if tidal times differ or information supplied is not sufficient. Conditions can change quickly and dramatically on the sea and there is no substitute for personal experience and judgement when kayaking or during the planning stages of a sea trip.

The guide is no substitute for personal ability, personal risk assessment and good judgement. The decision on whether to go out sea kayaking or not, and any consequences arising from that decision, remain yours and yours alone.

Acknowledgements

The authors would like to thank the following people for their support: J Alexander, Phil Berry, Barnaby Erdman, Bethany Erdman, Isaac Erdman, Derren Fox, Tam Hilditch, Johnny Johnston, Hamish Leslie, Lesley Mackay, Kirsty Murray, Angus Nicol, Mavis Robertson, Eric Schollay, Douglas Sewell, Christine Sewell, Graeme Sewell, Hiday Sharon, Norma Smith, Kye Valongo, all members of Shetland Canoe Club past and present. Doug Cooper for his help and suggestions with regard to tidal update information, his general assistance with the second edition of the guide and first hand observations from the kayak.

Photographs

A special thanks is due to those who allowed us to use their photographs. All photographs are acknowledged in the accompanying captions.

How to Use the Guide

To use the guide you will need an up-to-date tide timetable of the relevant area, the appropriate Ordnance Survey map and the knowledge to use them. Unlike many inshore journeys in the UK, T*he Admiralty Tidal Stream Atlas* is an important source of information for planning sea journeys. Admiralty sea charts and the '*Orkney and Shetland Islands* Clyde Cruising Club guide' are additional sources of tidal information.

Each of the fifty trip chapters is set out into six sections:

Tidal & Route Information - This is designed as a quick reference for all the 'must know' information on which to plan the trip.

Introduction - This is designed to give the reader a brief overview of what to expect from the trip and whet the appetite.

Description - This provides further detail and information on the trip including the coastline, launching/landing points, the wildlife and environment, historical information and places of interest to visit.

Tide & Weather – Offering further tidal information and how best to plan the trip which takes the tides, weather and local knowledge into consideration.

Map of Route – This provides a visual outline of the route's start/finish points, landing places, points of interest and tidal information.

Additional Information – This section provides further information (including Admiralty Charts and other useful maps) that will complement the trip, or be of interest if in the local area.

Using the Tidal & Route Information

Each route begins with an overview of pertinent details beginning with the following information: grade of difficulty, trip name, route symbols, and trip number.

Grade A | Relatively easy landings with escape routes easily available. Offering relative shelter from extreme conditions and little affected by ocean swell. Some tidal movement may be found, but easy to predict with no tidal races or overfalls.

Grade B | Some awkward landings and sections of coastline with no escape routes should be expected. Tidal movement, tidal races, overfalls, crossings, ocean swell and surf may be found on these trips. They will also be exposed to the weather and associated conditions.

Grade C | These trips will have difficult landings and will have no escape routes for the long sections of the trip. Fast tidal movement, tidal races, overfalls, extended crossings, ocean swell and surf will be found on all these trips. They will be very exposed to the weather and conditions, therefore require detailed planning and paddlers to be competent in rough water conditions. With this considered, the journey may require good conditions for the trip to be viable.

Distance	Total distance for the trip.
Time	Total average hours of paddling involved if paddling at an average of 5km an hour including short rest periods (this may take place over more than one day).
OS Sheet	Number of Ordnance Survey 1:50,000 Landranger map required.
Tidal Port	The port for which tide timetables will be required to work out the tidal streams.
Start	△ map symbol, name and six-figure grid reference of starting point.
Finish	○ map symbol, name and six-figure grid reference of finishing point.
HW/LW	The high and/or low water time difference between the local port nearest to the trip and the tidal port.
Tidal Times	Location or area of tidal stream movement, the direction to which the tidal stream flows and the time it starts flowing in relation to the tidal port high water.
Max Rate at Sp	The areas in which the tidal streams are fastest and the maximum speed in knots attained on the average spring tide.
Coastguard	Name of the relevant Coastguard Station.

MAP SYMBOLS

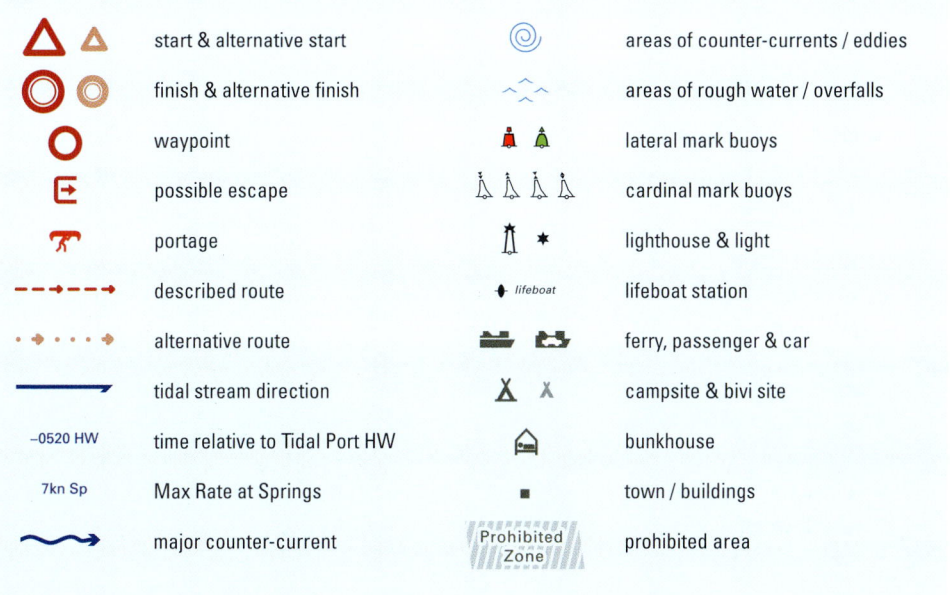

How to Use the Guide

About the Authors

Tom Smith

Tom was introduced to paddling by a relative on Loch Tummel in a home-made lath and canvas canoe. While doing youth work in Edinburgh he decided to join a course for instructors. During the course he found himself paddling out to the Bass Rock on a perfect summer evening. He has been a sea paddler ever since.

After a move to Easter Ross, early trips were mostly on the west and north coasts. A further move to Shetland followed in 1976. He spent over thirty years exploring the Shetland coastline.

Tom authored the first edition of the Shetland section of this guide and has now handed over the task of updating the Shetland section of the guide to Rachel Shucksmith.

Chris Jex

Chris has worked as an instructor, sea kayak coach, centre manager and outdoor practitioner in a wide variety of remote and beautiful outdoor locations in the U.K. and abroad over the past 35 years.

After initially visiting Orkney to climb the iconic rock stack known as the 'Old Man Of Hoy', Chris fell in love with the islands and its pace of life and moved to Orkney in 2000.

Before departing in 2008 he co-wrote the first edition of this book which was published in 2007.

After a 7 years period away from the islands, the lure, draw and charm of Orkney pulled him back to working for Orkney Islands Council as the Outdoor Education Advisor in 2015.

The amazing opportunity to live, work, play and explore in Orkney for the second time round has enabled him to gain an intricate understanding and knowledge of the coastline within the Orkney archipelago. Chris has even been known to venture to Shetland, to sample the equally amazing sea kayaking further north!

Tom Smith | Norma Smith

Chris Jex | Douglas Sewell

Rachel Shucksmith

Rachel learnt to sea kayak when she moved to Shetland to work as a marine scientist for the University of Highlands and Islands in 2003. Twenty years later Rachel still enjoys exploring Shetland's unique and wild coastline. She spends much of her spare time coaching and leading trips for Shetland Canoe Club.

Rachel has always enjoyed exploring some of the more remote coastlines of the UK, kayaking, diving and sailing and enjoys supporting others to experience the challenges and adventures of the sea. While fortunate to have dived across the world, she is passionate about exploratory diving and documenting the marine life of the more remote parts of the UK and northern Europe.

When she is not working or kayaking Rachel likes to spend time with her young family, introducing them to Scotland's seas and wildlife.

📷 *Rachel Shucksmith | Hamish Leslie*

📷 *The Old Man of Hoy | Mark Rainsley*

Fair Isle | Mark Rainsley

The Orkney Islands

An Introduction

Orkney is an archipelago of over seventy islands and rocky skerries, of which twenty are currently inhabited. The island's northerly position puts them on the same latitude as the southern tip of Greenland. Interestingly there is no landfall north, only the frozen sea-ice of the Arctic.

Orkney enjoys a relatively warm climate as a result of the Gulf Stream, seawater temperatures varying between 5°C in winter to 14°C at the height of summer. The driest months of the year are generally May and June with a settled period of weather towards the end of August and throughout September.

The land area of Orkney covers approximately 975km^2 measuring 80km from north to south, and 47km from east to west. The biggest island, which is referred to as the 'Orkney Mainland', has over three quarters of Orkney's population of 22,000 people.

Access to Orkney is usually by ferry from the south. Ferries run throughout the year from Aberdeen, Scrabster and Gills' Bay. If you have access to a sea kayak on Orkney, you can fly to the islands from several of Scotland's main city airports.

Orkney has benefited from the modern trappings of the 21st century, but distanced itself from many of the less appealing aspects of modern living. There are no traffic lights, fixed speed cameras, motorways or high-rise buildings, and crime levels are relatively low.

In stark contrast with Shetland, Orkney's topography is relatively low lying (except the island of Hoy). The fertile soils produce excellent grass for cattle and sheep but it is now the tourist and leisure industry which is the major source of revenue for many residents.

The land shows many traces and remains of original dwelling houses, religious sites and historical artefacts from people living in Orkney over 6,000 years ago. It is said "You only have to scratch the surface to find evidence of the past in Orkney". Due to the unspoilt nature of the Orkney landscape many sites are still to be discovered or excavated.

The earliest written reference regarding Orkney came from the Greek Explorer Pytheas who is thought to have circumnavigated the islands and who claimed to have seen 'the edge of the world'. The Romans visited Orkney for a short period of time during the 1st century AD but left scant remains or evidence of their stay. Since the arrival of the Vikings in the 12th century, Orkney's past has been well documented. Many stories and events are recounted within the Norse Sagas, which date from that period.

Orkney is predominantly made of soft sandstone which is prone to erosion from the wind and weather. This natural process has produced some amazing rock architecture along the high cliffs and coastal fringes. At peak bird breeding times in spring and early summer, many of the cliffs come alive with the noise, smell and sights of nesting birds flying back and forth collecting food and providing for their offspring. The low-lying shorelines are excellent places to spot mammals including the otter, grey and common seals, whales, dolphins and a variety of wading birds. Leatherback turtles have been found washed up on beaches and are thought to frequent these northerly waters in search of jellyfish, which are their favoured food. Although this guide concentrates on the coastline and information about sea kayaking, it is important to remember that, further inland, unique species of plants and animals may be found in Orkney.

Camping and accommodation in Orkney is relatively easy to find. Many of the wild camping locations may require permission from the local landowners who are generally more than happy to help and provide local information. A number of hostels, B&Bs and hotels are scattered amongst the islands and in the main towns and villages.

It is important to be aware of the exposed nature of the seas surrounding Orkney. Strong tidal waters, large sea swells and standing waves should always be respected. Prior planning, timing and a realistic evaluation of a personal ability should be taken into account for all these journeys. Poor weather alternatives or sheltered sections of coastline are available for most. It is important to have an alternative plan or escape route, should the forces of nature turn against you.

A remote walk, cycle, car journey, hop onto a ferry or short flight will provide memorable options during poor weather or rest days. These alternative ways of exploring Orkney will give the land-bound paddler a fuller and more balanced picture of life within these enchanting islands.

The journeys within this section are in order from south to north, from the South Isles of Orkney, through the Mainland, and into the North Isles.

SOUTH ISLES

The South Isles offer an array of adventurous challenges to all abilities Whether it be paddling beneath the towering sea cliffs and rock stacks of Hoy, tackling the swirling waters and overfalls within the Pentland Firth, or just relaxing on the sheltered sea within Scapa Flow, you will not be short of choices.

ORKNEY MAINLAND

The Mainland provides a variety of journeys depending on the state of the tide, weather and wind conditions. Access to the sea is never more than 8km in any direction.

Within the West Mainland a large and sheltered inland saltwater loch system offers superb panoramas across rolling hills. Historic monuments dating back over 5,000 years can be viewed up-close and easily visited from the water's edge.

The north and west coastlines of the Mainland are exposed to the ravages of the Atlantic Ocean, with remote cliffs and numerous caves to explore. The sea along these exposed shores is rarely flat due to rising or decaying ocean swell. Calm days on the west coast are to be taken advantage of!

To the south of the East Mainland the coastal fringes along the north shores of Scapa Flow offer excellent sheltered sea touring opportunities to all levels of ability, whereas the open sea further eastward has a number of powerful tidal races and overfalls formed by jutting headlands, shallow sounds and fast tidal streams. The varied coastline offers deep geos, blow holes, narrow caves and a plethora of historic sites which can be visited from the shoreline.

NORTH ISLES

The archipelago of islands to the north of the Mainland covers a land area of approximately 350km². The narrow sounds and currents between the islands are an excellent playground for intermediate level paddlers to test their open water crossing, navigation and tidal planning skills.

Muckle Skerry and lighthouse in fog | Chris Jex

Pentland Skerries

No. 1 | Grade C | 20km | 4-5 hours | OS Sheet 7 | Tidal Port Dover

Start	△ Burwick Pier (438 839)
Finish	○ John o'Groats Pier (379 735) or Gills Bay Pier (326 728)
HW	HW Burwick is 50 minutes before HW Dover.
	HW Duncansby Head is 1 hour 25 minutes before HW Dover.
	HW Pentland Skerries is 35 minutes before HW Dover.
Tidal Times	The SE going stream across the whole of the Pentland Firth starts 5 hours 5 minutes before HW Dover.
	At 03 hours before HW Dover, a strengthening S-SW going tidal stream builds in strength down and along the E and SE coast of South Ronaldsay.
	The strengthening and opposing tidal stream meets the E going tidal stream in the Pentland Firth and create a large anticlockwise swirling body of water (Liddel Eddy). The eddy extends up to three quarters of the way across the north channel between South Ronaldsay and Muckle Skerry (until HW Dover).
	The effect of the eddy is an almost continuous W going tidal stream around the SE and S coastline of South Ronaldsay.
	A short slack water period in the south channel between Muckle Skerry and Duncansby Head occurs approximately 1 hour after HW Dover.
	The W-NW going tidal stream across the Pentland Firth starts 1 hour 15 minutes after HW Dover until 5 hours before HW Dover.

Tidal current at Lother Rock, looking south | Chris Jex

Pentland Skerries

Max Rate at Sp	Between S Ronaldsay and the Pentland Skerries is 6-8 knots.
	Between Duncansby Head and the Pentland Skerries is 9 knots.
	Close to and S of the Pentland Skerries is 12 knots.
	Between John o' Groats and Gills Bay is 4 knots.
Coastguard	Shetland or Aberdeen

Introduction

The Pentland Firth (Pictland) journey has to be one of the most exposed and exciting open water crossings described within this book, if not within the UK. The short distance covered during this journey is potentially one of the most exhilarating rollercoaster rides any paddler will experience … if their tidal predictions are incorrect! A cool calculated approach is required to skilfully paddle and navigate through the swirling waters either side of the Pentland Skerries.

The paddle from the Pentland Skerries to Duncansby Head is relatively straightforward in comparison to the first half of the journey, but still requires careful tidal calculations to avoid the full force of the tidal stream which is squeezed around the most north-easterly point of the UK mainland. The 52m high lighthouse and old foghorn tower on Muckle Skerry act as important transit marks for both sections of the journey.

A committing paddle for experienced paddlers who have a good working knowledge of tidal streams and their effect!

Description

Access to the water and parking can easily be found next to the pier at Burwick. It is prudent to create and maintain good communication with the coastguard during the journey due to this area of water being a main shipping channel.

BURWICK TO MUCKLE SKERRY

OPTION 1 (FOR THOSE OF A NERVOUS DISPOSITION)

Depart Burwick about 6 hours before HW Dover and position yourself well upstream of Muckle Skerry by heading in a south-westerly direction for at least 3km. Time permitting, you may even choose to paddle to Swona before heading south-east towards Muckle Skerry. Once established within the main south-east going tidal stream, head towards the distinct twin towers of the lighthouse. A good transit marker is to keep the larger of the two lighthouse towers to the north (on the left as you head south-east). It is wise to try to arrive at Muckle Skerry on the most westerly point so as to avoid having to paddle across or through the overfalls and standing waves which are present along the north-west coast of the island.

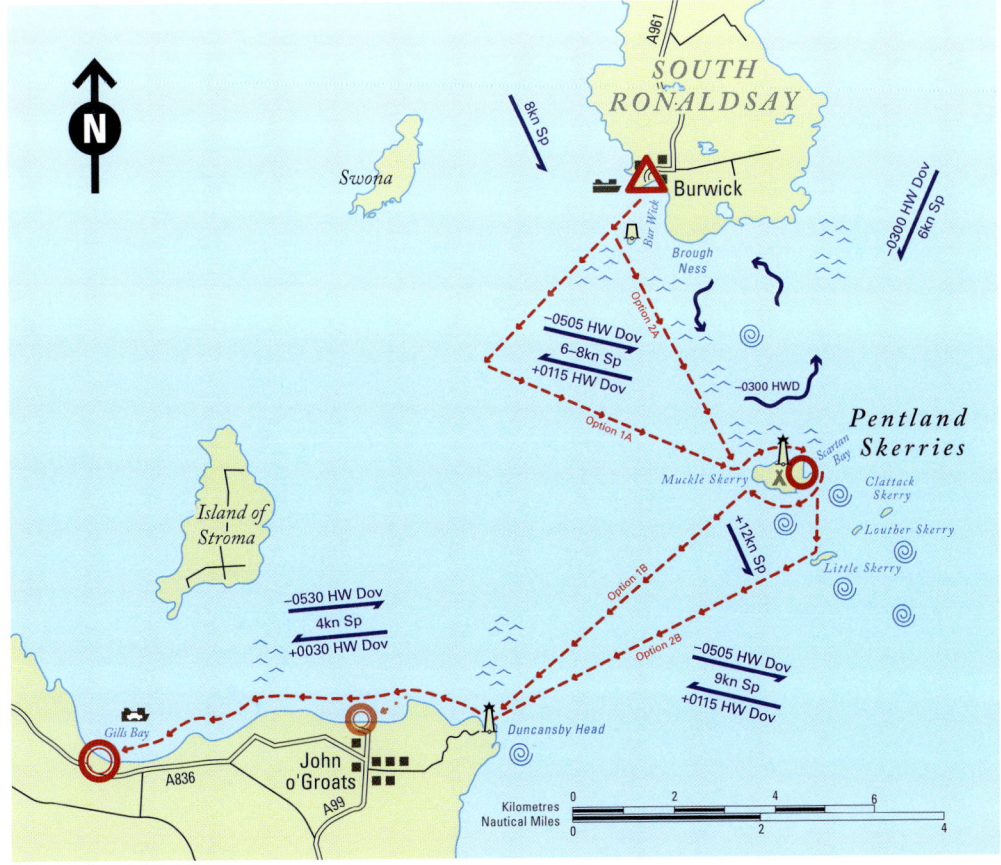

Pentland Firth marine traffic | Doug Cooper

OPTION 2 (FOR THE MORE CONFIDENT PADDLER)

Depart Burwick approximately 1 hour before HW Dover. It is prudent to head at least 1km west of Lowther Rocks, so as to best position yourself well upstream of the confused water. A direct compass bearing of 145° True from Lowther Rock points directly to the lighthouse on Muckle Skerry.

Staying well upstream of this bearing and making the best use of the main SE/E going tidal stream, navigate across the 5km of open water to Muckle Skerry. Transit markers as used in Option 1 are worth taking into consideration. There is an excellent but occasionally tricky egress at the steep sided harbour to the east of Muckle Skerry. A track from here leads to the lighthouse and buildings. An alternative get out point, if conditions are not favourable, is a narrow sheltered channel on the south coast just west of Rami Geo.

The lighthouse on Muckle Skerry is well positioned midway across the Pentland Firth to assist mariners entering from the east. This approach is known as Hell's Mouth for obvious reasons. The lighthouse became automated in 1994 and the keepers moved off the island. Please keep an eye on the time (and swirling waters to the north) whilst on Muckle Skerry, especially if you plan to continue on to the second section of the journey within the same day.

MUCKLE SKERRY TO JOHN O' GROATS

The second and less complicated half of the journey also has two options for getting to John o' Groats, depending on the time you wish to spend on the island, or time available after having completed the first half of the journey.

Arrival at John O Groats Harbour | Chris Jex

OPTION 1 (DIRECT ROUTE)

Depart Muckle Skerry's harbour at approximately HW Dover and paddle to the west end of the island using the eddy, which forms along the south side of the island. From here break into the main current (which should be decreasing in speed) and ferry glide the 7km across to Duncansby Head.

The powerful, wide tidal stream slows to a momentary halt just after HW Dover, only to start heading north-west, back the way it came. Using the lighthouses on Muckle Skerry and Duncansby Head as your transit markers, adjust your angle of attack as necessary.

OPTION 2 (INDIRECT ROUTE)

Depart from the sanctuary of the harbour at approximately HW Dover as the east going tidal stream is weakening. Paddle 1.7km (direct compass bearing: 180° True) arriving at Little Skerry in advance of the north-west going tidal stream.

A line of shallow rocky reefs and islets runs north-east from Little Skerry to Clettack Skerry. These rocky outposts of the Pentland Skerries are well recognised as a danger to all shipping where at HW only a small area of Little Skerry and Clettack Skerry remains visible above the water.

From Little Skerry the open water paddle involves just over 7km of unnerving paddling (direct compass bearing 242° True) across one of the most powerful tidal waters of the UK. Duncansby Head is generally reached within one to one and a half hours of paddling. Tidal movement north-west around Duncansby Head should be carefully negotiated as there may be associated overfalls along the coastline and around prominent headlands. If your tidal calculations are correct (for either option), a strengthening north-west going stream will push you around Duncansby Head, away from the impressive Stacks of Duncansby, and along the north coast of Scotland. The Bay of Sannick, a welcome sandy alcove, provides egress to the west of the lighthouse if required.

A relaxing 2km paddle will lead to a sheltered pier and harbour, close to the popular tourist spot at John o' Groats. Have an ice cream, take a photo standing next to the famous signpost, spend a penny or twenty at the public toilets (literally), contact the coastguard with the good news and arrange your return or onward journey from John O Groats.

If you choose to return using the vehicle ferry, another 5km of easy coastal paddling is required to get to Gills Bay. An overfall may be present between John o' Groats and Gills Bay. This may be avoided by staying close to the coastline.

Tide and weather

Tidal planning and a careful watch on the time during the journey are essential in order to benefit from any tidal movement and avoid the wrath of this unforgiving section of water. It is prudent to plan to complete the journey as close to the weaker neap tides as possible.

A light wind and settled weather window is best chosen for the journey. The sea area surrounding the Pentland Skerries is exposed to all wind directions. Rough water, standing white waves and difficult eddy lines may be present, even during good weather conditions.

Additional information

If choosing to camp or stop on Muckle Skerry, ensure you are self-sufficient and have all the tidal information required to complete the journey. Tidal stream times and speeds quoted are a guide. Speeds of up to 16 knots have been recorded SW of the Pentland Skerries.

The most efficient way to return to Orkney (if not by kayak), is with Pentland Ferries which depart on a daily and regular basis from the pier at Gills Bay. If this option is taken, take note that the ferry will return to St Margaret's Hope, and not Burwick Pier where you left your vehicle.

Admiralty Chart 2162, Imray Chart C68, and O.S. Explorer Map 451 & 461 cover this area.

The Haven' and old winding gear | Doug Cooper

Swona

No. 2	**Grade C**	**15.5km**	**4 hours**	**OS Sheet 7**	**Tidal Port Dover**
Start/Finish	Burwick Pier (438 839)
HW	HW Burwick is 50 minutes before HW Dover.
Tidal Times	For North Head on Swona and for making the crossing to the island, the SE going tidal stream starts 5 hours 30 minutes before HW Dover. The NW going stream starts 35 minutes after HW Dover.
	For the Pentland Firth and the S of Swona at The tails of the Tarf, the SE going tidal stream starts 5 hours before HW Dover. The NW going tidal stream starts 1 hour after HW Dover.
Max Rate at Sp	Between Swona and S Ronaldsay is 4-6 knots.
	The headlands to the N and S of the island can create overfalls and tidal streams of 9 knots. Large eddies extend to the E or W of Swona during tidal stream movement.
Coastguard	Shetland or Aberdeen

Introduction

The small, remote island of Swona (Sweyn's Island) lies directly in the path of the strong tidal waters that sweep through the Pentland Firth. Its position, 4km offshore from South Ronaldsay, makes it an excellent short journey for the experienced paddler.

The feral cattle, which now roam freely on this exposed island, should be given a wide berth to avoid confrontation. This relatively inaccessible island is an excellent place to observe puffins and Arctic terns, along with a host of other undisturbed wildlife.

Description

Burwick Pier has a rough stony launch area beneath the link-span. Access here will enable you to warm up and prepare for the 4.5km open water crossing to the island.

It may be prudent to walk from the car park area around the coastal path and up to the headland, which overlooks the relevant section of open water, in order to get visual confirmation of the conditions and tidal stream direction.

A short paddle along the coast to The Wing, a low-lying rocky reef, leads you into the clutches of the Pentland Firth. The area of water extending 0.5km west of The Wing can sometimes have conflicting tidal currents and a confusing eddy close inshore.

A long ferry glide heading on a bearing of 287° True leads towards The Haven, a small sheltered harbour on the north-east side of the island. It is wise to use a number of transit markers on Swona and South Ronaldsay, in order to check your progress across the strengthening or weakening tidal stream. If you plan to start the journey from Burwick at either 6 hours before HW Dover (before the start of the SE going tidal stream), or at HW Dover (before the NW going tidal stream), it may be sensible to paddle north along the South Ronaldsay coastline as far as Barth Head before starting the open water crossing. With the adrenaline pumping and an ever-watchful eye on your chosen transit markers, the crossing takes approximately 1 hour to complete.

The Haven is an excellent point to get out and stretch your legs. The rotting boat, rusting winding gear and a tractor give the visitor an idea of what life was like living on a remote island until the last people left thirty-three years ago.

Be aware of the very strong tidal currents which can build up around North Head and plan your circumnavigation to avoid the strongest tidal times which affect the headlands. Seals can usually be seen basking on the rocks and playing in the shallows along the short cliff-lined coast which leads around the headland to the rocky beach known as The Brook. The low-lying jagged beach of rocks and metal wreckage is an important nesting area for a large colony of Arctic terns. It is wise not to get out here as an attack by these persistent birds is not a pleasant experience.

The swirling areas of water known as the Wells of Swona (two large recirculating eddies which form to the west of both headlands during the west going tide) were in the past used by locals as excellent fishing spots. (Exciting during a spring tide!)

Heading south towards the Selki Skerry, be aware of the increasing strength of the current which can easily take control of your destination. As you head south towards The Tails of the Tarf it is prudent to keep close to the shoreline to avoid the tidal race and overfall around the headland. Respite may be found in amongst the skerries and clett at the south-east corner of the island, where a number of seals laze on the low-lying rocks.

The steep cliffs along the east coast host a large number of seabirds and colourful puffins, which take up residence along the top of the cliffs in burrows dug out of the sandy soil. Rafts of birds may be seen at the base of the cliffs resting or preening before heading out to sea to find food for their offspring. A cave and atmospheric gloup amongst the steep cliffs are worthy of exploration before heading back to The Haven.

The island is easily accessed from the natural harbour area. Caution should be given to going near any of the feral cattle which were abandoned here after the last people left. The animals are now recognised as one of only a few feral herds of Bos Taurus cattle remaining in the world and are of great scientific importance and interest. A walk amongst the well-preserved houses and south along the shoreline will lead you to the chambered cairn at the far end of the island. Listen out for the purring and high-pitched calls of the storm petrels which nest in the dry-stone walls.

It may be possible to stay overnight on the island but it would be wise to pitch your tent well away from the cattle, which roam freely. Access to a couple of the old houses close to the harbour area may provide cover if the weather is inclement. If you do choose to stay overnight it is worth walking to either of the headlands on the island and watching the powerful overfalls and standing waves that build when the tidal streams run in either direction within the Pentland Firth.

The journey back to Burwick needs to be carefully planned. Time spent on the island needs to be taken into account if choosing to head back to South Ronaldsay on the same day.

Swona's shipwrecks

The west side of Swona has been the downfall of a number of large ships especially during the 1930s. The *Pennsylvania*, *Gunnaren*, *Lord Percy* and the *Johanna Thorden* all suffered the same unfortunate fate after running aground or striking shallow reefs. The last ship mentioned incurred heavy loss of life whilst many of the crewmen tried to swim to the safety of the shore.

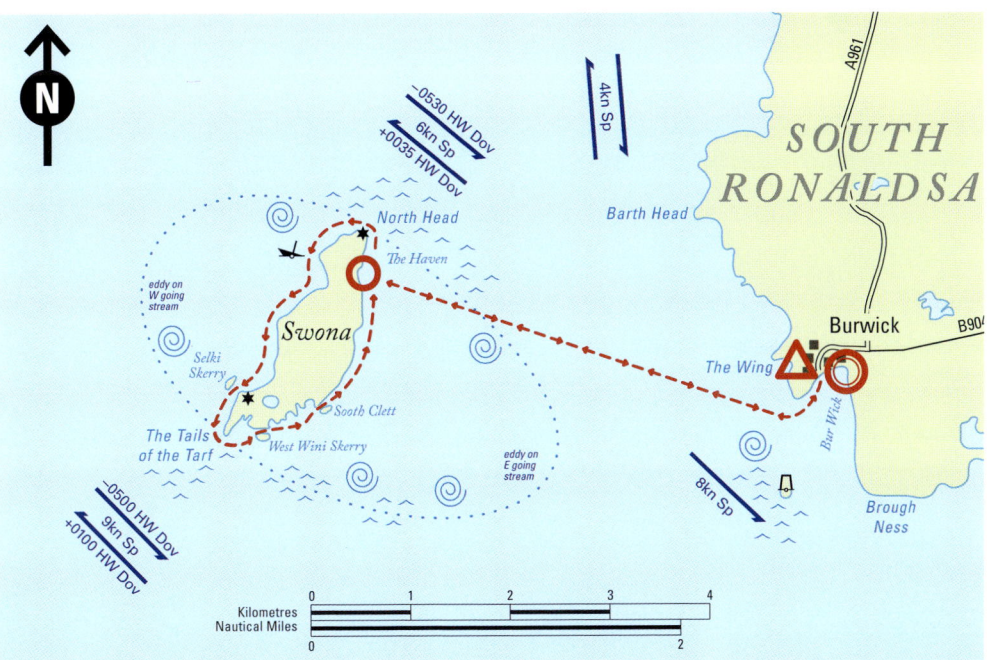

A good day's fishing, The Haven, Swona | Orkney Library & Archive

Tide and weather

The tidal races, overfalls and eddies within the Pentland Firth should always be treated with caution. Changes in direction and times of the tidal streams should be taken only as a guide as these are not always accurate. The paddler should always analyse and assess the water conditions and the current before committing to paddle in the tidal areas.

This open area of water is exposed on all sides and wind conditions may add to the difficulty of the journey. It is therefore important to check the forecast for the next couple of days before getting on the water.

A large eddy extends approximately 2-3km east of Swona on an east going tide. On a west going tide the eddy is smaller, approximately 1km to the west of Swona.

Additional information

On the West going tide, the tidal flow splits midway along the east coast of Swona at Sooth Clett. This creates a N and S going stream respectively, along the East coast of Swona.

Although the island is remote and uninhabited, it is privately owned. It is important not to damage or remove any of the building structure or contents. Camping here requires the paddler to be completely self-sufficient and remove all rubbish. Whilst walking around the island please be aware of exposed eggs or young chicks in camouflaged nests built on open ground.

It would be prudent to carry some form of mobile communication and the appropriate tidal information with you, in case of being stranded, or if deciding to change plans once on the water.

Admiralty Chart 2162, Imray Chart C68, and O.S. Explorer Map 461 cover this area.

Heading south, Halcro Head | Doug Cooper

South Ronaldsay

No. 3 | Grade C | 40km | 9-10 hours | OS Sheet 7 | Tidal Port Dover

Start/Finish	Car park at Churchill Barrier 4 (480 954)
HW	HW Burray Ness (E side) is 15 minutes after HW Dover.
	HW Burwick is 50 minutes before HW Dover.
	HW Widewall Bay (W side) is 1 hour 45 minutes before HW Dover.
Tidal Times	On the E coast of South Ronaldsay there is negligible N going tidal flow. The S going tidal stream starts at 3 hours and 30 minutes before HW Dover and continues until 5 hours 30 minutes after HW Dover. This is most noticeable at Grim Ness and Halcro Head.
	Due to the Liddel Eddy which forms within the north channel of the Pentland Firth, there is a W going tidal stream between Old Head and Brough Head starting approximately 4 hours before HW Dover until 5 hours 30 minutes after HW Dover.
	Slack water at Lother Rock is at 6 hours before HW Dover.
	A clockwise eddy forms between The Wing and Lother Rock near Burwick for 4 hours, starting approximately 30 minutes after HW Dover.
	The NW going tidal stream at Barth Head on the west coast of South Ronaldsay starts 35 minutes after HW Dover.
	The SE going tidal stream at Barth Head starts 5 hours and 30 minutes before HW Dover. North of Barth Head, the weaker SE going tidal stream starts approximately 1 hour later at 4 hours 30 minutes before HW Dover.

Barth Head, South Ronaldsay | Chris Jex

South Ronaldsay

3

	The S going (outgoing) tidal stream on the W coast of S. Ronaldsay at Hoxa Head starts 1 hour before HW Dover. This is short lived and reverts back to a weak N going tidal stream by HW Dover. The S going tidal stream reforms again 1 hour after HW Dover. The N Going (incoming) tidal stream at Hoxa Head, starts 4 hours after HW Dover.
Max Rate at Sp	Of the S going tidal stream passing Halcro Head on the E coastline is 6 knots.
	In the Pentland Firth is 6-8 knots.
	On the W side, close to Hoxa Head is 1-2 knots in either direction.
	Between Swona and S Ronaldsday is 4-6 knots.
Coastguard	Shetland

Introduction

The rugged South Ronaldsay (Rognvald's Isle) coastline is one of Orkney's best kept secrets. Both sides of the island have undisturbed wildlife, steep cliffs, caves and hidden, unspoilt beaches to explore. Some of the best examples of rock formations and geology in Orkney can be found along the coastline and are best viewed from the water.

The swirling, fast moving currents which sweep around the south coast are guaranteed to increase your heart rate. Sensory overload occurs as you edge closer towards the cauldron of white water, standing waves and battling currents which are clearly visible, audible and felt during each tide within the Pentland Firth.

This journey is best completed over two days allowing you time to absorb the beauty and magical atmosphere of this remote, historic and exciting coastline.

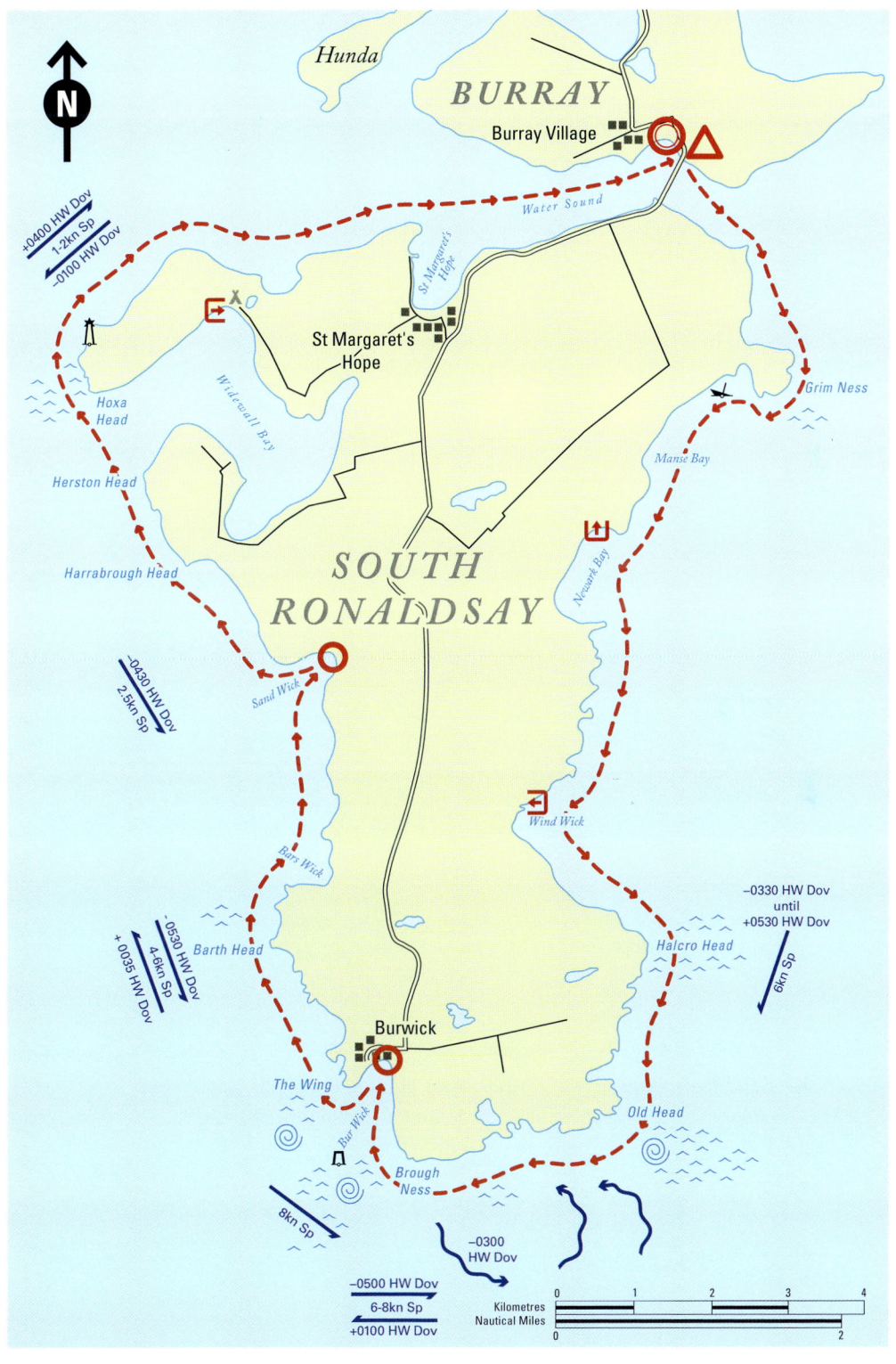

Description

Easy access onto the water can be made at the north end of Churchill Barrier No 4 next to the newly built toilet block. The sandy beach on the east side of the barrier has quickly accumulated golden sand and increased in size. Twenty years ago, you were able to walk amongst the visible rusting remains of the blockships and masts, now they are completely buried.

After the headland at Grim Ness and just past the Stack of Kame, there is an excellent sheltered beach which is worth visiting to see the beautiful array of wild flowers which appear on the headland during the spring and summer.

An infamous shipwreck

A Liberian steamer called *Irene* was washed onto the rocks of South Ronaldsay during a strong south-easterly gale in 1969. Her ill-fated distress call, broadcast to the Longhope and Kirkwall lifeboats, resulted in a lifeboat capsizing with the loss of all on board. The crew of the *Irene* were eventually rescued from the shore. Rusting pieces of the wreck can still be seen scattered along the coastline below South Cara.

The steep grassy-sloped coastline leads to the beautiful and secluded sandy beaches at Manse Bay and Pool of Cletts. The restored St Peter's Church with its crowded walled cemetery dates back to 1642 with earlier remains from the 8th century. The interior of the church is unusual in that the seating is arranged along the length of the building with the altar positioned along the side wall. Looking from the sea, a prominent carved stone cross (with a hole in it) can be seen south-east of St Peter's Church

The next 3km of coastline has some of the most awe-inspiring and beautiful cliff scenery in Orkney. A host of birdlife including guillemots, razorbills, cormorants and fulmars all compete for space along the narrow ledges on the towering cliffs. The coastline is a marvellous sight during the breeding season when thousands of birds congregate here. A large number of caves, arches and tunnels can be explored along the towering coastline.

The rock stack known as the Clett of Crura marks the point close to the area where two British destroyers, HMS *Narborough* and HMS *Opal*, ran full steam into the cliffs in poor visibility in January 1918. Of the 181 people on board the two ships, only one person survived. A memorial plaque in the car park above the beach at Windwick commemorates this sad loss.

The impressive cliffs continue towards Halcro Head with amazing rock arches, caves and a tunnel leading into a gloup where a shaft of light penetrates the back of the tunnel via a collapsed roof 100m inland. The tidal current around Halcro Head can cause some exciting standing waves and clapotis and is an indication of stronger currents to come further south.

The coastline of rock walls and deep geos lead to the well preserved archaeological site known as The Tomb of the Eagles which was found in 1958 by the local farmer. A large number of human bones and sea eagle claws were found along with some amazingly well preserved artefacts dating back to about 3000 BC. At the time of the guidebook update (2025), the Tomb of The

'The Altar' Harrabrough Head | Chris Jex

Eagles Museum was sourcing community funding in order to re-open to the public. It is possible to get out at Ham Geo to stretch your legs.

The dull rumbling noise and the white crests of standing waves indicate your approach to the Pentland Firth. The currents here should not be underestimated, approach with caution, keeping close to the rocky shoreline. The pebble beach close to Banks is a perfect place to watch the seals and listen to the swirling waters as they funnel through the narrow entrance of the Pentland Firth.

Further west the navigation light on Lowther Rocks marks the shallow reef which guards the bay at Burwick. Interestingly, the granite rocks used to build the pier and breakwater were shipped from Norway! This is a good place to stop off and stretch your legs before heading up the west coast. The west coastline continues to impress the paddler with a stunning vista across to the islands of Swona and Switha and west towards the hills of Hoy.

A large number of grey seals give birth to pups in this area amongst the secluded rocky beaches during late September through to November. Paddlers are advised to give a wide berth to the adults and pups during this time, so as not to disturb or frighten the mothers away. Porpoise and otters are common along this coastline, as the area is infrequently visited by humans.

The west facing cliffs and steep chiselled rock wall at Barth Head display some impressive contorted rock strata. Respite from the sea is available at Barswick where a small archway in the headland and a rock stack provide a picturesque backdrop to the remote, rocky beach. A small accessible beach at Sandwick is overlooked by Weems Castle, a ruined broch south of the bay.

At The Altar at Harrabrough Head an interesting collection of interconnecting archways have been carved out the headland. Large numbers of puffins nest in burrows along the top of the cliffs.

At certain states of the tide the entrance to Widewall Bay may have a weak tidal flow. Further east the Sands of Wright provide an excellent location for a campsite or a break.

During both the World Wars, Hoxa Head was an important strategic location used to protect the entrance to Scapa Flow. Ammunition bunkers, gun mountings, look out posts, searchlight platforms and the remains of a camp are still in evidence. The new glass fibre, square shaped lighthouse above Scarf Skerry was built in 1996, replacing the original lighthouse built in 1901.

The coastline now eases to low lying fields and a rocky shoreline with a distinct burial mound and broch, west of the Dam of Hoxa. Buried within the large mound is reputed to be Thorfinn Skullsplitter who died in AD 963. Skullsplitter's name continues to live on, as it is the name of one of the many popular beers produced by the Orkney Brewery.

Entering Water Sound and the final 5km of paddling, the picturesque village of St Margaret's Hope can be seen nestled at the back of a sheltered bay. The Hope is neatly laid out with a number of fine houses and narrow winding streets. A number of pubs, local food and craft shops, and an excellent café await your custom. This bay is where, in 1263, King Hakon Hakonson's fleet of over 120 ships sheltered before heading on to mainland Scotland.

A low-lying seaweed strewn shoreline leads to Burray pier and village where the Sands Hotel (serving food and beer) can be found next to the refurbished boat yard and slipway. After passing the pier, egress off the water back to the start point and the other side of the 4th barrier is via a small flight of steps at the north end of the blocks which make up the 500m long barrier. Take care when crossing the barrier as there is a blind bend in the road for vehicles travelling south.

Tide and weather

Tidal streams around the east, south, and west coastlines can be difficult to paddle against at certain states of the tide and the east and south coastlines are prone to large sea swells following strong onshore winds. The exposed cliffs and steep coastline require paddlers to commit to the water with no escape for up to 5km at a time before egress may be found. That said, there are many small beaches and areas along the coast where it is possible to get out and curtail the journey if required. This option should not be relied upon in poor sea conditions as landing may become more difficult when there are rough seas.

Additional information

The journey can be split into smaller sections depending on the tides, time available or prevailing weather conditions. Wild camping is available at a number of locations including sheltered bays and open fields close to the coastline. Permission to camp in fields or fenced off areas should be sought, if possible, due to livestock.

Admiralty Chart 2162, Imray Chart C68, and O.S. Explorer Map 461 cover this area.

Bay of the Tongue, Kame of Hoy | Chris Jex

Hoy

No. 4 | Grade C | 63km | OS Sheet 7 | 15 hours | Tidal Port Dover

Start/Finish	△○ Houton (318 040)
HW	HW at Stromness is approximately 1 hour 45 minutes before HW Dover.
Tidal Times	The S going tidal stream through Gutter Sound starts 5 hours before HW Dover. The N going tidal stream starts 5 hours after HW Dover.
	The SSE, (outgoing) tidal stream within Cantick Sound starts 1 hour 50 minutes before HW Dover. The NNW (incoming) tidal stream starts (and rapidly increases in strength) 4 hours and 50 minutes after HW Dover.
	The S-SE going stream along the SW coast of Hoy starts 5 hours 30 minutes before HW Dover. The NW going tidal stream starts 30 minutes after HW Dover.
	The E going (flood) stream in Burra and Clestrain Sound starts at about 6 hours after HW Dover. The W (outgoing) stream begins at around HW Dover.
Max Rate at Sp	Of the tidal streams to the W of Rysa Little, Fara and Cava is up to 2 knots.
	On the W and SW facing coastline of Hoy is up to 2 knots, more around the prominent headlands.
	At Tor Ness, Brims and at Cantick Head is 6-7 knots.
	In Clestrain Sound is 8.5 knots.
	In Burra Sound is 4.5 knots.
Coastguard	Shetland or Aberdeen

© Ward Hill (479m), Orkney's highest point, Hoy | Chris Jex

4 Hoy

Introduction

The journey around Hoy (High Island) is an exhilarating and spectacular experience, which should be on every adventurous sea kayaker's shortlist of places to visit. The awe inspiring cave riddled cliffs which surround Hoy include St John's Head, one of the tallest cliff faces in the UK, and Orkney's most recognisable landmark, the Old Man of Hoy.

Approximately two thirds of the Hoy coastline consists of remote steep cliffs. Although they do not offer easy escape to roads or emergency assistance, they do allow the paddler to get out for a break (swell permitting) onto numerous rock and boulder-strewn shorelines. The other third of Hoy's coastline does not disappoint. It provides superb views of Scapa Flow to the north-east and an ever changing view of deserted islands and picturesque beaches.

The journey is best completed over two to three days depending on how much time you wish to spend exploring.

Description

The journey should start with good planning and the ability to forecast the conditions which may prevail on the open W-SW coastline. Contact with Shetland coastguard should be made as a matter of course.

Access onto the water is next to a large car park to the west of the pier on the edge of the Bay of Houton. After leaving the shelter of the bay, paddle south-west across the open water known as Bring Deeps towards Scad Head where an impressive gun emplacement, observation tower and lookout posts remain. There is a suitable beach at Chalmers Hope Bay to the west to get out, stretch your legs and explore the ruins, or find a wild camping spot.

Once around Green Head, the stunning turquoise waters of Lyrawa Bay come into view. The next bay, Pegal Bay, has a hidden deep gorge leading down towards the sea. A profuse variety of native trees and bushes grow within the gorge, which also shelters a number of rare dragonflies.

A small amount of tidal movement may occur between the small islands of Fara, Rysa Little, Cava and Hoy. The red (port channel marker) buoy within Gutter Sound leads you past Mill Bay, where there is an ice cream shop, café and bistro (at Millhouse), and on to Lyness Bay where there is the newly refurbished Scapa Flow Museum (free entry) with an excellent interpretation centre with world war exhibits, historic wartime remains and a café.

On the south shore of Switha Sound there are two prominent martello towers. The second tower at Hackness is open as a museum. Both were built in 1813 during the Napoleonic Wars and were designed to protect Baltic convoys from being raided by US warships and privateers.

Bay of Quoys, Outdoor Education kayaking | Chris Jex

Keep a look out for the inquisitive resident population of porpoise within Switha Sound and along this section of the coastline.

Lyness

The naval base now lies dormant and is a shadow of its former glory when over 30,000 troops were stationed there during the two world wars. This prime location was chosen because it offered a strategic deep water anchorage able to accommodate large warships.

The pump-house and one of the former oil storage tanks have been turned into an interpretation and visitor centre with an excellent indoor and outdoor display of war artefacts, wartime memorabilia and displays relating to Scapa Flow during the First and Second World Wars. The café here also serves great coffee and food. The Scapa Flow Museum is well worth visiting and access can be made via the slipway to the south-west of the main ferry terminal and pier area.

Once past the Cantick Head lighthouse and overfalls within Cantick Sound, the west going current will whisk you past the cliffs which form the southerly coastline of South Walls. A number of impressive gloups, caves and arches are hidden in amongst the steep cliffs.

© Rackwick Bay and cliffs in evening light | Doug Cooper

If, due to poor weather or rough seas, you wish to avoid or abandon the committing paddle along the west coast, it is possible to cut short the journey by paddling north into Aith Hope, passing the old lifeboat station, and portaging across The Ayre into North Bay. The shallow sandy beach is also a good place to camp.

The tidal currents and overfalls become more predominant towards the low-lying, rocky headlands at Brims Ness and Tor Ness. The steep standing waves clearly visible to the south of the headlands give the paddler an idea as to the power of water which is forced through the Pentland Firth with each tide. From here you can push on around Tor Ness towards the towering red cliffs at Berry Head, or take time out at the beach and sand dunes close to Melsetter. The beach provides an excellent camp but it is important to be aware of livestock in the field behind the dunes.

The next section is one of the highlights of this amazing journey but it has few egress points during its 13km duration. A small number of rocky beaches may give access to the shore but once out of your kayak there is a 5km walk before any assistance can be found. It doesn't get more remote than this in Orkney.

After passing a number of grey seal colonies and the steep storm beach at Hawick, the eroded sandstone walls lead to the much higher and more spectacular cliffs beneath The Berry with its scruffy rock stack known as The Needle. The overhanging, deep red and orange coloured rock walls create an imposing setting, especially when paddling directly beneath the cliff face. This section of coastline will leave you with some amazing memories and a crick in your neck … it's simply amazing!

Rinnigill Pier, remains of wartime hydrogen plant | Chris Jex

A rocky egress or an 'uneven' camp is possible at Little Rackwick. Shallow reefs need to be given consideration when landing here if there is any swell. The photogenic waterfall, which freefalls over the cliffs and into the sea north of Little Rackwick has a glorious backdrop of bright green algae, making it easy to spot whilst heading north-west towards Sneuk Head. The intricate rock walls and gullies culminate in a pyramid of steep, cream coloured rock which dominates this punctuated section of coastline. A long tumbling waterfall to the north of Sneuk Head provides another stunning backdrop.

The indented ochre coloured cliffs lead to calmer turquoise water within the Bay of Rackwick, a tranquil location with its own microclimate and some of the best beach and cliff scenery in the whole of Orkney. A bothy and sheltered camping area are located mid way along the boulder-strewn beach. The safest egress is on the sandy beach south of the burn outlet. Beware the beach may have pronounced surf when a west to south-westerly swell is forecast.

Rackwick Bay may also be used to curtail your journey if conditions or circumstances are not as expected. The camp area and bothy has (non-drinkable) water, toilet and a fireplace. Listen out for the grinding, rasping call of the corncrake especially towards dusk, as it has been heard within the pasture areas on a number of occasions. Be warned! In nil wind or damp conditions, Rackwick can be a haven for the Orcadian midge!

The short paddle west towards Rora Head hides the next amazing cliff-lined section of this journey. The chiselled rock headland of Rora Head has a small archway and cave with a tidal race off its steep headland. Be aware of a large anticlockwise recirculating eddy to the south of

The Old Man of Hoy | Doug Cooper

Rora Head which develops on the south-east going tide. Tidal flow around Rora Head in either direction will have associated clapotis and an overfall.

A small amount of tidal movement may be felt around the headland at the Old Man of Hoy, but should not present a problem as long as you keep close to the coast. A wide variety of seabirds including fulmars, puffins, kittiwakes, guillemots, cormorants, razorbills, Arctic skuas and the ubiquitous great skua (known locally as the bonxie) may be seen playing in the updrafts or resting on the water.

Continuing north past Hendry's Holes, a deep chasm and gully, you come to one of the steepest and highest continuous cliff faces in the British Isles. St John's Head, at just over 300m high, was first climbed in 1969, the route taking a number of days and nights to complete!

The Old Man of Hoy

The prominent rock stack is one of Orkney's iconic features. In total it stands at a height of 137m with a solid grey base of volcanic basalt, which has so far saved it from collapsing or being eroded away.

If paddling during the drier months of the year it may be possible to see climbers scaling the landward side of the rock stack which offers the least resistance to attaining its summit. Historic drawings show the rock stack as part of an archway which once linked it to the headland. The question on everybody's lips is "When will it fall over?"

The Kame of Hoy is a steep, angular headland where an exciting paddle through an archway and a tunnel further east leads to calmer waters. The receding cliff line and waterfall east of The Kame lead up to the remote buttresses beneath the Cuilags (433m), the second highest peak in Orkney. At Muckle Head a rock stack dominates the bay with a fresh water stream and rock slabs plunging into the sea.

After passing the remains of a rusting boiler washed up from one of the many shipwrecks along this coastline, the entry into Burra Sound requires careful tidal planning. Burra Sound has a number of low-lying skerries along the south-west side of the channel which are home to a number of curious seals. These may join you as you head east around the rocky reefs and shoreline towards the pier at Moness. The pier gives easy access to public toilets, water and a waiting room. A café aptly named Beneth'ill Cafe serves locally sourced food and great coffee at Linksness.

A brisk walk up the road to the Hoy Interpretation Centre (open 24/7) and the Hoy Centre (4 star Hostel Accommodation) offers options for those taking the paddle around Hoy at a more leisurely speed.

Paddling east into Scapa Flow offers some excellent picturesque views southwards into the deep glaciated valleys and up to the lofty peak of Ward Hill (479m), the highest point in Orkney. The cliffs, rock formations and stacks between Sea Geo and the Candle of the Sale are a spectacular finale to the journey around Hoy.

Upon reaching Chalmers Hope, head north across Bring Deeps back to the Bay of Houton. Entry into the Bay of Houton may be possible over shallow reefs to the west of the Holm of Houton, at certain states of the tide.

Tide and weather

Departure from Houton at approximately 2-3 hours before HW Dover will enable you to use the south going tidal stream out past Fara and towards Cantick Head. It would be wise to be at Tor Ness at approximately HW Dover to avoid the large overfalls which build around the headland during the first two hours after HW Dover.

Strong tidal movement through the Pentland Firth, especially when combined with an Atlantic swell and an opposing wind direction, can produce some extremely rough and difficult conditions along the exposed south-west to north-west coastline of Hoy. In these conditions egress onto rocky shores and beaches is almost impossible.

Departure from Rackwick (if used as an overnight camp) should be at least 5-6 hours after HW Dover so as to give you the benefit of the east going tidal stream through Burra Sound and back to Houton.

Tidal stream times in the Clestrain and Burra Sound can be up to 30 minutes either side of the stated times in this guide due to the prevailing wind direction, swell from the west, and size of the tidal range.

Additional information

Admiralty Charts 2162, 2249, 2568, 35, Imray Chart C68, and O.S. Explorer Map 462 cover this area.

Looking west from South Ronaldsay towards the island of Flotta | Chris Jex

Flotta

No. 5 | Grade B | 27km | 6 hours | OS Sheet 7 | Tidal Port Dover

Start/Finish △○ Sands of Wright (423 935)

HW HW at Widewall Bay is 1 hour 45 minutes before HW Dover.

Tidal Times The N going stream within the Sound of Hoxa starts 4 hours after HW Dover. About 6 hours after HW Dover a large anticlockwise eddy forms in the area between Flotta and Hoxa Head until HW Dover.

The S going stream runs down the E side of Flotta, starting 6 hours before HW Dover, gaining strength and eventually extending across the whole of the Sound of Hoxa by 1 hour after HW Dover.

Two large opposing eddies form S of Flotta, within Switha Sound; both start approximately 5 hours after HW Dover and continue until 2-3 hours before HW Dover.

An outgoing SSE tidal stream within Cantick Sound starts 1 hour 50 minutes before HW Dover. The NNW ingoing tidal stream starts (and rapidly increases in strength) 4 hours and 50 minutes after HW Dover.

In Weddel Sound the direction of tidal flow changes every 2-3 hours. The weaker incoming N going tidal stream flows for up to 2 hours, starting 4 hours after HW Dover and 4 hours before HW Dover. The stronger S going tidal stream is dominant at all other times.

Wartime barrage and submarine netting Flotta | Douglas Sewell

Max Rate at Sp	In the Sound of Hoxa is 2 knots.
	Around Stanger Head and to the E of Switha Sound is 3 knots, easing to 1.5 knots in Switha Sound.
	In Weddel Sound is up to 2 knots in either direction.
Coastguard	Shetland

Introduction

The island of Flotta (Flat Isle) has a unique and varied history. Being surrounded by sea and in a geographically prime position as a lookout point at the entrance to Scapa Flow, it has had to suffer the attentions of the military in both World Wars. The building of a major UK oil terminal during the 1970s has kept this small but less frequented island a lucrative resource for Orkney and the UK oil industry. The island may yet see further development in the near future with possible plans for a new green Hydrogen Hub and Electrical Substation connected to large offshore windfarms to possibly both the east and west of Orkney.

Nonetheless, Flotta is a peaceful island with a wealth of interesting places to visit and explore. The unusual currents and complexity of the tides make the journey an interesting planning exercise in crossing tidal waters and using the tide to full advantage. One of the many highlights of this journey is the possibility of sighting the harbour porpoises, usually resident within Switha and Hoxa Sound.

Description

The anticlockwise journey starts and finishes from a beautiful beach known as the Sands of Wright, located 3km west of St Margaret's Hope in South Ronaldsay. Every August the flat sandy area is host to the colourful 'Boys Ploughing Match' during which boys and girls dress in traditional horse and ploughing costumes. The beach has a toilet block and ample parking areas.

The northern coastline of Widewall Bay has undulating, steep grass and rocky cliffs leading to the headland at Bloie Geo.

The Hoxa Head Battery, with its strategically placed lookout posts, underground ammunition bunkers and gun emplacements has a prime view of the south entrance to Scapa Flow. The currents within the Sound of Hoxa are unique in that there is an anticlockwise two-way flow of water. This can assist progress on one side of the channel, but hinder it on the other!

The 2.5km open water crossing towards Stanger Head may seem a little daunting, but does benefit from a number of excellent navigational transit markers to help paddlers gauge their position mid channel. At Stanger Head the imposing coastal defences look out over the deep geo and arch at the Hole of Row. Two rock stacks known as The Cletts are reputed to have come alive, moved out of the geo and never returned!

The next 4km section of coastline is where most sightings of the resident pod of harbour porpoises occur. Kirk Bay has a small chapel and cemetery tucked in close to the shoreline with possible egress on the east side of the bay. Switha Sound is the meeting point of three

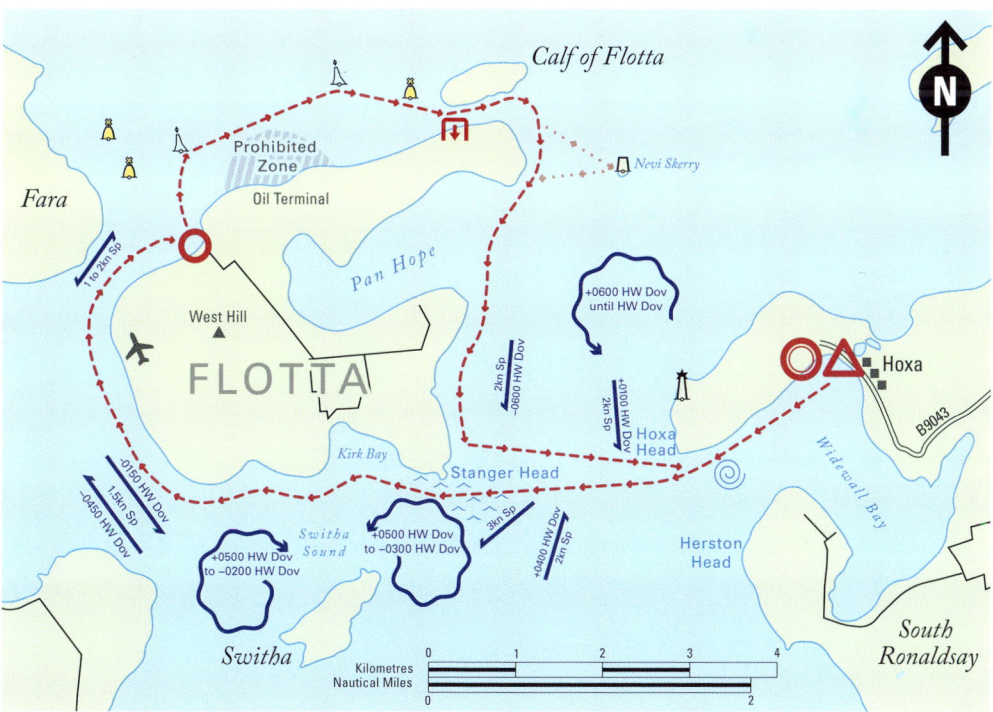

Kayak rescue, oil tanker | Kye Valongo

tidal currents and, like the Sound of Hoxa, has a number of large eddies forming within it. The turbulent currents in this area rotate in opposite directions, at the same time bringing food and rich nutrients into the Sound from a number of directions. This is probably the reason why the harbour porpoises are regularly seen in the area.

The start of the rocky south-west shoreline of Flotta is marked by the impressive Innan Neb coastal battery which housed a twin 12 pounder gun used to defend the southern entrances to Scapa Flow. The rest of the low-lying coastline before Weddel Sound is relatively flat and remote except for an overgrown landing strip parallel to the shore.

North Sea oil

From sea level very little of the Flotta oil terminal can be seen, which is a testament to the monumental landscaping task which was required during its construction. The oil terminal is fed by underground pipes. These run under Churchill Barrier No 4 to the oil field located along the east coast of mainland Scotland.

The oil tankers in Scapa Flow collect or transfer oil and gas. The local Harbour Authority's fleet of tug boats and pilots will generally assist when the huge oil tankers are performing ship to ship transfers and when arriving or departing via the Sound of Hoxa.

Hoxa Head Battery and Lookout point, South Ronaldsay | Chris Jex

On the south side of the channel it is possible to pick out the distinct shape of the Cantick Head lighthouse and the two round-shaped martello towers, the latter having been built during the Napoleonic war to withstand attack from American privateers. Once through Weddel Sound the gas flame, burning high above the oil terminal, dominates the horizon.

The two piers, west of the oil terminal, provide good shelter from the wind. The easterly pier has good beach access next to the ferry waiting room and toilets. The sheltered beach west of here is an excellent place to see seals. Behind the pier lie the remains of a large cinema, which held up to 1500 army and navy personnel.

Important information

East of the main pier area is a large jetty used for oil and gas transfers. This sensitive area is marked on charts as a *Restricted Area* and vessels should not pass within 450m of the oil terminal jetty. In order to adhere to this notice, a good rule of thumb is to head approximately 1km north from the passenger ferry pier, towards the Easterly Cardinal Buoy (black/yellow/black). From here it is safe to head ESE towards the Calf of Flotta, 3km away.

The Calf of Flotta is a small island cut off by Calf Sound. It contains a mountain of rusting boom netting, scrapped and dumped here at the end of the Second World War.

The Golta peninsula, as well as housing the flame tower, has a number of excellent wartime sites. These include a First World War jetty and roadway (leading to Stanger Head), the YMCA building (identifiable by its tall, lone chimney) and the remnants of a rocket battery which once housed over sixty-six launchers within the now derelict triangular huts.

From Roan Head, at certain states of the tide, it may be possible to paddle to and get out on the rocks below the navigational beacon at Nevi Skerry.

The route now heads south past the entrance to Pan Hope and a number of wartime lookout posts along the Flotta coastline. It is worth staying close to land here to view the wonderfully wind sculpted rock formations and avoid any shipping which may be entering or leaving Scapa Flow. Once across the Sound and past Hoxa Head, the less turbulent waters lead you back to the Sands of Wright and a well-earned rest.

Tide and weather

The tidal movement for this journey can be difficult to judge due to the number of channels which meet in the area between the Sound of Hoxa and within Switha Sound. If you plan to complete the journey in 6-7 hours, it is best to depart 2-3 hours after HW Dover using the south-going tide to ferry glide across the Sound of Hoxa. Tidal movement during approximately 4-6 hours after HW Dover will assist your journey around the south and west coast of Flotta and through Weddel Sound. The northern coastline of Flotta is relatively unaffected by tidal movement until entering the Sound of Hoxa from the north. Keeping close to the Flotta shoreline it is possible to head south using the large anticlockwise eddy which forms within the Sound of Hoxa, then confidently ferry glide east across open water towards Hoxa Head.

Additional information

Tidal planning and timing is essential in order to complete the journey described.

There is an exclusion zone extending in a semicircle around the oil terminal pier. The area is clearly marked on the chart and should be observed at all times. Large oil tankers in this area are to be given a wide berth.

The circumnavigation of Flotta can also be completed by starting from the ferry port of Lyness on Hoy, or could involve a return journey from the Bay of Houton on the Mainland of Orkney.

Admiralty Charts 2162 and 35, Imray Chart C68, and O.S. Explorer Map 462 cover this area.

Hunda Reef, Burray | Chris Jex

Burray & Hunda

No. 6 | Grade A | 20km | 4-5 hours | OS Sheet 7 | Tidal Port Dover

Start/Finish	△◯ Car park at Churchill Barrier No 4 (480 954)
HW	HW Burray (Scapa Flow) is 1 hour 40 minutes before HW Dover.
	HW Burray Ness (E side) is 20 minutes after HW Dover.
Tidal Rates	Burray Ness on the E side of the island may be affected by weak tidal movement in either direction.
Coastguard	Shetland

Introduction

Burray (Brochs Island) is an excellent introduction to day or weekend coastal paddling. The island has an exciting mix of beaches, short sections of low-lying cliffs and rocky headlands. A number of archaeological remains and historic sites along the shoreline can be easily accessed by kayak during the journey.

The circumnavigation of Burray requires a short portage across Churchill Barrier No 3. This portage enables the paddler to absorb the amazing panoramas and views to Copinsay on the east, and Flotta and Scapa Flow to the west.

Barrier 3, Glimps Holm island | Chris Jex

Description

Access onto the golden sandy beach on the east side of Barrier No 4 can be made from the small car park and toilet facility at the north end of the barrier. The sands, which have built up along the east side of the barrier, have formed a stunning crescent shaped bay. The area marked by a wooden totem pole, at the north end of the beach, is an excellent camping spot.

The first section of paddling, around the east side of the island, leads you away from the clear aquamarine waters of the bay and north along a gentle shoreline of rocks and seaweed, passing the rocky inlets of Sea and Wife Geo. The low-lying finger of rock at Burray Ness can produce some surprisingly large and unpredictable waves, if the wind is blowing on-shore or there is any swell from the east. It is worth giving the headland a wide berth if conditions are rough. A small amount of tidal movement may be felt at Burray Ness as water either empties out of Holm Sound or is deflected around the rocky underwater promontory.

The tranquil and infrequently visited beach at South Links provides respite from the open ocean. Behind the dunes there is a small ruined church and cemetery at its south end. The area around the church and dune area is covered in a technicolor show of wild flowers and vivid natural colour during the warmer months of the year.

Heading north and around the headland, a single, large wind turbine dominates the horizon. The energy efficient blades overlook a number of historic sites including the remains of two brochs situated north-west of the headland. These well-placed, defensive sites would have been an imposing sight to an invader, reaching up to 10m in height. A number of First World War gun emplacements and lookout posts are scattered along the north shoreline. These were positioned to protect the entrances into Scapa Flow before the Churchill Barriers were built. Interestingly, the prominent First World War lookout tower and gun emplacements were built on top of one of the brochs, proving that the view from here was strategically as important to those defending the island during the 20th century as it was in the Iron Age.

Weddell Sound, now blocked by Churchill Barrier No 3, has a number of excellent sandy areas which, like those at Barrier No 4, have built up to form a sheltered sandy coastline. The broken remains of the *Reginald*, a three masted schooner, provide an excellent backdrop to a picturesque lunch spot on the beach.

To access the west side of the 3rd Churchill Barrier, it is possible to portage across the roadway at either end; the south end being slightly easier. The north end requires kayaks to be lifted over a locked gate. Please be aware of traffic. On the west side of the barrier a number of blockships are easily visible at low tide. Two of the ships, the *Martis* and *Empire Seaman*, are well worth exploring. Shallow water and easy access to the sunken wreckage make it a prime location for new scuba divers practising their skills and exploring the underwater wreckage. It is wise to keep your distance from their air bubbles which may be seen from the surface.

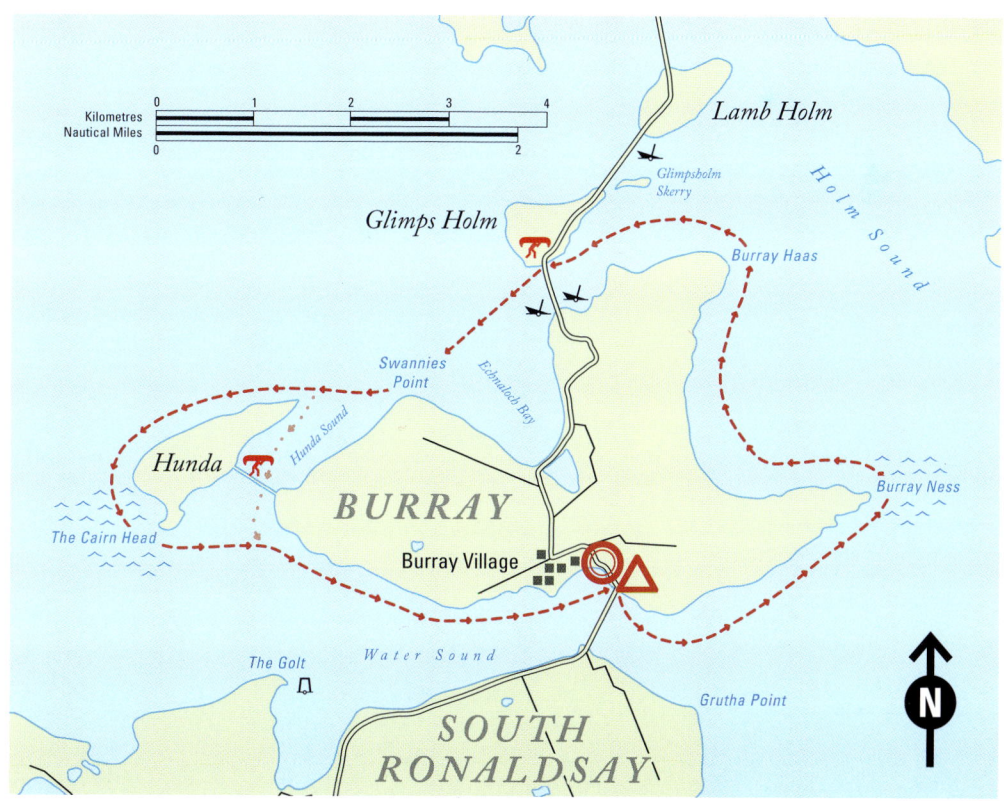

Barrier 3 blockship remains, Scapa Flow | Chris Jex

Depending on the open water conditions it is possible to either paddle directly to Swannies Point, or follow the shoreline towards Echnaloch, where there is a freshwater loch with a number of resident wading and nesting birds. The west side of the island is higher and less cultivated than the east, with steep, broken cliffs and a rocky shoreline. Possible egress may be found via a small slipway with a steep track leading to a single-track road, just beyond, and south-west of Swannies Point.

Hunda (Dog Island) is a haven for a variety of wildlife including otters, seals and birds. It is joined to Burray by a natural rocky reef with a concrete causeway on top of it. The causeway, built as part of the boom defences, now gives access to pasture land and livestock on the island. A ruined cairn at the south promontory on the island is clearly evident.

Paddling around Hunda can be an exciting experience, especially if there is a westerly onshore wind which can produce large areas of clapotis. In these conditions, a shorter and less exposed option is to portage over the easterly end of the causeway, avoiding the 3km paddle around Hunda.

The south facing bay at Wha Taing is home to a playful colony of common seals which are usually found lazing around the headland close to the causeway. The last 4km of paddling, along Water Sound, leads past a number of steep broken cliffs, wide open bays and picturesque cottages close to the water's edge.

Fresh fish for supper! Burray | Chris Jex

Burray and the herring industry

The village of Burray flourished and developed during the 19th century, predominantly as a herring fishing community. At the height of the industry over half of the island community were involved in fishing. Unfortunately, a change in people's preference for fresh rather than cured fish, and the fact that larger boats based on the Scottish mainland were more economically viable, meant that by 1880 the herring industry was in decline. Close to the pier, the two storey building (the Sands Hotel), was the main building used for packing and curing the herring.

At the close of the Second World War, when the barriers were completed, any remaining fishing boats were forced to relocate due to the sea passageways between the islands being blocked.

Duncan's Boatyard, next to the hotel, continues to provide a boatyard and repair workshop, and is a family business, that has been managed by successive generations. It is the last remaining dedicated facility for boat repair within Orkney.

Leave the water at the north end of Churchill Barrier No 4 via a small flight of steps leading steeply up towards the road. At low water a small sheltered sandy beach is exposed. The portage across the road requires a high degree of care, as traffic travelling south cannot be easily seen.

Burray village, Barrier 4 beach | Chris Jex

Tide and weather

Tidal movement around the headlands of the island is relatively weak and does not affect the journey. Wind from the north-west through to south-west can produce windblown swell within Scapa Flow and clapotis along the steeper shoreline cliffs. Ocean swell and wind from the east through to the south can funnel into Holm Sound causing rough water around Burray Ness and the beach start point on the east side of Barrier No 4; therefore, winds from the north to north-east are preferable for this journey.

Additional information

Possible camping areas around Burray include the beaches at Barrier No 4, South Links and the shoreline to the east of Barrier No 3. Permission to camp on the land close to Hunda should be requested from the landowner.

Admiralty Charts 2162, 2249, 2250, 35, Imray Chart C68, and O.S. Explorer Map 461 cover this area.

The Italian Chapel on Lamb Holm | Chris Jex

Lamb & Glimps Holm

No. 7 | **Grade A** | **8.5km** | **2-3 hours** | **OS Sheet 6 & 7** | **Tidal Port Dover**

Start/Finish	N end of Churchill Barrier No1 (483 012)
HW	HW Burray Ness (E side) is approximately 15 minutes after HW Dover. HW Scapa Flow (W side) is 1 hour 40 minutes before HW Dover.
Tidal Times	The journey is unaffected by tidal streams.
Coastguard	Shetland

Introduction

The circumnavigation of Lamb Holm and Glimps Holm and portage across Churchill Barriers Nos 1 and 3 is a delightful short trip for all levels of paddler. The journey is steeped in history with the remains of wartime buildings and sunken blockships amongst the many sights along the way. Contorted cliffs, sandy beaches and numerous sea birds all add up to an excellent half-day of paddling. There are a number of access points throughout the journey.

© Barrier 2 & 3 looking NW towards Scapa Flow | Chris Jex

Description

Easy access to the water can be found next to a convenient lay-by at the north end of Barrier No 1 via a shingle beach. Following the west side of Barrier No 1 and shoreline of Lamb Holm, evidence of wartime buildings, landing stages and rock quarrying is still clearly visible. After about 1.5km a stone pier and rocky beach at the north end of Barrier No 2 give shelter from the west and easy egress off the water for a quick break.

The next section of the journey leads you along the 10 ton blocks of Barrier No 2 towards Glimps Holm. Throughout the year you may see groups of eider duck sheltering on the water close to the barrier, as well as a number of small wading birds feeding off the shoreline at low tide.

The north side of Glimps Holm has a steep muddy bank and boulders along its shoreline making egress difficult. The scenery soon changes once around the headland due to the contorted rock strata embedded in the cliff. There is an excellent pebble beach below the highpoint of the cliff, which enables the paddler to get out and have a closer look at the spectacular strata and folds in the rock. Heading along the rocky shoreline and around the headland of Tarri Clett can sometimes be exposed to wind-blown waves, when there is an onshore wind.

As you paddle ever closer to Barrier No 3 you will notice the rusting remains of two sunken blockships. These are the *Martis* and the *Empire Seaman*. Keep a look out for fishermen along Barrier No 3 who may cast their lines near the wrecks in hope of enticing the large pollock, conger and wrasse which shelter around the wrecks. Other sightings may include cormorants and shags, which can often be seen atop the rusting ledges drying their wings.

The Churchill Barriers

On the 13th October 1939, the German U-boat *U47* was skilfully manoeuvred through Kirk Sound, passing the blockship defences undetected and into the open waters of Scapa Flow. The subsequent torpedo attack resulted in the sinking of the battleship HMS *Royal Oak* and tragic loss of nearly all the ship's crew. In 1940 Winston Churchill decided to close the sea passages for good by constructing four causeways which would link up each of the islands along the east side of Scapa Flow.

Some 1700 men (mostly Italian POWs) were involved in blasting and relocating over 1 million cubic metres of rock. In total more than 36,500 blocks weighing 5 tons, and 15,000 blocks weighing 10 tons, were formed and carefully placed to clad the outside of the barriers and fortify them against the pounding waves and fast moving currents which once flowed between each of the islands.

In 1945, almost at the end of the war, the barriers were finally completed after more than four years of construction and costing in excess of £2.5 million.

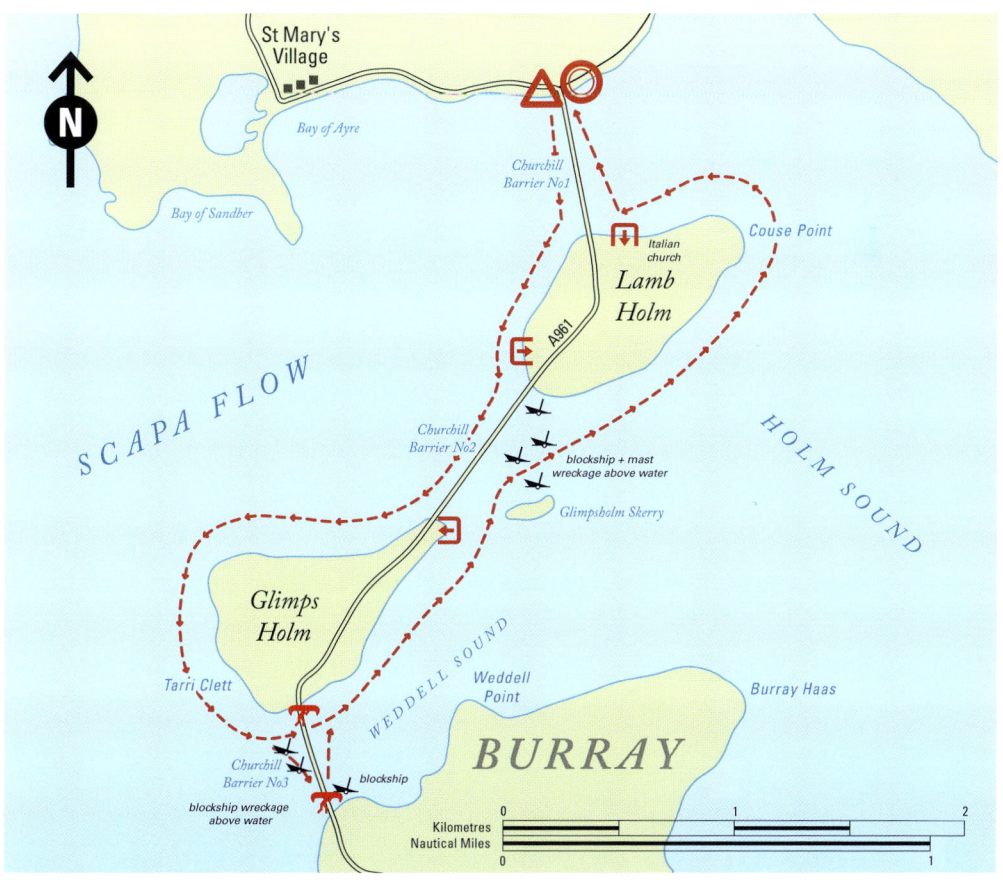

© Wreck of 'Reginald' with lobster pots, Barrier 3 | Doug Cooper

To access the east side of Churchill Barrier Number 3 it is possible to portage across the roadway at either end, the south end being slightly easier. The north end now requires kayaks to be lifted over a locked gate and down obvious steps to the beach. Please be aware of traffic from both directions when crossing the road.

The dazzling white sands within Weddell Sound have slowly built up to create one of Orkney's most accessible and sheltered beach areas. When the sun is shining this coastline can provide a spectrum of stunning colours, with golden sands and aquamarine water reflecting the blue skies above.

To the south of Weddell Point there are a number of lookout posts, coastal defences and gun emplacements used during the two world wars. Further on, beyond Boats Geo, are the remains of two large fortified brochs, which stood guard over the shores of Burray during the Iron Age. Beautiful beaches and a tranquil coastline lead you north towards Glimpsholm Skerry.

At Barrier No 2 the angular mast provides a focal point to aim towards. The shallow water area gives the paddler the opportunity to explore and paddle amongst the rusting engine and boiler sections of yet more sunken blockships. The *Emerald Wings*, *Lycia*, *Ilsenstein*, *Cape Ortegal* and the *F/C Pontoon* all lay beneath the HW water line. Barriers Nos 2 and 3 are popular scuba diving sites. If you happen to see air bubbles appearing on the surface, please keep clear and be aware of divers below!

A 'groatie buckie' – rare finds on Barrier 3 beach | Chris Jex

A number of wartime lookout posts and interesting low-lying cliffs and geos lead along the east side of Lamb Holm towards Round Point.

The last section of the journey takes you west towards the south end of Barrier No 1. At a sandy beach and slipway there is the opportunity to stretch your legs, sample the 'John Gow' Rum which is distilled on the small island, visit the Italian Chapel (small entry fee), and then head for the finish point at the north end of Barrier No 1. The rocky beach is seaweed covered at low tide and care should be taken when carrying kayaks.

Tide and weather

For access on and off the water and the portage across Barrier No 3, it would be advantageous to complete the journey close to HW. The disadvantage, however, is that the blockships will be less visible due to them being underwater. This consideration apart, the journey is unaffected by tidal flow and requires no tidal planning.

During moderate or strong winds from either east or west it is possible to paddle from Barrier No 1 to Barrier No 3 keeping to the lee-side of the islands and barriers as they provide excellent shelter. The east side of the barriers can be prone to heavy sea swell after, or during, strong onshore winds.

East coast, Barrier 2 wrecks (remains of blockships) | Doug Cooper

Additional information

Please be aware of livestock on both Lamb Holm and Glimps Holm. Ensure that gates are shut and avoid getting close to grazing animals.

A scenic walk around Glimps Holm and a visit to the beach at Churchill Barrier No 3 is an excellent alternative for non-paddlers in the group or for those who wish to take photos. Entrance to the Italian Chapel, a popular tourist attraction located on Lamb Holm, entails a small charge and can be busy when coaches and tourists are present.

Walking along the roadway at Barrier Nos 1, 2 and 3 is *not* recommended due to the narrow lanes and busy traffic, especially during the summer months.

If you have time, a wetsuit and an inclination for getting wet, take a snorkel and mask on the journey to get a stunning underwater view of the sunken blockships.

Admiralty Charts 2250, 2249, 35, Imray Chart C68, and O.S. Explorer Map 461 cover this area.

Copinsay, east-facing cliffs and lighthouse | Doug Cooper

Copinsay

No. 8	**Grade B**	**16km**	**4 hours**	**OS Sheet 6**	**Tidal Port Dover**
Start/Finish	Slipway on the W side of Newark Bay (568 041)
HW	HW Burray Ness is 15 minutes after HW Dover.
Tidal Times	In Copinsay Pass the SW going stream starts about 4 hours 55 minutes before HW Dover. The NE going stream starts about 15 minutes after HW Dover.
Max Rate at Sp	In Copinsay Pass is 3 knots. In Horse Sound is 4 knots.
Coastguard	Shetland

Introduction

Copinsay (Kolbein's Island) and its outlying islands were given the status of an RSPB nature reserve in 1972. Paddling around the island is an exhilarating journey especially during the spring and early summer period when there are over 40,000 nesting birds perched precariously on the narrow cliff edges. The circumnavigation of Copinsay is a relatively short paddle, but it is worth spending time exploring the island on foot and even including an overnight camp so as to soak up the atmosphere and noise of the seals and birds in the late evening. You may also be lucky enough to hear or see the elusive and rare corncrake, which is known to nest here.

Copinsay island and Deerness slipway | Chris Jex

Description

Access, to the west side of Newark Bay, is from one of the best slipways in Orkney. The area has two slipways for either high or low water launching and a higher car parking area, which should always be used so as not to block the slipways.

An easy paddle across the shallow waters of Newark Bay and along a low rocky coastline for 2km brings you to Point of Ayre at the south-east corner of the Deerness peninsula.

The open water paddle across the Copinsay Pass is approximately 2km and can easily be negotiated by crossing at slack water. In poor visibility it is possible to paddle from the Point of Ayre on a bearing of 140° True direct to the sandy bay and jetty on Copinsay. Alternatively, a determined paddle well upstream of any rough water ensures the pulse rate is kept high. The Barns of Ayre on the hillside to the north, and Black Holm to the south, act as excellent markers to determine your position whilst crossing the open water channel.

Once across the channel, the tidal current eases as you follow the rocky coastline into North Bay, which has a small jetty and farmhouse buildings close to the shore. On landing, the island comes alive with the sound of sheep, birds and seals, giving the island a magical atmosphere.

The old farmhouse still retains its charm and is now an information point for the infrequent visitors to the island. It is an excellent place to rest or shelter if the weather is not favourable.

The short but steep hike up the metalled track to the top of the island will repay you with spectacular views to the west across the Orkney Mainland. From the high point of the island (64m) close to the lighthouse wall, it is possible to (carefully) peer over the stunning cliffs on the east side of the island and get a glimpse of what lies ahead if you choose to paddle beneath the spectacular rock walls. During the breeding season, the updraft from the cliff brings with it the potent scent of bird guano coming from 'Seabird City'. From the stunning vantage point of the lighthouse, it is worth heading north along the cliffs passing a helicopter landing pad. The view will give you an idea of the direction of flow and strength of the tidal stream through Horse Sound; this is especially important if you plan to visit the Horse of Copinsay as part of your journey.

Once back on the water, a short paddle around the north coast of Copinsay, passing a number of picturesque sandstone arches and bays, brings you into Horse Sound. Crossing Horse Sound in either direction should not be taken lightly as the flow through this shallow gap can reach substantial speeds (up to 4 knots). Standing waves and difficult currents need to be safely assessed and tackled, or respectfully left until the tide slackens … or another day.

The barren rocky outcrop of The Horse of Copinsay is worth a visit to see the infamous Blaster Hole, which spouts water when there is a strong onshore wind. The barren rocky outcrop is home to a colony of great black backed gulls and a small colony of immature gannets. It used to be said that atop the small barren island "there was enough grass to fatten one sheep, feed two or starve three".

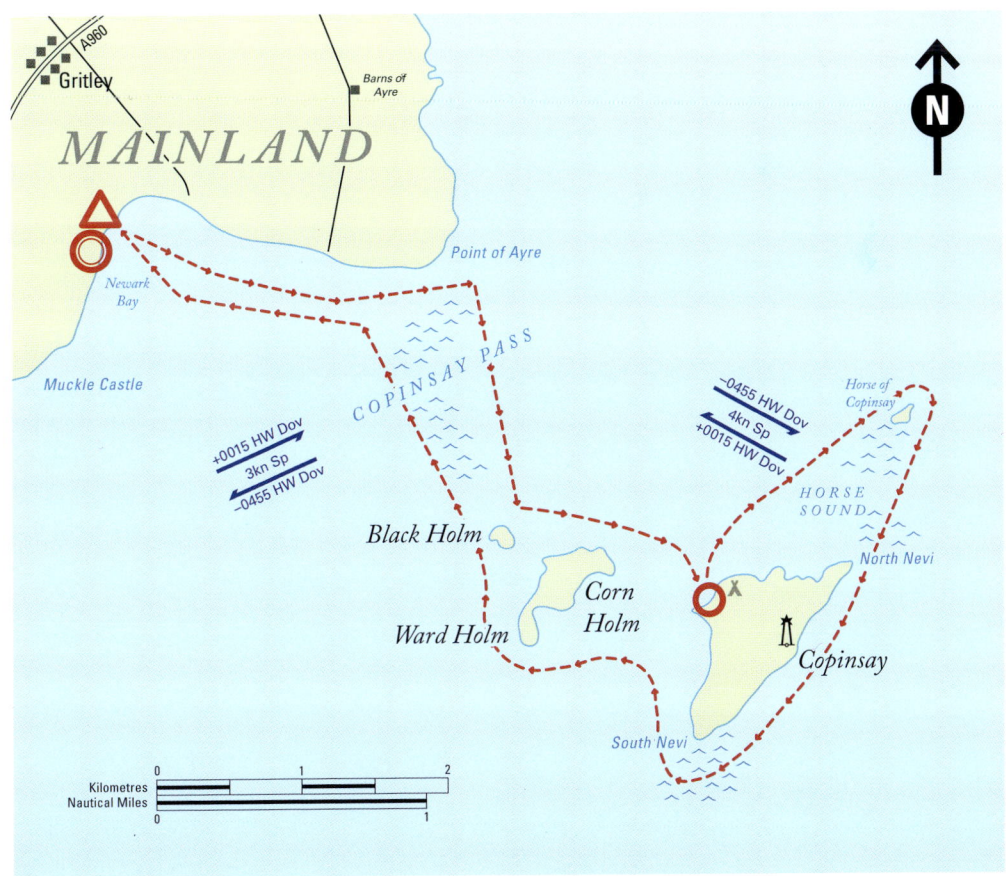

Once around North Nevi on Copinsay, the imposing east coast cliffs come into view. From sea level, the overhanging cliffs look even more spectacular than from above. Kittiwakes, guillemots, razorbills, cormorants and puffins are all crammed in organised lines on the narrow cliff ledges. At the base of the cliffs during nesting times, large rafts of seabirds congregate to preen and rest from gathering food and feeding their young. Passing under the lighthouse, the cliffs slowly ease in height with a number of steep geos at the south end, close to South Nevi. Be aware of a number of rocky skerries at the south end of the island, which lie just beneath the surface.

At low water, the Holms (islands) to the west of Copinsay are joined by a rocky and seaweed covered isthmus, which gives access to a small ruined chapel and a number of cairns on Corn and Ward Holm. On Scarf Skerry there is thought to be the largest colony of oyster plants in Orkney. Heading west towards Ward Holm, keep watch for a large colony of playful grey seals that seem to follow the kayaks and congregate along the shoreline on this side of the islands.

From the west side of Black Holm it is wise to carefully re-assess the state of the tide and the speed of the tidal waters in Copinsay Pass before heading into open water. The 2km paddle back across the sound towards the Orkney Mainland makes for an excellent finish to a relatively short journey, which packs in a lot of sights, sounds and memorable experiences. These can now be savoured whilst you relax and head back to the sandy shoreline of Newark Bay and the finish of the journey at the concrete slipway.

Tide and weather

The tidal stream within the Copinsay Pass combined with an opposing wind can create difficult conditions. At stronger states of the tide, a clear line of boils along an eddy-line, a distinct glassy wave and a set of short standing waves mark the shallow depth of water across the whole of the channel (averaging only 3-5m deep). During the SW going tidal stream the speed of water on the south side of Copinsay Pass (close to Black Holm) is more pronounced than the north side due to water being pushed onto the island chain and around the headland of Black Holm.

Tidal streams may affect the headlands to the north and south of Copinsay, forming obvious rough water, and clapotis around North and South Nevi.

The east facing cliffs on Copinsay can be prone to very heavy clapotis and sea swell when there is a moderate onshore wind.

The best weather conditions for the journey are after a settled spell of weather, when there is a light WNW wind, as this wind direction is unlikely to create any significant sea swell.

Additional information

If you choose to walk on the island please be aware of the well-camouflaged and delicate bird nests, which lie on open ground due to the lack of predators. It is worth staying away from the central field and walled areas on the island during early spring and summer so as to avoid being attacked by the very protective black backed gulls that reside here.

If you do plan to stay overnight on Copinsay, you will need to be fully self-sufficient. Please respect the RSPB Bird Reserve area by taking all rubbish away with you when departing.

Admiralty Chart 2250, Imray Chart C68, and O.S. Explorer Map 461 cover this area.

Departing with a smile from the Bay of Houton, Scapa Flow | Chris Jex

Cava & the Barrel of Butter

No. 9 | Grade B | 13km | 3 hours | OS Sheet 6 & 7 | Tidal Port Dover

Start/Finish	Houton Pier (319 039)
HW	HW Stromness is about 1 hour 50 minutes before HW Dover.
Tidal Times	The incoming E going stream starts 6 hours after HW Dover. The outgoing W going stream starts at HW Dover.
Max Rate at Sp	There is a weak tidal flow through Scapa Flow of 1 knot in either direction.
Coastguard	Shetland

Introduction

The historic natural harbour of Scapa Flow offers the paddler a varied coastline, small deserted islands and a large but sheltered area of open water for exploration. The triangular journey visits the island of Cava (Calf Island) and the rocky outcrop known as the 'Barrel of Butter' where a colony of common seals is resident throughout the year.

61

Heading for 'The Barrel of Butter' within Scapa Flow | Chris Jex

The journey passes over an area of water where a large number of warships of the German high sea fleet were scuttled in 1919. The huge rusting remains of three battleships and four light cruisers now lay hidden 30-40m beneath the surface. Scapa Flow is recognised as one of the top ten most popular wreck diving sites in the world.

Description

Access to the water is best found down a short grassy track west of the house and pier area. If open, the ferry terminal building has a toilet and waiting room.

The Bay of Houton and the Holm of Houton create a relatively enclosed, sheltered area of water. This provides an excellent harbour area for small creel boats and the vehicle ferry which services Flotta and Hoy. Houton Bay was a strategically important location during both world wars and was used as a base for flying boats and as a strategic supply depot for the Navy. Heading south-east out of the Bay of Houton be aware of other boats, especially at the mouth of the bay where shallow water restricts their passage through the narrow entrance.

From the entrance to the bay, head on a bearing of 174° True for 2.6km towards the lighthouse on the island of Cava. The area of water to the north of Cava was where the interned German Fleet was detained and subsequently scuttled in June 1919. In all, fifty-two ships were sunk and seventy-four ships beached or damaged as the Germans attempted to ensure that the captured ships would never fall into enemy hands. The original lighthouse on Cava was built in 1898 and replaced with a new, more prominent structure in 1988.

The journey continues around the west side of Cava, in an anticlockwise direction past The Ayre, a narrow neck of land. There are a number of ruined dwellings to the south. The island, which had a population of twenty-four people in 1841, is now uninhabited and left to grazing sheep and wildlife. Various egress points can be found along the shoreline if you wish to explore the island, which used to have a narrow gauge railway around its perimeter during the war.

Once around the Point of Ward at the south-west tip of the island, the journey continues to follow the rugged coastline towards the Point of Tuberry. From here, a bearing of 46° True enables you to set your sights on the next 2.3km of open water and towards the navigational beacon on the Barrel of Butter. During this part of the journey it is important to remember you are crossing the South Isles ferry and Flotta oil terminal launch boat route. It would be wise to remain vigilant for other watercraft, including dive boats, within the area.

The Barrel of Butter, which was originally called Carlin Skerry, gained its name from the time when men from the Orphir area would pay an annual rent of a barrel of butter to the laird. In return, local men were allowed to kill the seals on the island. Thankfully, the seals still remain in large numbers. If time allows, donning a wetsuit, mask and snorkel is an excellent way of getting up close to the seals in their natural habitat. Arctic terns are known to nest here in small numbers.

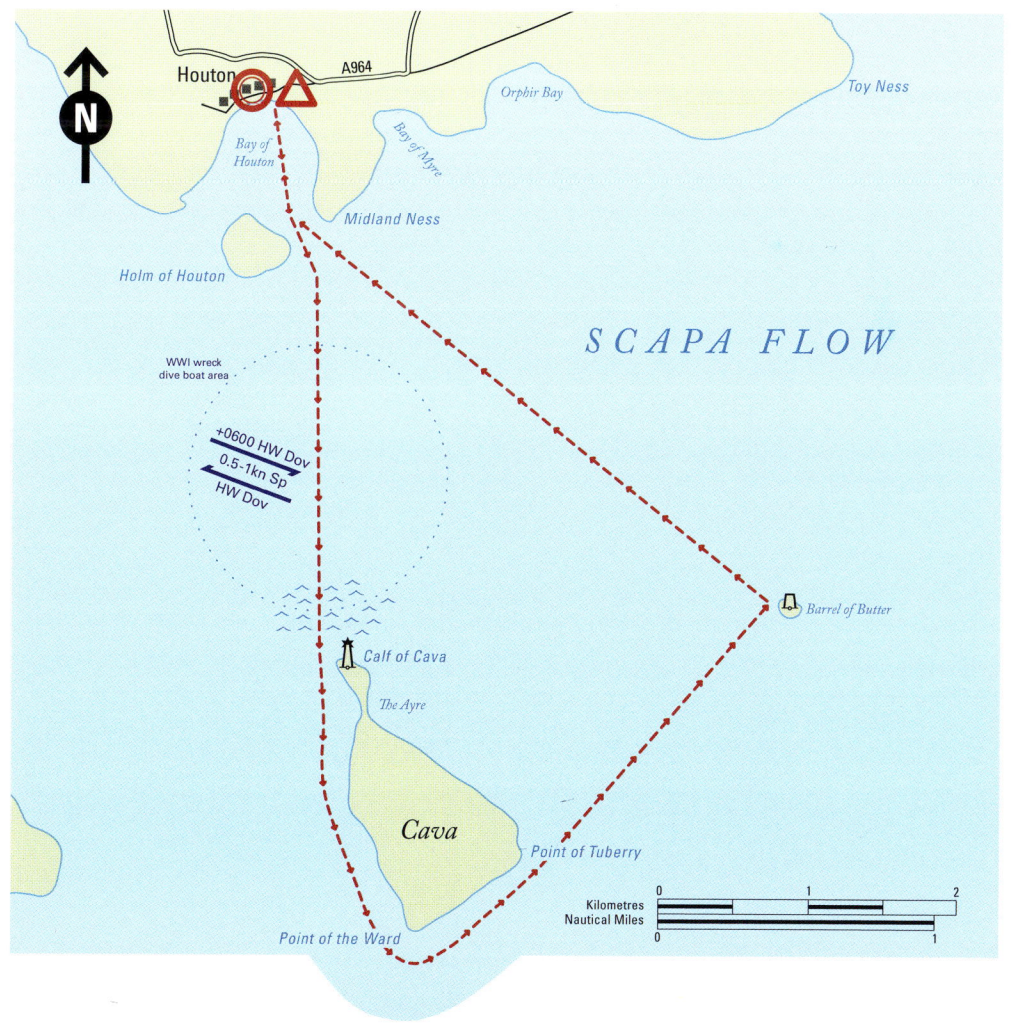

Grey seal pup, Barrel of Butter | Chris Jex

The final 3.9km open water crossing on a bearing of 305° True, will lead you directly into the Bay of Houton. As you head closer towards the mouth of the bay why not practice using a number of navigational transits, by lining up the red navigational lights on the foreshore and hillside at the back of the bay. This will enable you to steer an accurate course through the deep-water channel and to the left of the green starboard marker buoy inside the bay.

Tide and weather

Scapa Flow is a relatively sheltered natural harbour area with two main entrances to the south and west. Although the tidal movement in the deep water areas is negligible, the water conditions should not be underestimated when there is a wind of Force 4 or more from any direction.

Up to 1 knot of tidal current may be found north of the island of Cava. This is more noticeable if there is an opposing wind, which may create an area of choppy waves.

Additional information

Optional journeys include travelling further south to Rysa Little and/or Fara. The water channels around the islands may have moderate to light tidal currents at various states of the tide but good shelter from a W/SW wind. Prior tidal planning is advised if heading south of Cava.

The ferry terminals at Lyness (Hoy) or Flotta provide the paddler with a number of alternative finish points, or escape options, if unable to return to Houton due to deteriorating weather. Ferry timetables vary throughout the year and are worth checking before setting off from Houton.

Admiralty Charts 2249, 35, Imray Chart C68, and O.S. Explorer Map 462 cover this area.

Paddlers taking a rest, Bay of Sandber | Doug Cooper

Holm & Rose Ness

No. 10 | Grade B | 23.5km | 5-6 hours | OS Sheet 6 & 7 | Tidal Port Dover

Start	△ Beach or slipway at Scapa Bay (442 086)
Finish	◯ Dingieshowe Beach (549 033)
HW	HW Scapa Bay is 1 hour 40 minutes before HW Dover. HW Burray Ness (E side) is 15 minutes after HW Dover.
Tidal Times	The SW going tidal stream at Rose Ness starts 5 hours and ten minutes before HW Dover. The NE going stream starts at HW Dover.
Max Rate at Sp	Around the headland at Rose Ness is up to 2 knots.
Coastguard	Shetland

Introduction

The journey from Scapa Bay to Dingieshowe Beach is an excellent full day introduction to coastal paddling. Added excitement may be obtained by paddling offshore to visit the war grave and final resting place of the warship HMS *Royal Oak*.

Archway and collapsed cave (gloup) south of the Bay of Semolie, Rose Ness | Chris Jex

Description

Easy access to the water can be made from either the slipway at the pier or numerous parking areas along the beach at Scapa Bay, close to the public toilets. This bay is home to the Orkney Islands Council Harbours Department headquarters (the pyramid shaped building) and is the main port for the pilot vessels which assist the oil tankers' safe passage in and out of Scapa Flow. Above the pier lies a mass of pipes and tanks which were used to store oil and fuel during the war. Further up the hillside are the striking pagoda shaped chimneys of the Highland Park Distillery.

Highland Park single malt whisky

Highland Park is well recognised as one of Scotland's, if not the world's, best single malt whisky. The 12, 18 and 25-year-old single malts have gained a number of awards and accolades all over the world by those who judge or write about the 'water of life'.

The distillery is still the most productive distillery in Orkney, and is situated slightly further north than the Scapa Distillery which is situated less than 1km to the south-west. The site was chosen for the clean water supply which comes from a walled-off field above the distillery known as High Park. After much illicit distilling and hiding of the prized whisky from the excise men, the distillery was eventually legalised in 1825.

The distillery is unusual in that it still produces approximately 20% of its own malt, which is dried over a traditional peat fuelled fire in the pagoda-shaped kilns which overlook Scapa Bay and Kirkwall.

The distillery has its own visitor centre, shop, audiovisual show and tour of the distillery.

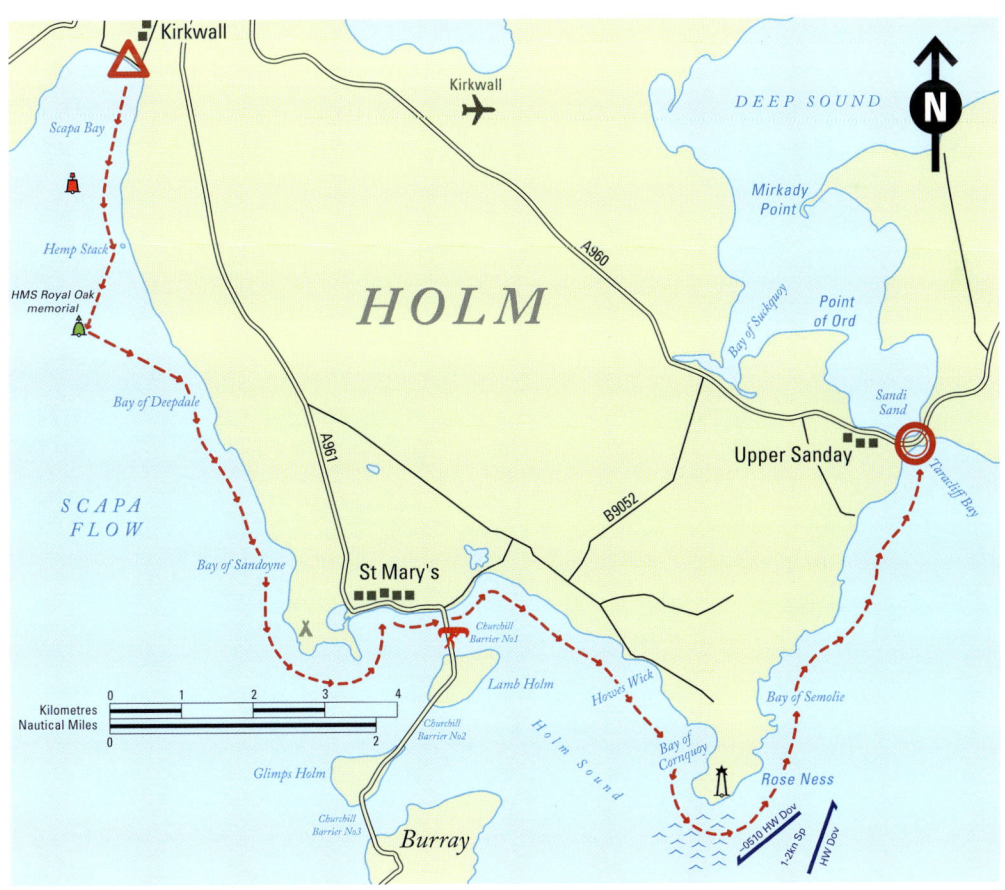

The Old Beacon on Rose Ness | Doug Cooper

The relatively remote, steep and rocky coastline which runs parallel to the A961 (Kirkwall to St Mary's) is infrequently visited from land, but has a number of rocky egress points below the cliffs, well suited for taking short breaks. The first major feature is Hemp Stack. From Hemp Stack take a bearing of 215° True for 1.3km into open water heading towards the green starboard navigational buoy which marks the location of the final resting place of HMS *Royal Oak*.

HMS *Royal Oak*

A memorial plaque on the buoy commemorates the tragedy that occurred when, at 1 am on the night of October 13-14th 1939, the German U-boat *U47* entered Scapa Flow through a narrow tidal channel and fired three torpedoes. This resulted in a direct hit and the sinking of the battleship within 15 minutes. The loss of 833 out of the 1200 seamen aboard was a horrendous toll on the British Navy.

Each year a short memorial is attended by survivors and family members of those who died. A book of remembrance is displayed within St Magnus Cathedral in Kirkwall; each day a page is turned to reveal the names of those that perished on that fateful October night. An ongoing reminder of the event is the small leak of oil which may be smelt and seen floating on the waters above the wreck on a calm day.

From the navigational buoy head (SSE) back towards Deepdale where a stream enters the sea over a rocky shoreline. Deepdale is being developed as a renewable marine development area, with plans for a large deep water pier and storage area. Please be aware of any water traffic or work being undertaken in this area. The easier angled rock and grassy foreshore lead you past the circular fish farms dotted along the coastline towards the open Bay of Sandoyne and a steep shingle beach, north of Howequoy Head. During the Second World War this was one of many locations where mine loops were strung across vast expanses of water to prevent enemy attack. From the bay just north of the headland, the defence netting was strung across the eastern entrances to Scapa Flow and secured at Swannies Point on the island of Burray, over 3km away!

Heading east into St Mary's Bay *(Haven)* a small line of cottages and a rock built pier come into view. In the early part of the 19th century St Mary's was a busy herring-fishing village. A public toilet is located near the end of the pier. Passing the jewellery workshop, shop and café, the north end of Churchill Barrier No 1 has an information board and sheltered lunch spot next to the concrete blocks which mark the egress point.

Portaging kayaks across the main road requires some care, as does the access back onto the water via the seaweed-strewn rocks east of the barrier. A paddle along the east side of Barrier No 1 and a short walk take you to the Italian Chapel, one of Orkney's most visited attractions. Alternatively, a pleasant paddle along the south facing coastline towards the small sandy bay at Graemeshall may reward you with sightings of wading and shoreline birds. The imposing coastal battery further east became obsolete after the Churchill Barriers were built. The remains are relatively intact and can be visited from the shoreline.

Continuing along the coast a number of pleasant sandy beaches are popular areas for bird watching, and spotting grey and common seals hauled out at low water. The headland at Rose Ness has a prominent stone pillar and navigational light at its high point. The headland section can produce confused clapotis when there is an onshore wind and an overfall below the navigational light. Beyond the headland there are numerous geos and steep black cliffs, which continue for about 2.5km. Most notable is the atmospheric gloup or sunken cave just south of the Bay of Semolie. The cliffs along this section of coastline are an excellent area for climbing, and are often frequented by local climbers and walkers.

The short, open water paddle towards Dingieshowe heads towards an amazing section of cliff, with a subterranean tunnel, archways and a number of small caves between Forse and Notster. Guillemots can be seen closely huddled on the smallest of ledges during the breeding season. The last 2km of paddling enables the kayaker to relax and absorb the stunning views east out to the island of Copinsay. It is worth assessing the landing at Dingieshowe, which may be tricky if there are waves breaking over the shallow reef in the centre of the bay.

Access to the car park and toilet is via a small track right of centre between the dunes. During late spring the grass area behind the dunes is carpeted with colourful wild flowers, including primrose and orchids.

Cliffs and caves at Forse | Doug Cooper

Tide and weather

The Scapa Flow (west) side of the barriers has no tidal movement but can be rough if a moderate to strong westerly wind is present. The water and exposed headland on the east side of the barriers can be subject to heavy sea swell after, or during, strong onshore winds.

Starting the journey about 1 hour before HW Dover will provide HW access onto the water at Scapa Beach and give the paddler a favourable north-going tidal stream once you have reached Rose Ness, and along the cliffs towards Dingieshowe.

The journey is best completed when the wind is from the north-west. This gives a down wind paddle for the first half of the journey which then enables the paddler to follow a sheltered shoreline during the latter part of the journey.

Additional information

The pier at Scapa is best given a wide berth if there are large pilot vessels manoeuvring nearby.

Entrance into the Italian Chapel entails a small charge. Wet clothing should not be taken into the chapel.

Please do not walk along the barrier. There is no access due to the narrowness of the road.

If the conditions around the headland at Rose Ness are too difficult, due to onshore winds, tidal movement or clapotis along the cliffs, the journey can be amalgamated with journey No. 7 Lamb and Glimps Holm as an alternative paddling option.

Admiralty Charts 2250, 35, Imray Chart C68, and O.S. Explorer Map 461 cover this area.

Heading south from Mull Head | Doug Cooper

Deerness

No. 11	**Grade B** | **22km** | **6 hours** | **OS Sheet 6** | **Tidal Port Dover**
Start/Finish	△◯ Car park at Dingieshowe Beach (549 034)
HW	HW in Deer Sound is 30 minutes before HW Dover.
Tidal Times	At Mull Head the SE going tidal stream starts 4 hours 30 minutes before HW Dover. The NW going tidal stream starts 1 hour 20 minutes after HW Dover. In the Copinsay Pass the SW going stream starts 4 hours 55 minutes before HW Dover. The NE going stream starts 15 minutes after HW Dover.
Max Rate at Sp	Around Mull Head is 2.7 knots. In Copinsay Pass is 3 knots.
Coastguard	Shetland

Introduction

The Deerness (animal shaped) peninsula is almost separated from the Orkney Mainland, except for a narrow isthmus of sand dunes lying parallel to the road. This location provides excellent access to the water on either side of the road. Paddling around the peninsula gives a unique viewpoint of the rugged coastline, which is dotted with a myriad of deep geos, caves, sandy beaches and important historic sites.

Description

The car park and toilets are well signposted as you drive along the narrow isthmus of land (on the A960) which joins Deerness to the rest of the Orkney mainland. Planning your start time near to HW on the north side of the isthmus will ensure a short walk across the shallow bay within Peter's Pool. An easy and sheltered first section of paddling north into Deer Sound leads you past a ruined broch then east round Mirkady Point, where shallow rocks and a shingle shoreline lead to the open sea. The paddling becomes a little more exposed as you pass by the Covenanters Memorial, which boldly dominates the southern skyline like an oversized chess piece.

Covenanters Memorial

The Covenanters Memorial was built in 1888 to remember those who drowned whilst being shipped across the Atlantic to America to be sold as slaves. The cause of the ship being wrecked on the jagged reefs and eventually sinking was put down to the anchor cable breaking during a storm. Many of the crew above deck escaped, leaving the covenanters below deck behind battened hatches. Fortunately one crew member did assist, and 47 out of the 257 on board escaped. Unfortunately those that reached the shoreline were soon re-captured and shipped across the Atlantic.

After passing Denwick Bay the cliffs at Swin-Ber signal a change of scenery. Weathered sandstone cliffs and geos lead to the impressive cliffs and caves at Mull Head. Be aware of the effects of the tidal water which accelerates around the exposed headland. It is not unusual to find standing waves and clapotis along this coastline especially when there is an onshore wind from the north or east.

Before rounding the headland it is worth stopping off at a sheltered bay just below the summit trig point (marked on the OS map). Here the rock walls and caves overhang significantly, dwarfing the kayaks below. Take the time to savour the magical atmosphere created by the noise and smells of this 'seabird city' before heading back into the tidal current. Fulmars and black backed gulls are often seen soaring along the cliff tops using powerful updrafts of air to show off and perform effortless aerobatics whilst keenly scanning the sea and cliffs below for an easy meal.

Heading south towards the Brough of Deerness, check out an amazingly deep and narrow geo north of Howan Lickan (torch useful). The chasm eventually ends in a narrow dark slit in the rock, barred by a well-jammed buoy. Beyond the buoy, the boom and hiss of distant water at the end of the fissure enlivens the imagination and encourages a quick paddle back towards the sunlight. Many of the rocky coves, geos and beaches dotted along this section of coastline have an assorted selection of flotsam, including pieces of a washed up yacht (a reminder that the sea is not always friendly to mariners).

Access from the water to the Brough of Deerness is via a hidden bay (south of the island), which has a cave on its left which can often be full of seals. The Brough of Deerness can be accessed via a narrow cliff path and roped handrail along its south side. Once on top, it's possible to view the remaining walls of a monastery and numerous circular dips and ridges of an ancient settlement. The small monastery was a place of pilgrimage during the 17th century, and it is reported that male pilgrims would walk in circles around the chapel, chanting and scattering water and sharp stones on the path!

Yet more steep cliffs and some interesting rock arches will lead the paddler to 'The Gloup', a subterranean sea vent which has eroded inland along a fault line. Paddling through the cave entrance and into the main amphitheatre gives the paddler an exciting and unique view of the sheer rock walls. A small cave at the back is guarded by a waterfall.

Heading south for 1km, passing rocky inlets and a small rock stack, will lead you into Sandside Bay where there is a pleasant sandy beach to stretch your legs and take a break. An alternative get out is a small concrete pier close to the chapel and shallow reefs further south. The Skerries to the east of the bay are home to a playful colony of seals.

The steep cliffs past Tammy Tiffy sport yet more excellent caves and archways carved out of the soft sandstone just beyond the Back of the Breck.

At Point of Ayre check out the unusual volcanic rocks (basalt) before tackling the tidal currents which pass around the headland.

A low rocky shoreline and field boundaries lead to a wonderful beach at Newark Bay, which has stunning clear blue water and golden sands. There is excellent egress off the water from either a small car park area at the east end of the beach, or a recreational slipway facility owned by the Deerness Small Boat Owners Association, further west.

The last section of the journey follows broken cliffs past Muckle Castle (a small volcanic rock stack), a small cave and an archway before the end of the journey at Dingieshowe Bay. Dumping swell and a shallow reef in the centre of the bay may alert you to carefully selecting your exit point especially if the wind or swell is onshore.

Tide and weather

Be aware the tide goes out a long way on the north side of Sandi Sand, if you arrive there 3 hours either side of low water.

The tidal streams around Mull Head should be treated with caution. Tidal planning would be prudent, to ensure you are not fighting against fast moving water. Some tidal movement and an ever present weak north going eddy is felt along the rocky coastline between the Point of Ayre and Mull Head.

During strong winds from the north, east and south the exposed headlands and cliffs may be affected by standing waves and clapotis, which can cause difficulty for inexperienced paddlers. Therefore the journey described is best completed when there is a light to moderate wind from the WNW.

Additional information

An alternative start to the journey may be made from Northquoy Point (at the north end of the B9051) where there is a hidden and unspoilt sandy beach with easy access onto the water. Please park considerately at the beach access point as there is limited space.

The circular coastal path starting at The Gloup is an excellent way to see a number of the points of interest described within the journey. It is recommended as a superb walk if conditions for paddling are not suitable.

A short half-day paddle and exploration along the east coastline, from Sandside Bay heading north or south, is an excellent alternative for a shorter 'out and return' journey.

Admiralty Chart 2250, Imray Chart C68, and O.S. Explorer Map 461 cover this area.

Tankerness coastline | Doug Cooper

The String & Tankerness

| No. 12 | Grade B | 19km | 4-5 hours | OS Sheet 6 | Tidal Port Dover |

Start △ Slipway W of Kirkwall harbour (448 113)

Finish ◯ Mill Sand, Tankerness (513 077)

HW HW Kirkwall is 45 minutes before HW Dover.

Tidal Times The E going tidal stream within The String and Shapinsay Sound starts 5 hours 15 minutes before HW Dover.
The W going tidal stream within The String starts 45 minutes after HW Dover.
Slack water to the E of The String is approx 1 hour after HW Dover.

Max Rate at Sp In The String is 3.9 knots.
In Shapinsay Sound is 2.8 knots on an E going tide and 1.3 knots on a W going tide.

Coastguard Shetland

Cannon at The Ness, Tankerness | Chris Jex

Introduction

This memorable journey is ideally suited to the accompanied beginner or intermediate paddler. It takes in superb views of lighthouses, modern day castles, cliffs and a stunning view east towards the remote windswept island of Auskerry. The journey enters the notorious channel of water known as 'The String', passing a number of protruding headlands and along a superb rocky coastline.

Description

The journey starts from the slipway used by the ferry which heads back and forth between the island of Shapinsay (Helping island for ships) and Kirkwall (Kirk Bay). An adjacent car park, waiting room and toilets allow you to kit up and get onto the water in relative comfort. Once on the water, caution and a wide berth should be given to all other shipping within the busy area close to the pier. When clear of the harbour it is worth stopping to look back towards Kirkwall to admire the skyline, which is dominated by the spire of St Magnus Cathedral.

The coastline along the first section of the journey is low-lying farmland, the Kirkwall Bay Touring Park and a scattering of houses, which disperse as you near Iceland Skerry. The obvious low islet, which guards the entrance into The String, is known as 'Thieves Holm'. The small scruffy island is now equipped with a new navigational beacon/light on its high point. The sea area around the headland and Thieves Holm can be notoriously rough in windy conditions as this is where the tidal stream builds up speed as it is forced over an uneven shallow seabed.

Thieves Holm

It is said that those who had been tried and found guilty were condemned to die on this island because it was cheaper than having to hang them on the gallows. At one time it was customary to leave the corpses of wrongdoers clearly visible as a warning to all seafarers entering the harbour.

Thankfully this practice ceased some time ago and all you will see now are a few seals basking on the rocks with gulls, fulmars and eider ducks sheltering along the lee shoreline.

The next section of paddling whisks you through The String, past a cluster of wartime buildings and the Bay of Carness to the south. To the north is the prominent lighthouse on Heliar Holm and the prestigious Balfour Castle. In the foreground of the castle, close to the shore, is an unusual round tower which once housed a sea water shower (The Douche) and dovecot.

At the Head of Work you will find a small chambered cairn, just north of the 15m highpoint. A short rest here will enable you to prepare for the 5.5km open water crossing within the widening expanse of water known as the Shapinsay Sound. The tidal stream here is still very much in

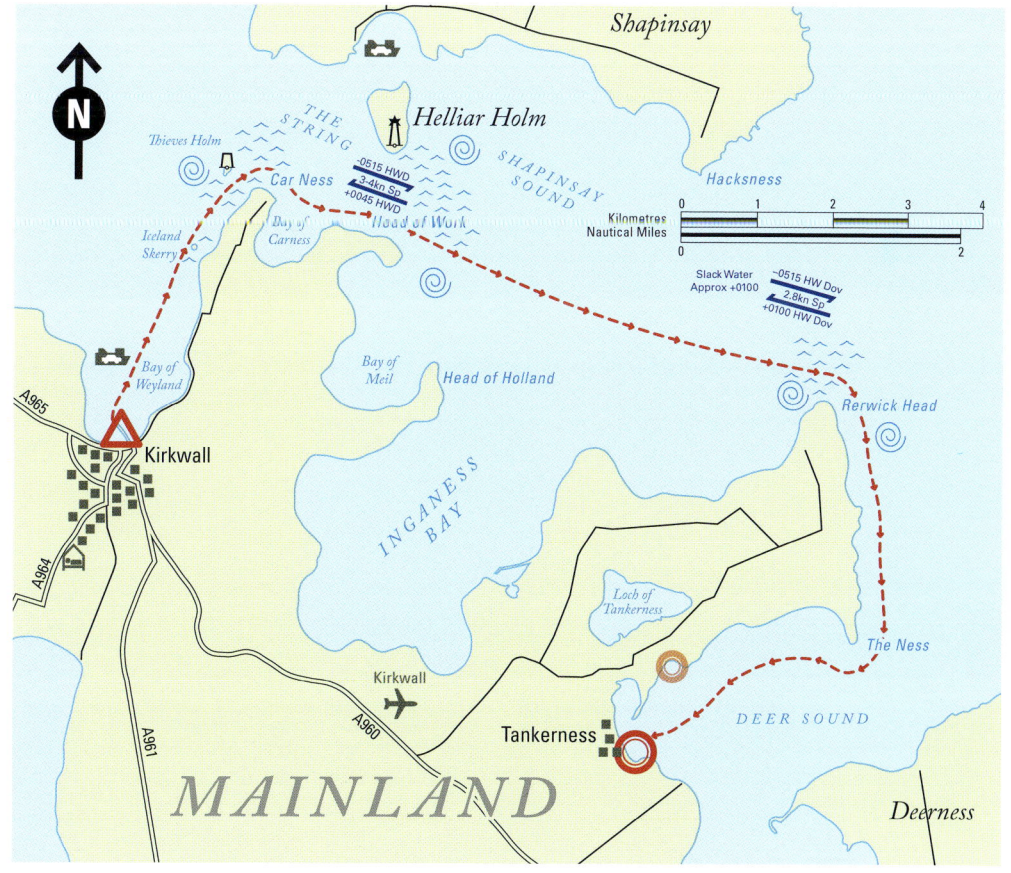

control, and paddlers should ensure they stay in close proximity to each other for safety. A long wide eddyline to the south of the main flow of water can create minor upwellings and confused water as you head ESE towards the low-lying headland of Rerwick Head.

Access at Rerwick Head, for visiting the Second World War gun emplacements and lookout buildings, is best found via the shingle beach west of the headland. If exploring the historic buildings, please be aware of your safety as many are now in a ruinous state. Look out for the calibration marks on the floor where the six-inch guns were mounted and the thick reinforced walls of the underground bunkers where ammunition was once stored.

The view north from here encompasses the steep cliffs along the east coast of Shapinsay, the wind turbines on Stronsay and the low lying island of Auskerry to the east, with its distinctive white lighthouse.

Once around the headland, the coastline leads the paddler along a steep rocky coastline. Here you can explore an amazing variety of caves, tunnels and rock stacks. These are particularly fine around the Hole of Roo, situated about 1km south of Rerwick Head.

At the end of the east facing shoreline there is an excellent egress point on either side of the peninsula. Here you can find the remains of a circular stone structure and a rusting cannon.

Deer Sound is home to waders and sea birds that gather in large numbers to feed in the shallow bays and remote sandy beaches along the sheltered south-facing coastline. This makes for a gentle warm-down before reaching the imposing Hall of Tankerness (possible get-out at low water).

The tidal egress point at Mill Sand is next to the sharp bend in the road and south of the de-consacrated church, now housing Sheila Fleet's jewellery workshop, gallery and café (marked on the O.S. map as a church).

Tide and weather

The tidal stream extending from Thieves Holm to Rerwick Head may need to be approached with some caution during strong winds and poor weather. The strength of the tide through the confined area within the channel should not be underestimated.

A small tidal overfall with standing waves may be present around Rerwick Head. The worst of this rough water can be easily avoided by staying close to the shoreline.

Additional information

Kayakers should be aware of busy water traffic in and around the Kirkwall harbour area and within The String.

The journey described requires either two vehicles or a well-timed and remote hitchhike to enable you to return to the start point.

During the spring and summer months large cruise ships regularly visit Kirkwall Bay. A wide berth should be given and caution exercised.

Admiralty Charts 2249, 2250, Imray Chart C68, and O.S. Explorer Map 461 cover this area.

Scapa Flow, rainbow over Graemsay | Chris Jex

Scapa Flow

No. 13 | Grade A | 27km | 6 hours | OS Sheet 6 & 7 | Tidal Port Dover

Start	△ Marina slipway, Stromness (256 094)
Finish	⭕ Beach or slipway at Scapa Bay (442 081)
HW	HW Stromness is approximately 1 hour 45 minutes before HW Dover.
Tidal Times	The incoming, E going stream at Houton Head starts 6 hours after HW Dover. The outgoing, W going stream starts 25 minutes before HW Dover.
Tidal Rates	In Clestrain Sound is 5 knots. This quickly reduces to 1 knot S of Houton Head.
Coastguard	Shetland

Introduction

The journey along the coastline of Scapa Flow (Ship Isthmus Bay) between Stromness (Tidal Stream Point) and Kirkwall (Kirk Bay) is a popular introduction to many paddlers who visit Orkney. There are numerous cliffs, golden sandy beaches and waterfalls to be explored along this enclosed and relatively sheltered section of coastline which, like the whisky produced close to the finish of the journey, should never be rushed.

Tug boats, Scapa Pier | Chris Jex

Stromness

Stromness or Hamnavoe (the Haven), as it was once known, was visited between 1690 and 1815 by a growing number of merchant ships. They chose the longer but safer northerly sea route to avoid privateers in the English Channel. The Hudson Bay Company used the town to re-supply their sailing ships, which were en route to and from Canada, where they traded for furs with the indigenous people of the north. The company had a head office in the town and employed a substantial number of Orcadian workers during the 18th and 19th Centuries. During the same period over 30 whaling boats would visit each year to replenish supplies before heading back to Greenland to fill their holds with whale meat and oil.

The herring boom at the start of the 20th century attracted over 400 fishing boats, which, during the short two month season, caught bountiful supplies of fish which were salted, barrelled and taken to fish markets throughout Scotland.

Description

The slipway (opposite the car park and public toilet as you head south into Stromness) north of the marina provides an excellent departure point. Once on the water, the numerous stone piers, waterfront houses and slipways squeezed in along this busy shoreline give the paddler a glimpse of the history and maritime importance of Stromness. The ferry traffic, tourists and visitors to the marina continue to make good use of the excellent amenities, cosmopolitan atmosphere and hospitality available in the town.

Once past the Inner and Outer Holm islands, the paddler has the choice of either heading east out into open water or following the low-lying, north shoreline into the shallow but pleasant Bay of Ireland.

If heading into open water it is wise to plan to travel with the tidal current as it becomes constricted between Stromness and the island of Graemsay. If choosing to follow the north coastline, be aware of a large, slow-moving back-eddy within the Bay of Ireland. This flows anticlockwise around the shoreline, starting from the Skerries of Clestrain, during the incoming east going tide.

The low-lying coastline leads the paddler past the starboard buoy at Peter Skerry and past the high ground known as Houton Head. High on the headland a number of old searchlights and gun emplacements overlook the westerly entrance into Scapa Flow. A number of smaller lookout posts can be seen lower down on the shoreline.

Arctic explorer – John Rae

The square shaped Hall of Clestrain, close to the Skerries of Clestrain, was the birthplace and home of the courageous Arctic explorer John Rae (1813-1893). John Rae was condemned by the 'establishment' because of his controversial report regarding the survivors of the Franklin expedition in1845, which stated that the hungry men had turned to cannibalism in order to survive. It is now accepted that his report was relatively accurate.

John Rae is now rightly recognised as the person who helped discover the final route through the inhospitable frozen wastelands of the Northwest Passage.

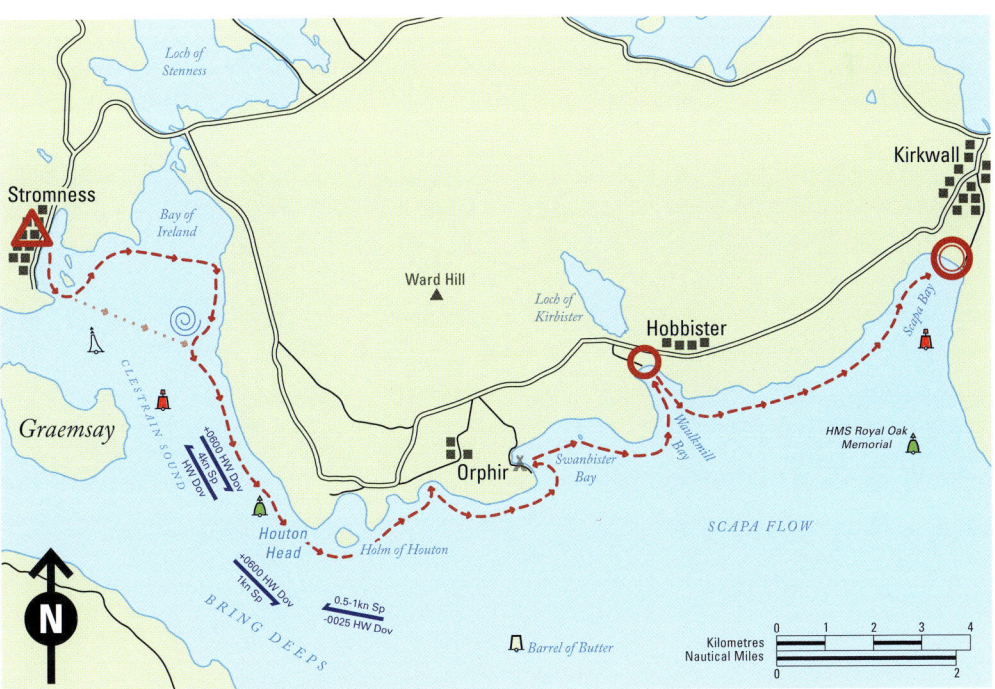

St Magnus Cathedral | Mark Rainsley

Scapa Flow

13

The tide, having spent all its energy within Clestrain Sound, now slows to a mere half knot as you paddle past the Holm of Houton which is home to a resident colony of seals. The Bay of Houton provides a superb sheltered anchorage due to the narrow deep water entrance. The Vikings moored their fighting warships here in 1263 after a foray to the Clyde. The biggest was said to be rowed by at least 100 fighting men.

During the two World Wars, Houton Bay was used as a major base for restocking warships and as a base for flying planes. Remains of broken slipways and the foundations of a number of large aircraft and air balloon hangers are still evident.

The 'Grand Scuttle'

While absorbing the view south across Scapa Flow, try to picture the scene on 21st June 1919 when over seventy captured German battleships were scuttled on the orders of Admiral Von Reuter. Many of the large battleships 'turned turtle', coming to rest upside down on the seabed. Many others were left beached or partially submerged.

The immense job of recovering the precious metal was carried out by a number of determined salvage companies; their work continuing until the end of the 1970s.

Out of over seventy scuttled ships there are now only three battleships, four light cruisers and four destroyers left on the seabed. Scapa Flow is widely recognised as one the best wreck diving locations in the world.

Sandstone strata near Roo Point | Chris Jex

Continuing past the Bay of Myre you arrive in Orphir Bay. Here a worthwhile visit to the Orkneyinga Saga Centre and the 'Earl's Bu' enables you to watch a free audiovisual display about the Norse Earls, many of whom lived in Orkney.

The steepening shoreline leads past the headland at Toy Ness, an attractive sandy beach west of Smoogro Skerry and the heather clad headland at Ve Ness. The shallow skerry below the headland, known as The Lash, gives way to one of Orkney's most beautiful hidden beaches. Depending on the state of the tide, Waulkmill Bay is either a large area of drying sand or a beautiful sheltered bay full of azure coloured water. A toilet block at the top of the steps to the east of the bay gives access to a clean water supply.

The maritime heath and heather clad hillside to the east of Waulkmill Bay is owned by the RSPB, who manage the Hobbister Nature Reserve. The steep coastline has a picturesque waterfall and a number of small rocky bays. In many places, especially near Roo Point, the soft eroded cliffs show an amazing array of red, orange and yellow hues. They also provide suitable nesting sites for cormorants, guillemots and fulmars.

At the entrance to Scapa Bay a number of shallow, sandy bays provide a sheltered anchorage for small yachts. Egress off the water can be made via the crescent shaped beach or the slipway on the north side of the pier.

The sight of the whitewashed Scapa Distillery building to the left of the beach, the pyramid shaped Orkney Harbour headquarters and the protruding spire of Kirkwall Cathedral straight ahead, indicate that you are at the end of this journey. On the skyline, to the west, the distinct shape of the Highland Park distillery beckons you onto terra-firma for a toast to a good day's paddling.

Overnight camp, Stromness and ferry | Mark Rainsley

Tide and weather

Tidal planning is required for the first section of the journey, especially if planning to paddle within Clestrain Sound. Paddling against the strong tidal current here is not advised. The best time to start the journey is approximately 6 hours after HW Dover, whilst the east-going tidal stream is still weak. The journey is relatively sheltered from any ocean swell and the open sea, but be aware of short steep wind blown waves which build quickly from the south.

The journey from Houton to Scapa is best completed when there is a northerly wind, the shore is then sheltered except for the area within the Bay of Ireland.

Additional information

The journey described requires two vehicles or the use of the regular bus service which runs between Kirkwall and Stromness.

Before heading north-east into Scapa Bay it is possible to extend the paddle by visiting the Royal Oak Memorial Buoy situated on the east side of the bay. Details regarding this historic landmark can be found within Chapter 10 (Holm and Roseness) which may also be used as a continuation to your journey.

The route can be split into several smaller journeys and there are numerous options for camping or egress en route.

Admiralty Charts 35, 2249, 2568, Imray Chart C68, and O.S. Explorer Map 462 & 463 cover this area.

Sunset over Loch Harray | Chris Jex

Lochs of Stenness & Harray

No. 14 | **Grade A** | **16.5km** | **4-6 hours** | **OS Sheet 5**

Start	△ Track close to The Ness (259 151)
Finish	○ Merkister Hotel (297 190)
Tides	No tidal streams affect this area.
Coastguard	Shetland

Introduction

The Loch of Stenness (Stone Point) and Loch of Harray (Inland District) are recognised as one of the UK's largest tidal estuaries. There are over 43km of unspoilt shoreline around the inland sea estuary, which is one of Orkney's most popular inland bird breeding areas. There is also a diverse range of wildlife and excellent historic sites. The water within the inland sea lochs may be shallow, especially in the Loch of Harray, where in some places it is possible to stand up in the middle of the loch!

Looking south across the Loch of Stenness | Chris Jex

As recognition of the area's important archaeological status the Ring of Brodgar, the Watch Stone and the Standing Stones of Stenness (all easily visited from the water) were given UNESCO World Heritage Site status in 1999.

Description

The starting point for the journey is in the north-west corner of the Loch of Stenness, opposite two small islands next to the land promontory called The Ness. Access onto the water is via a grassy track leading off the narrow road west of the houses. Vehicle drivers should park considerately and not block access to the fields or house driveways.

The first section of the journey follows a low shoreline south-east for 2.5km. After this relatively easy section, an open water crossing of the loch will bring you to the Unstan Chambered Cairn.

Access to the cairn can be made via a hidden sheltered lagoon on the left, 50m past the white house. From the lagoon carefully access the public track and path which lead to the cairn. The Unstan Cairn was excavated in 1844 revealing one of Scotland's largest ever finds of Stone Age pottery (now housed in the Royal Museum, Edinburgh). During the excavation two human skeletons were found buried in a crouching position.

The entrance to the loch is frequented by seals, otters and a host of birdlife. This is mainly due to the slow moving sea water flowing in and out under the Bridge of Waithe. A 1.5km paddle north-east across to the north shoreline of the loch brings you to a shallow bay and a fenced pathway leading to the mystical Ring of Brodgar. This impressive stone circle has in place twenty-seven of the original sixty standing stones, an outer ditch and a number of outlying standing stones and cairns. The high ground on top of the rounded cairn to the west makes an excellent viewing point.

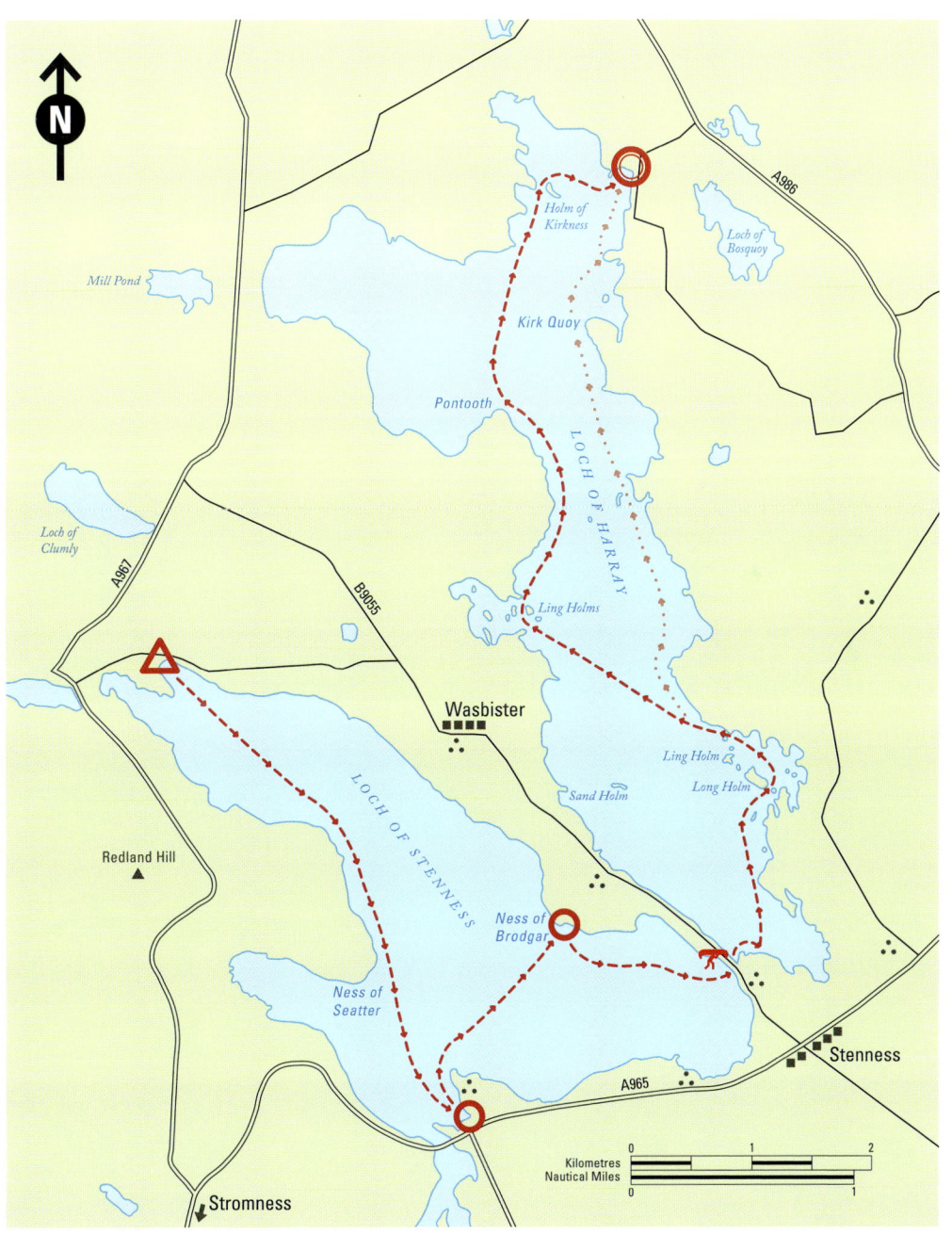

The Ring of Brodgar | Chris Jex

Festivals in Orkney

A wide variety of public events and social gatherings take place throughout the year in Orkney. These include: the Orkney Jazz Festival (late April), the Orkney Nature Festival (mid May), the Orkney Folk Festival (late May), the St Magnus Festival (late June), Stromness Shopping Week (late July), various mainland and island agricultural shows (July & August), the County Show (mid August), the Orkney Rock Festival (early September), the Orkney International Science Festival (September), the Orkney Blues Festival (late September), the Orkney Story-telling Festival (october), the Kirkwall Christmas and New Year Ba' (traditional street ball game), and the Stromness Yule-Log Pull (December).

Following the shore eastwards, head towards the imposing standing stone. The Watch Stone (5.5m high) stands sentinel over the causeway, marking the portage point across the road. Access is easiest at the south end of the causeway, where the adjacent lay-by can be used to safely shuttle kayaks across the road. The portage provides an excellent opportunity to observe the amazing number of mute swans and the occasional lazing seals which frequent the shallow water at this end of the loch.

After the short portage, follow the southerly shoreline east for approximately 200m. At a convenient grassy get out point you can visit the Burnhouse Settlement. The well-preserved foundations and remains of a majestic feasting hall, and many small dwellings, are clearly outlined. The

Loch of Stenness – storm approaching | Chris Jex

settlement is thought to have been built and used at the same time as Skara Brae, Orkney's other UNESCO World Heritage site and well-known Neolithic settlement.

A pathway heading south-west leads you to a majestic stone circle known as the Stones of Stenness. The remaining four out of twelve tall stones are testament to human skill and ingenuity over five thousand years ago.

The southerly corner of the Loch of Harray hosts a wide range of migratory and nesting birds. Keeping a watch amongst the shallow reed beds may reward you with a sighting of an elusive otter. The journey follows the shoreline north towards a sheltered area of water and islands known as Ling and Long Holm. To the east of the islands is a small picnic area.

Those still interested in exploring should paddle along the east shoreline for about 500m and then head WNW across the open shallow water to the other side of the loch, where the remains of an ancient broch lie on a distinct promontory of land. The large area of tall reeds within the bay to the west is another prime site for spotting otters.

From the west shore of the Loch of Harray head north towards the Holm of Kirkness passing the visible remains of the Burrian Broch on the easterly shoreline. This ruined broch is one of many hundreds dotted around the shores and coastlines of Orkney.

The last kilometre of paddling leads you to the final get out point and the welcome sight of the Merkister Hotel. Egress from the water to the road and hotel can be made next to a small boathouse adjacent to the road or a rough slipway within the Hotel grounds. The hotel is well known for its hospitality, superb food and well stocked bar.

Burnhouse Settlement | Chris Jex

Tide and weather

The Loch of Stenness is affected by a very small rise and fall of the tide. Water flows in and out of the loch via a shallow channel under the Bridge of Waithe. The Loch of Harray is unaffected due to a one way sluice in the dam constructed under the causeway.

The low lying land gives very little protection from the short, choppy waves, which quickly form as the wind increases.

Additional Information

The journey described requires a vehicle shuttle to get back to the start point. Alternatively, plan your journey to return back to the start point.

Access to all the archaeological sites mentioned is free of charge. Visitors are requested to respect these sites and not cross fences or marked off areas within them. Please take all rubbish home or use the bins provided at the sites.

Each year in July/August, there is an annual round up of the swans on the loch. The purpose of this exciting event is to ring and count the juvenile birds. If you are in Orkney during this time, and want to take part in the round up, contact the RSPB office in Stromness for information. The more kayakers on the water, the better!

Please be aware of nesting birds during the breeding season in spring/summer.

Please be courteous to the fishermen who may be seen along the shoreline or in boats on the water during the fishing season when the lochs are regularly used for competitions.

Admiralty Chart 2249, Imray Chart C68, and O.S. Explorer Map 463 cover this area.

Black Craig, Billia Croo | Doug Cooper

Stromness to Skaill

No. 15 | Grade C | 18km | 4 hours | OS Sheet 6 | Tidal Port Dover

Start	△ Sailing Club Slipway, Stromness (254 081)
Finish	○ Beach at Skaill Bay (235 192)
HW	HW Stromness is approximately 1 hour 45 minutes before HW Dover.
Tidal Times	In Hoy Sound, between Ness Point and Graemsay, the W outgoing tidal stream begins at HW Dover. The E incoming tidal stream begins 6 hours after HW Dover.
	At 6 hours after HW Dover there is a weak S going coastal tidal stream between Row Head and Breck Ness. This is caused by the offshore E going tidal stream dividing N and S at Row Head.
	At HW Dover the coastal tidal stream along the W coast becomes a weak N going tidal stream and more affected by localised eddys.
Max Rate at Sp	In Hoy Sound is 8.5 knots.
	To the W of Hoy Sound is 4 knots.
	Along the W coast is up to 1 knot in either direction
Coastguard	Shetland

Stromness | Mark Rainsley

Introduction

This delightful journey involves an exciting paddle through one of the fastest flowing sea channels within Orkney, which gives access to the open sea and the remote west coast. Along this storm battered coastline, paddlers will be rewarded with some of the most spectacular and imposing headlands, cliffs and caves to be found in Orkney.

Description

Access onto the water may be found at the sailing club's slipway close to the municipal camp site at the Point of Ness. Once on the water, paddle past the campsite. At low water, give the shallow skerries at the Point of Ness (marked by the prominent navigational light) a wide berth.

Depending on the state of the tide, the journey through Hoy Sound can vary from glassy, flat calm water to a wild roller coaster of waves and confused current. If at this stage of the journey the direction of the flow in Hoy Sound is not in your favour, start from the beach access point, and car park at Warebeth, further west.

The shoreline alongside the golf course has a number of military lookout posts and an army barracks high on the hill overlooking the westerly entrance into Scapa Flow. Shallow reefs at Kirk Rocks, just after the cemetery, and at Braga, just before the headland at Breck Ness, can produce big waves from a seemingly flat sea. Caution should be observed when close to these reefs.

The prominent ruined walls of Breckness House, built in 1633 by Bishop Graham at Breck Ness, mark a change of direction leading you towards the looming cliffs of Black Craig. In the

The Castle of North Gaulton | Doug Cooper

boulder strewn bay before the cliff there is a substation, built to oversee the European Marine Energy Station. The deep water area to the west is clearly marked with the associated cardinal buoys warning shipping to avoid this sensitive test area.

The next 5km of coastline from Black Craig to Yesnaby consists of continuous cliffs, allowing little respite for paddlers. The cliffs are riddled with small caves, testament to the power of the strong westerly storms which lash this coast during the winter months.

Neban Point marks the halfway point on this 18km journey and is prone to a small amount of tidal movement. North of the headland you will discover an amazing rock stack called North Gaulton Castle. From the landward side, the jagged east arête soars steeply out of the water. Approximately 1km further north, a square cut headland marked as the Point of Lyregeo leads to a long steep north-facing wall of rock, and an interesting geo and cave.

The next headland, Inga Ness, marks the start of a popular coastal walk and area known as Yesnaby. This picturesque coastline attracts a large number of locals, tourists and climbers throughout the year due to its rocky headlands, secluded bays and magnificent rock pinnacle in Garthna Geo (to the south of the car park area). The rock stack, known as the Castle of Yesnaby, was first climbed in 1967 by the adventurous climbing team who also climbed a number of major new routes on the Old Man of Hoy. Numerous caves indent this impressive coastline. Within the bay there is a smaller rock stack still clinging to the mainland via a precarious archway. A long south facing wall and offshore reef lie adjacent to the wedge shaped headland. On the headland's north side a number of small bays show the scars of a once productive quarry area; the stone being cut for millstones. A deceptively deep through-tunnel and cave can be explored in the second of the small bays, at mid to low water.

Skara Brae

This unique and well-preserved Neolithic settlement lies at the south end of Skaill Bay. The site was revealed after a storm and unusually high tide, which washed and blew away the dune system protecting the ancient site which was buried for over 4,000 years.

Excavation started in 1860s but did not fully uncover the whole site until the site was re-opened in the early 20th century, when it came into state care. In total, seven well preserved houses, a workshop and linked narrow corridors and alleyways reveal an immense amount about how our ancestors lived, worked and survived.

Detailed excavations revealed forms of damp-proofing (raised clay flooring), drainage, guttering and fine stonework in the form of dressing tables, porches, internal shelving, cells and beds. Artefacts including bone tools and jewellery were found. A number of skeletons were also found underneath one of the walls.

An interpretation centre with museum of artefacts and audiovisual presentation is an excellent way to understand and interpret how our past ancestors lived their lives. A replica house close to the visitor centre and admission to Skaill House museum (an excellent bad weather option) is included in the price of visiting this popular and important UNESCO World Heritage site.

After all the exploration and excitement it is worth stopping at either of the small sheltered bays after the steep headland of the Brough of Bigging. Give a wide berth to the reefs just offshore especially if there is a westerly swell running. The view of the Old Man of Hoy and St John's Head to the south rewards those who walk up to the cairn atop the prominent headland. Once back on the water it may be possible to paddle under a leaning rock archway north of the bay. Open caves and steep cliffs lead to the windswept Broch of Borwick, and a small rocky beach.

Further north, the black cliffs lead to the deep geo known as the Ness of Ramnageo where a number of waterfalls spill over the cliff edge into the sea. The entrance into the geo is hidden from view, so closer inspection is required. The steep black cliffs either side of the geo give the paddler a welcome break from the swell.

The final set of cliffs leading up to, and beyond, Row Head (55m) offer an opportunity to explore deep and spectacular caves, one of which is cathedral-like with its high roof and long deep fissure. At the back of Yettna Geo, to the right, is an ominous and deep recess with a cavernous interior. The final headland before turning east into the Bay of Skaill has an impressive round archway. During strong south-west to west winds or when there is a large swell, water is forced through this hole providing an exciting spout. A fine spectacle for those on land, but more worrying for those brave enough to be on the sea!

The Bay of Skaill has two reef breaks at each side of the bay. Be careful not to hug the coastline too close when heading into the bay, otherwise you may find yourself surfing the steep clean waves towards shallow rocks. The sandy seabed and steep boulder backdrop of the beach give easy egress to a toilet block, fresh water tap, car park and road.

Tide and weather

The best time to complete this paddle is after a consolidated spell of calm weather. Low pressure systems far out in the Atlantic to the south-west through to north-west may affect the sea swell along the west coast of Orkney, even when wind and weather seem calm.

Due to the inaccessibility of the coastline and lack of egress points, it is advised that paddlers realistically assess their ability to cope with exposed and open water conditions.

It is imperative to plan and check the tidal currents at the start of the journey, due to the fast moving and unforgiving currents which race through Hoy Sound. Tidal stream times can be up to 30 minutes before or after the stated times in this guide depending on the prevailing wind direction, swell from the west, and size of the tidal range. Departing Stromness at approximately HW Dover is advised.

Additional information

Please be careful not to block access to the slipway in Stromness.

Carry snacks and safety equipment close to hand whilst on the water so as not to get dehydrated, hungry or caught out if an emergency arises.

Many of the caves are only accessible at certain states of the tide. Be aware of low lying reefs and quick building ocean swell when close to the coastline.

Admiralty Charts 2249, 2568, 35, Imray Chart C68, and O.S. Explorer Map 463 cover this area.

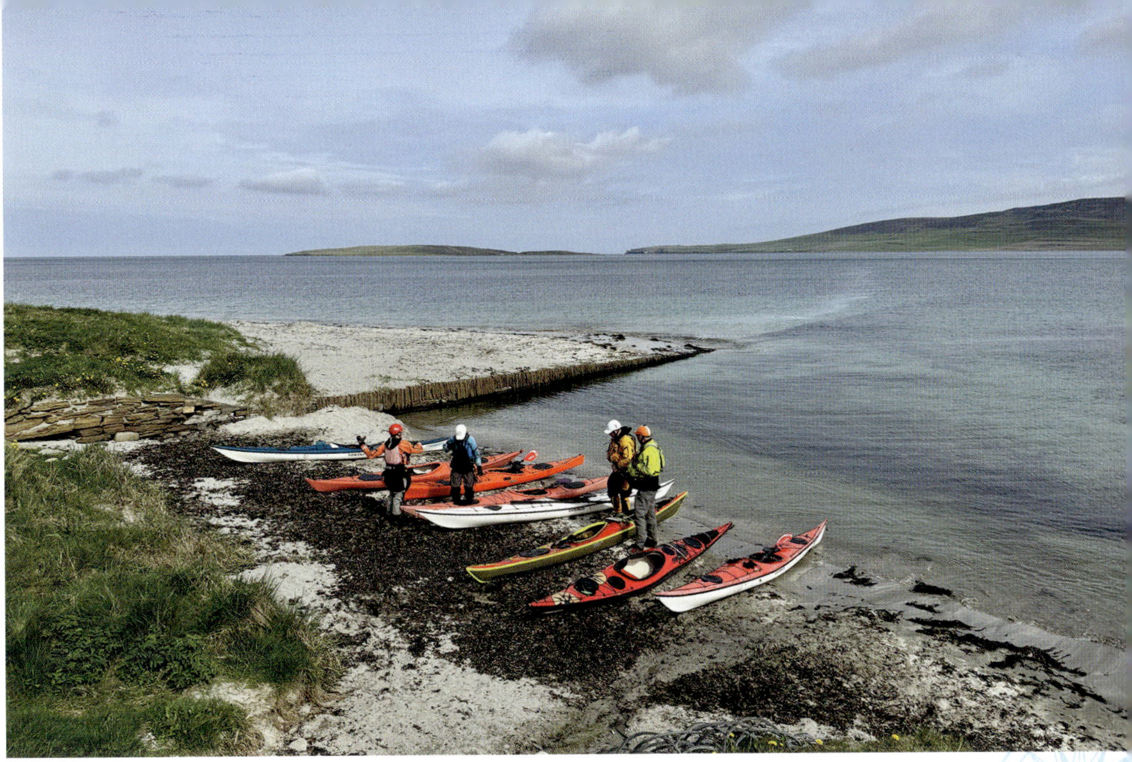

Evie to Marwick

No. 16 | **Grade C** | **23km** | **5 hours** | **OS Sheet 6** | **Tidal Port Dover**

Start	△ Car park at Broch of Gurness (380 268) or pier at Sands of Evie (373 266)
Finish	⭕ Beach at Marwick Bay (229 241)
HW	HW Eynhallow Sound is 1 hour 40 minutes before HW Dover.
Tidal Times	The W going tidal stream at the Point of Hellia starts at HW Dover. The E going stream starts 6 hours before HW Dover.
	At Burgar Rost (shallow channel S of Eynhallow) the outgoing NW stream starts 30 minutes after HW Dover. The incoming SE stream starts 5 hours 30 minutes before HW Dover
	Slack water at Brough Head is approximately 6 hours before HW Dover.
Max Rate at Sp	In Eynhallow Sound is 3.3 knots.
	In the shallow channel S of Eynhallow is 7 knots.
	Around Costa Head, Standard Rock and Brough Head is 2 knots.
Coastguard	Shetland

Common seal colony, The Brough of Birsay | Mark Rainsley

16 Evie to Marwick

Introduction

Paddling along the north-west coastline of Orkney, from Evie (Back Current in a River) to Marwick via the Brough of Birsay (Island of the Enclosure or Rampart), enables you to experience the grandeur of the north coast's spectacular cliffs. The cliffs spurn the pounding Atlantic swells and this journey takes in some of the most exposed and remote paddling to be found within Orkney waters. Paddlers should be confident at handling sea swell, awkward clapotis and the lack of egress available en route.

Description

Access to the water is from either a large car park area next to the Broch of Gurness or via a small lane leading to the west end of the beach at the Sands of Evie (public toilet and small pier). A short paddle and warm up lead you to the tidal race and overfalls located between the island of Eynhallow and the Orkney Mainland.

At the headland named Haafs Hellia the mixture of confused water, clapotis and tidal waters cause the sea to rear up in confusion as the water rushes around the headland and along the base of the 150m high cliffs. Getting close to the cliffs to inspect the caves and dark recesses can be a tricky business; the sea state and swell should be given healthy respect.

The scale of the cliffs creates an eerie atmosphere as you paddle onwards to one of the most picturesque rock pinnacles in Orkney. Standard Rock is festooned with nesting birds during spring. At its base there is an underwater tunnel and the seabed is full of scoured rocks and

round boulders. The sea state around here is rarely calm, but it is worth paddling through the gap between the stack and the cliffs. When you reach the calmer waters on the other side of the stack you can relax a little, take sanctuary from the bouncing swell, and have a slightly less tight grip on your paddle!

Close behind the rock stack there are a number of deep caves. One of them is cathedral like in height and depth, and worth paddling to the back of, to take in the amazing view when looking back out to sea.

High above the caves and cliffs, on top of Costa Hill, lie the remains of a wartime lookout point and remnants of the UK's first ever aero-generator (built in the 1950's). Its remains, and a wartime lookout point, are all that is left on the windswept peak. The cliffs continue for another 1.5km until they drop in height to a small rocky bay with a short pinnacle on its east side. This low lying area of land is marked as Oyce on the OS map. Egress here is marginal but possible over a shallow rocky seabed close to a small rock stack (extreme care needed when there is any ocean swell).

The next 4km of paddling eases slightly, allowing you to absorb this rugged, barren coastline where a number of ill fated ships, sailing in rough or foggy conditions, have foundered onto the rocks beneath the imposing cliffs. The small headland and outlying submerged reefs at Whitaloo Point enable you to explore a deep geo, which extends 250m inland. As you head back out of the geo, have a look for a cave entrance on the westerly headland. This opening (if there is not too much swell) will lead you through a dog-leg shaped tunnel underneath the headland and out through the other side (not for the faint hearted).

Continue along the coastline past a number of large easy angled rock slabs. At Skipi Geo a shelving pebble beach enables you to get a well deserved break, stretch your legs and take a closer look at the Fishermen's Hut and the 'nousts', once used to store fishing boats during the winter months.

Deep cave and Standard Rock | Chris Jex

At Brough Head there is a concrete causeway across the isthmus, which is only accessible during periods of LW. If you choose to take a shortcut and paddle between the Brough and the Headland, be aware of the concrete pathway which can form into an unfriendly weir when submerged!

On the west side of Brough Head an automated lighthouse faces out to sea overlooking the precipitous cliff edge. In calm weather search out a number of deep geos and caves below the lighthouse which will entice the kayaker inwards to explore. On the sheltered east side of the island a well preserved Viking settlement and chapel dating back to the 6th or 7th century are a popular tourist attraction at low water. The Brough of Birsay is also a well known location for cetacean spotting due to its height and location which is also especially appealing to the the comical clown-like puffins, that nest in burrows along the north side of the island. Be aware of a rising tide if you decide to walk across the causeway; otherwise you may get stranded!

The change in paddling direction, after rounding the Brough of Birsay, leads you past the village of Birsay and a sandy shoreline. Within the village are the walled remains of the Earl's Palace, a stronghold of the Earls of Orkney during the 12th century. The striking skyline to the south marks the start of Marwick Head. The towering sandstone cliffs and the Kitchener Memorial (a stone tower at the highpoint of the headland) lie within the impressive RSPB reserve.

Across the shallow sandy bay can be seen the bright green algae and dripping waterfall which marks the first of many caves. The cacophony made by swooping fulmars, guillemots, razorbills, puffins, soaring kittiwakes and diving gannets can be deafening. The number of birds congregating here during the breeding season has to be seen to be believed. This is one of Orkney's most impressive and hidden sights. The sea swell and associated clapotis in this area need to be given

Brough of Birsay | Doug Cooper

respect, as shallow rocky reefs lurk beneath the precipitous cliffs. On calmer days it is possible to paddle behind a long drying reef (beneath the memorial tower), giving shelter from the swell.

The Kitchener Memorial

The striking square shaped tower was built to commemorate Field Marshall Lord Kitchener, who died along with all but twelve of the crew of HMS *Hampshire* on the 5th June 1916, when the warship hit a German mine in open seas west of the cliffs.

The warship and the Minister for War were posted on a secret mission to talk with the Russian government. The rescue of survivors who were washed ashore was greatly delayed due to the warship's journey being under the cover of night; part of the measures taken to prevent information about the mission reaching Germany.

As you leave the main amphitheatre the guano streaked cliffs give way to easier angled rock and the Bay of Marwick, where a rocky reef protects an inner sandy lagoon at low water. Be wary of the reef if paddling over it during shallow water periods. The car park is situated at the south end of the bay. If you arrive after the outer reef is revealed, be prepared to complete a short portage over slippery rocks to gain access to the lagoon and final egress point. Alternatively, get out to the south of the car park area and portage the kayaks along a well worn track.

Tide and weather

A period of calm weather leading up to the journey will ease the swell and increase the comfort of paddling along this superb but exposed coastline. The journey is best avoided if the wind has been in excess of Force 3-4 from the west, north or north-east … or if such conditions are forecast.

Tidal streams affect three main areas: Eynhallow Sound, Costa Head/Standard Rock and Brough Head. These will all have either standing waves or clapotis during tidal movement in both directions. There is a noticeable easing of tidal movement when paddling close to the north coastline (when the tidal stream is heading west). This is due to the tidal stream being deflected WNW out into the Atlantic.

There is negligible tidal movement at Marwick Head. Be aware of any prevailing Atlantic swell and the lack of egress after leaving Birsay Bay.

Additional information

Taking into account the small number of get out points, it is wise to carry emergency equipment, food and water close to hand, as you may need them whilst in your kayak.

A visit to Eynhallow may be included in the itinerary if time allows. The island (a Nature Reserve) contains the well preserved and decorative remains of the earliest known Benedictine monastic settlement in Orkney. The island is populated by a large number of seabirds and seals.

Be wary of paddling through the channel to the east of the Brough of Birsay as there may be shallow rocks and a concrete walkway submerged under the shallow fast moving water. If sea conditions are marginal or too rough around the Brough of Birsay, an alternative safer egress can be found at Skipi Geo along the north coast.

It is possible to shorten the journey by getting out at a sandy beach and slipway on the south side of the concrete causeway at Birsay, after rounding the Brough of Birsay.

Admiralty Chart 2249, Imray Chart C68, and O.S. Explorer Map 463 cover this area.

Auskerry Lighthouse | Phil Berry

Auskerry

| No. 17 | Grade C | 31km | 7 hours | OS Sheet 5 & 6 | Tidal Port Dover |

Start/Finish	Sandside Bay (589 069)
HW	HW in Deer Sound is 30 minutes before HW Dover.
Tidal Times	The SE going tidal stream starts 4 hours 30 minutes before HW Dover, turning S about 1 hour after HW Dover. The NW going stream starts 1 hour 20 minutes after HW Dover.
Max Rate at Sp	NE of Mull Head and around the coastline of Auskerry is 2.7 knots.
Coastguard	Shetland

Introduction

The open sea crossing to Auskerry (East Skerry) involves a committing 10km journey in order to reach one of the least visited islands in Orkney. Auskerry is home to a single dwelling where a family occasionally lives during the warmer months of the year. The 34m high lighthouse, partly converted into a summer retreat, towers over the small low lying island offering a welcome sight to any mariner entering Orkney from the east. Once on the island (after asking permission if the landowners are in residence) a well deserved circular walk should include the lighthouse, the ruined chapel, the Bronze Age house remains and a number of standing stones.

South Geo, Auskerry | Chris Jex

Description

Access to the water is via a rough track (just after a small bridge on the single lane road) leading to Sandside Bay. The beautiful sandy beach offers excellent access to the east coastline of the Deerness peninsula. The first 3km of paddling along the cliff-lined coastline towards Mull Head acts as a good introduction and warm up for the crossing to Auskerry and is an excellent short paddle in its own right.

The crossing is on a bearing of 52° True when aiming from Mull Head to the lighthouse at the south end of Auskerry. These two prominent landmarks give the paddler excellent transit markers with which to gauge their position once in open water. Although this is not a busy sea passage, be aware of large vessels heading in or out of Kirkwall Bay or along the east side of Orkney. There are regular sightings of porpoise, minke and killer whales in this area especially during the spring and summer months, so it is worth keeping an eye open for rising dorsal fins, especially on calm days.

Head anticlockwise around the island taking in the rugged, rocky east coast first. Here you can still see the rusting remains of the *Hasting County,* driven onto shallow rocks in 1926. The rocky, angular reefs give way to shallow waters and a number of rocky beaches at the north end of the island. On the west side of the island there is an excellent get out point at South Geo, next to a sheltered inlet and jetty. In the past, the jetty was the lifeline link between Kirkwall and Auskerry and was used to unload weekly mail and essential provisions for the islanders and lighthouse keepers.

If you are visiting during the summer months, you may not be alone. The family who live on the island at this time of year will no doubt be busy crofting and looking after the unique North Ronaldsay breed of sheep which are bred and reared on the island. If you pass by, a courteous chat and friendly hello is always appreciated. Other visitors known to regularly visit are those studying the bird migrations and nest sites on Auskerry. Of particular interest are the 3,600 pairs of storm petrel which reside underground in burrows, only coming out to feed during late evening or at night. A more easily spotted bird is the common tern, of which there are over 780 pairs in residence during the spring/summer nesting period.

If staying overnight the best campsite (ask permission from landowner if present) is close to the lighthouse walls. With luck you will be able to see the storm petrels around the lighthouse area at dusk and in the beam of the light at night. This spectacle along with the eerie crying of seals on the shoreline makes for an atmospheric overnight stop.

After the open water crossing back to the Deerness peninsula, it is worth exploring the superb steep coastline incorporating a visit to the Brough of Deerness and The Gloup before returning to Sandside Bay. A more detailed description of this section of coastline is described within chapter number 11.

VARIATIONS

An alternative journey is to continue north across the shallow, and at times rough, Auskerry Sound. You can then paddle nothwards around the east side of Stronsay (chapter 20). The main attractions of this option are the impressive cliffs of Lamb Head, Burgh Head and Odness. Once

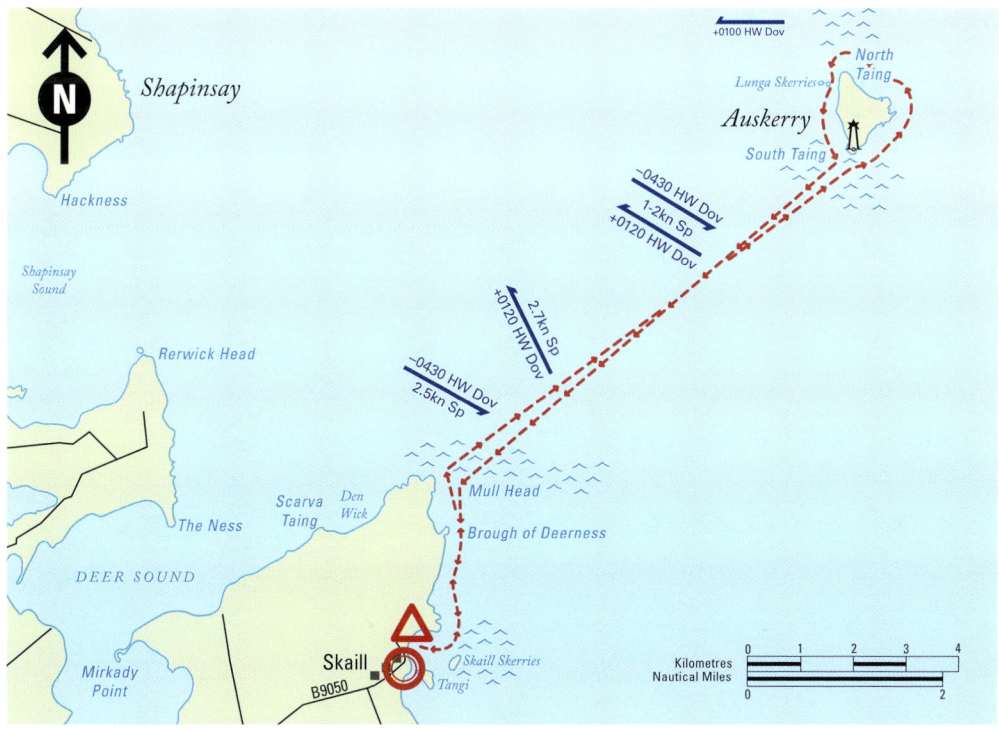

Departing Mull Head for Auskerry | Chris Jex

Auskerry

past Mill Bay head into Papa Sound to the village of Whitehall, from where you can catch a ferry back to Kirkwall or continue on your adventure within the North Isles.

Tide and weather

The 10km open crossing is best planned either side of slack water, so as to avoid the strongest part of the tidal stream. Tidal overfalls and faster moving water may be present close to Mull Head. The rest of the open water crossing, wind and tide prevailing, is relatively easy going.

Moderate to strong wind from the east or south-east will create an uncomfortable sea swell.

If you are planning to continue your journey to Stronsay, be aware of submerged reefs and shallow water within Auskerry Sound. These are known to cause considerable standing waves and a strong tidal race between the islands during poor weather.

Additional information

Please respect the wishes of the family living on the island. If possible ask permission before camping or walking amongst livestock.

Auskerry is a remote island. For the majority of the year there will not be any residents on the island. Plan to be self-sufficient should the weather change while you are out there.

When parking at Sandside Bay ensure you do not obstruct access onto the beach, as it is sometimes used for hauling out boats.

Admiralty Chart 2250, Imray Chart C68, and O.S. Explorer Map 461 & 465 cover this area.

Caves and arches, Taings of Berstane, Shapinsay | Chris Jex

Shapinsay

No. 18 | **Grade B** | **37km** | **8 hours** | **OS Sheet 6** | **Tidal Port Dover**

Start/Finish	△○ (Slipway) W side of Kirkwall harbour (448 113)
HW	HW Kirkwall is 45 minutes before HW Dover.
	at Shapinsay is 55 minutes before HW Dover.
Tidal Times	The E going stream within The String and N of Shapinsay starts 5 hours 15 minutes after HW Dover. The W going stream starts 45 minutes after HW Dover.
	Slack water to the E of The String is approximately 1 hour after HW Dover.
	An E-SE going stream rounding the Ness of Ork and along the E coast starts 5 hours before HW Dover. The NW stream starts 1 hour after HW Dover.
	The S going stream past 'The Galt' starts 5 hours 30 minutes before HW Dover.
	The S going stream through Vasa Sound on the W side of the island starts 6 hours before HW Dover. The N going stream starts 15 minutes after HW Dover.
Max Rate at Sp	In The String is 3.9 knots.
	In Shapinsay Sound, the E going stream is 2.8 knots and the W going stream is 1.3 knots.
	On the W side of Shapinsay is 2.9 knots.
	Over and around Vasa Skerry is 5 knots.
	At Ness of Ork and to the E of Shapinsay is 4.3 knots.
Coastguard	Shetland

Launching at the slipway, Kirkwall | Chris Jex

Introduction

Shapinsay (Helping Island for Boats) is only a stone's-throw away from the Orkney Mainland, but has managed to preserve a friendly and laid back island atmosphere. There is an abundance of bird and wildlife throughout the year.

The island has a number of prominent headlands, offshore islands and reefs which create fast moving tidal streams and overfalls. Careful tidal planning is required especially when crossing The String to the south of the island.

The circumnavigation, starting at Kirkwall (Kirk Bay) harbour, can be completed in a day or a more leisurely approach could include an overnight camp.

Description

Access to the water is easily made at the slipway opposite the small roundabout along the harbour road. A toilet, ferry waiting room and car park are close by.

The first 4km of paddling follows the east coast of the Bay of Kirkwall passing Iceland Skerry and on towards Thieves Holm. This route is regularly used by the Shapinsay ferry and a number of creel boats each day, so it is important to be aware of your position whilst heading north. Crossing The String will take about 20 minutes, during which time a determined ferry glide may be required.

Continuing north towards Grukalty Pier (where the Romans are thought to have landed and anchored their ships) a number of small skerries close to the coastline are home to cormorants, Arctic terns, greylag geese and the elusive otter. Pleasant paddling past Vasa Loch may enable you to spot the whooper swans which regularly visit this inland water site. If you arrive here and there is an oncoming tide be aware that it can reach up to 5 knots around Vasa Skerry. Further north, within the Bay of Furrowend, a large number of terns nest on the shingle shoreline. This area of beach below the house is best left undisturbed during nesting times.

The narrow peninsula of land to the north has a steep muddy bank along its west shoreline and a number of World War II lookout points and gun emplacements. The views out to Gairsay, Rousay and the western Mainland of Orkney provide a stunning panorama before heading around The Galt peninsula. The shallow skerry and tidal stream here can create interesting overfalls and fast moving water.

Veantrow Bay has some wonderful remote sandy beaches next to The Ouse and Lairo Water, where you may want to search for the unusual 2m square stone known as the Odin's Stone. Most paddlers will choose to head east across Veantrow Bay, passing a number of fish farms and onwards to the Ness of Ork.

At Ness of Ork, yet another strong tidal stream may be experienced as the sea is forced around the prominent headland. Easy access to the Broch of Burroughston on the east side of the island enables a worthwhile visit to this well-preserved Iron Age fortification. The site includes an impressive ditch, rampart and a small enclosed settlement with a corbelled cell and stone steps leading down to a well. About 2.5km to the south at Linton are the remains of a small chapel dating from the 12th century, dedicated to St Catherine.

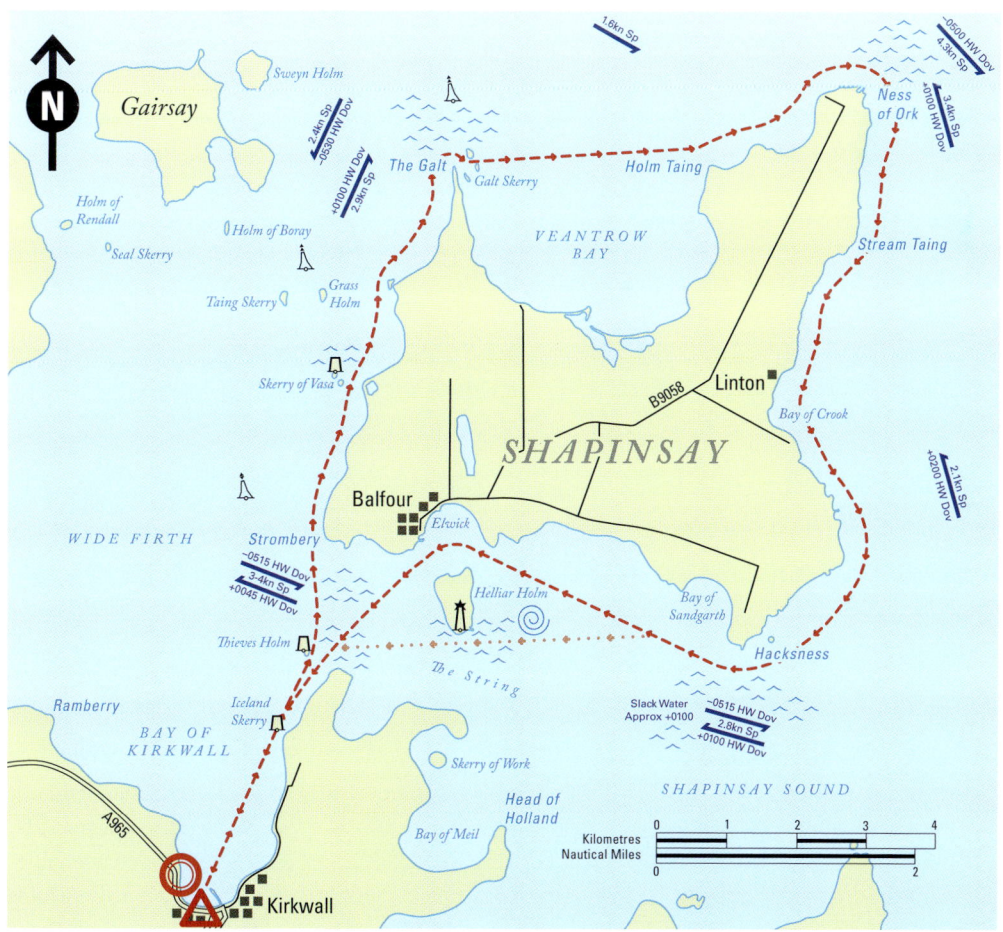

The String and Helliar Holm Lighthouse, Shapinsay | Chris Jex

Balfour Castle

Balfour Castle proudly displays an array of quintessential Scottish Baronial architecture. Completed in the mid 19th century it has a total of 12 outside doors, 52 rooms and 365 window panes (one for each day of the year), a Victorian affectation referred to as a 'Calendar House'. A round tower close to the shoreline is known as the Dishan Tower or Douche. Its ornate design conceals a dovecot and an ingenious seawater shower, which was the height of luxury in the mid 19th century. The castle is now an exclusive hotel and private home. It possesses the enviable title of 'The most northerly castle in the world'.

At Dog Geo a small rock stack signals the start of an impressive section of cliffs. A number of deep caves and geos can be explored. The area marked on the OS map as 'The Foot', where there is a narrow archway through the headland, is particularly interesting.

The low lying coastline close to South Skerry shows signs of extruded basalt lava (volcanic rock), which is unusual in Orkney due to the predominance of sandstone. As you round the southerly headland there is good access to a stalled cairn at Haco's Ness, which has six upright stones contained within a low chamber. A beautiful sandy beach, a favourite amongst locals, can be found at the Bay of Sandgarth.

Further west is the island of Helliar Holm with its prominent and strategically important lighthouse. This was built to assist mariners in finding safe passage into Kirkwall Bay. Built in

Elwick Bay and Helliar Holm island, Shapinsay | Chris Jex

1893 it became automated in 1967, leaving the keeper's house and building in disrepair. Access to the outside of the lighthouse may be made from some stone steps directly beneath the light. The north shores of Helliar Holm are home to a large colony of common seals.

Depending on the height of the tide it may be possible to head into the sheltered Elwick Bay from the east side. If that is not an option you will have to pass around the south side of the lighthouse and into the bay from the deeper south-west channel. Elwick Bay is famous for being the location where King Haakon of Norway assembled his fleet of over 100 galley ships in 1263, before heading south to the battle of Largs to lay claim to the Norse ruled lands within Scotland.

The two piers at Shapinsay village allow easy access to a picturesque line of old workers' cottages, the gatehouse and old sea-washed toilets! The small village has retained a unique charm and tranquillity. There are a number of places to visit including the The Smithy restaurant and café and Heritage Centre, the old stone gasworks tower and the largest watermill in Orkney; Elwick Mill is situated 400 metres along the coast road, east of the school and community centre.

When you are finished with your *terra firma* adventures, check the state of the tidal flow in The String before heading south-west out of the sheltered bay, and across the short but fast moving tidal channel. Passing between Car Ness headland and Thieves Holm, the bright lights and built up area of Kirkwall will be in sight, marking the end of a memorable circumnavigation of Shapinsay.

Volcanic rock, Shapinsay | Douglas Sewell

Tide and weather

Depending on your time of departure there may be overfalls and standing waves around all the major headlands of Shapinsay. Rough water can form through The String, especially north-east of Thieves Holm, where competing tidal streams collide and are forced over a shallow reef.

Clapotis may affect the E/SE facing cliffs and coastline during an onshore wind, or when swell is present from the east.

Additional information

The ferry service from Shapinsay to Kirkwall leaves on a regular basis throughout the day. This is a useful option if you want to shorten the journey or if The String is too rough for the return crossing.

The journey can also be started or finished from Carness Bay (north of Kirkwall), Rerwick Point (Deerness) or the Rendall coastline (West Mainland). These alternative options may assist with tidal planning, enabling the paddler to use preferred tidal times/streams to complete the journey.

Admiralty Charts 2249, 2250, Imray Chart C68, and O.S. Explorer Map 461 covers this area.

In the tidal stream, south of the Holm of Boray | Chris Jex

Gairsay

No. 19 | Grade A | 11km | 3 hours | OS Sheet 6 | Tidal Port Dover

Start/Finish	△○ Hall of Rendall/Dovecot car park (423 207)
HW	HW at Tingwall is about 1 hour 35 minutes before HW Dover.
Tidal Times	The SE going stream between Gairsay and the W Mainland of Orkney starts 5 hours 30 minutes before HW Dover. The NW going stream starts 30 minutes after HW Dover. The N going stream to the E of Gairsay starts 30 minutes after HW Dover, turning S approximately 5 hours before HW Dover.
Max Rate at Sp	Between Gairsay and the Orkney Mainland is 2 knots. E of Hen of Gairsay is 2.9 knots.
Coastguard	Shetland

Introduction

The journey around Gairsay (Garek's Isle) is a great introduction to circumnavigating the many smaller islands within Orkney. The coastline around the island is generally low lying and rocky with contrasting scenery between the uncultivated and wild heather slopes of the north, and the green fields and grassland areas to the south. A short walk to the top of the 102m summit will

113

Paddling past the dovecot at The Taing, Gairsay | Phil Berry

19 Gairsay

reward you with one of Orkney's best 360° panoramas, looking out over the myriad islands to the north and east. There is an adventurous feel to paddling around this remote island, which is infrequently visited as there is no easy public access or boat service.

Description

The small car park used to access the Dovecot can be used to prepare equipment and kayaks before getting onto the water. A short portage gains easy access to the sea along a rough track and shallow stream bed south of the farmhouse and buildings at the Hall of Rendall.

From the sheltered bay head north along the coastline, past a ruined broch, until level with a distinct small square building. From here it is worth ensuring the tidal stream is still heading in the preferred direction and at a manageable speed. The short ferry glide across the 1km of open tidal water to Gairsay will bring you close to The Taing with its intriguingly shaped tower/dovecot. The square building on the Orkney Mainland and the dovecot on Gairsay can be used as markers to ascertain your position whilst crossing the tidal channel. This is a bearing of 060° True.

The farmer frequently visits and occasionally resides at the large farmhouse marked as Langskaill on the OS map. Langskaill farm is thought to stand on the site of the great drinking hall of Sweyn Asliefsson, a notorious Viking warrior who lived on Gairsay. The main drinking hall would have housed over eighty of Sweyn's fighting men.

Following the low west-facing coastline, head towards Odin Ness and around the north coast. The rocky shoreline has a steep mud and grass slope where fulmars may be seen nesting in holes within the soft mud cliffs.

North Head is a distinct promontory of land. Its two sided pebble beach, ruined sheepfolds and brackish loch are an excellent place for exploring or having lunch. From here, it is an easy walk up to the high point of the island for an amazing 360 degree view of Orkney (without disturbing the inhabitants or livestock on the south side of the island).

Once rested and back on the water, continue around the headland and into Russness Bay. Here there are a number of small cairns and inland lochs marked on the OS map. These features are worth exploring and offer good cover for you whilst spotting the bird and wildlife along the shoreline. The number of seals in this bay can exceed well over 100, providing an impressive natural spectacle as you paddle amongst their bobbing heads and frequent splashes.

To the north-east of Gairsay is a small island called Sweyn Holm, a quiet and sparsely vegetated place with a small ruined dwelling on its south shore. This island is named after Sweyn Asleifsson.

Tidal flow and clapotis can form along the short, steep cliffs leading towards the Ness of Gairsay, making sea conditions quite difficult during a moderate onshore wind or during poor weather. From the Ness of Gairsay head south-west across open water to the Holm of Boray. The guano covered rocky island is host to a large colony of cormorants, black-backed gulls and fulmars.

For the last section of the journey it is worth heading west towards the navigation light on Seal Skerry. This will enable you to be upstream of the Holm of Rendall. The last 2km of open water paddling, if timed right, will allow you to make use of the following and increasing tidal stream, which heads north-west approximately 1 hour after HW Dover.

The tidal streams around Seal Skerry and the Holm of Rendall flow over a shallow seabed and reef system. This greatly accelerates the speed of the water, forcing you north and to ferry glide

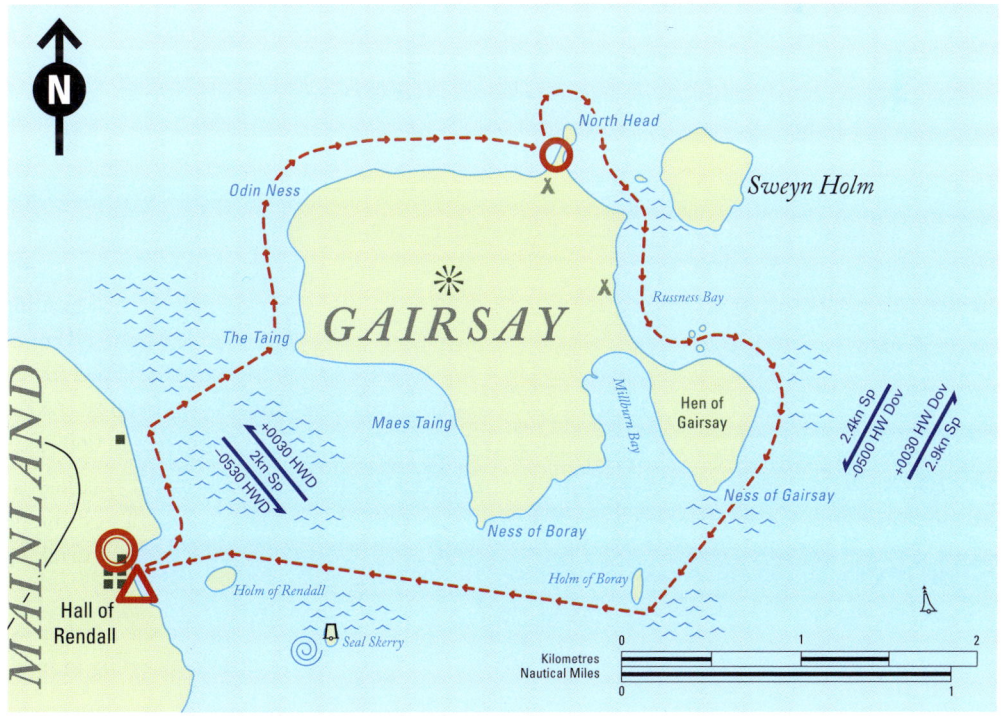

Rockpool life, Gairsay | Chris Jex

across the quickening current in order to break out behind the Holm of Rendall. From here a short paddle west takes you to the journey's end.

Tide and weather

The circumnavigation can be paddled in either direction, taking into consideration the tidal stream with an open crossing to Gairsay, and the often exposed coastline and tidal flow to the east of 'Hen of Gairsay'. The relatively short paddle is sheltered from the open sea but can still be affected by onshore winds and the effect of wind against tide.

Additional information

Please be aware that there may be grazing animals and livestock on the island. Arctic and great skuas breed on the moorland; they can be very territorial during nesting times.

A visit to the Dovecot next to the car park area is an additional highlight to the journey. Built in 1648 it is an unusual beehive shape, and is the oldest one of its type remaining in Scotland.

For those wanting to get away from the shore and flat sheltered water, the tidal water between the Orkney Mainland and Gairsay and around the small islands to the south provides some exciting tidal movement and standing waves.

Admiralty Charts 2249, 2250, Imray Chart C68, and O.S. Explorer Map 461 cover this area.

Burgh Head, Stronsay | Chris Jex

Stronsay

No. 20 | Grade B | 43km | 9-10 hours | OS Sheet 5 | Tidal Port Dover

Start/Finish	△○ East Pier at Whitehall village (658 285)
HW	HW in Papa Sound is 1 hour 40 minutes before HW Dover.
Tidal Times	The S going stream on the W side of Stronsay starts 4 hours before HW Dover. The N going stream starts 2 hours after HW Dover.
	The E/NE going stream around the SE corner of Stronsay starts 5 hours after HW Dover. The W/SW going stream starts 1 hour after HW Dover.
	An E going tidal stream flows between the smaller islands to the N of Stronsay starting about 6 hours after HW Dover.
	The SW going tidal stream in Spurness Sound starts 50 minutes before HW Dover.
	The SE going tidal stream around the headland at Rothiesholm starts 5 hours before HW Dover. The NW going tidal stream starts 1 hour after HW Dover.
Max Rate at Sp	On the W side of Stronsay close to Rothiesholm Head is 4.3 knots.
	Between the small islands NW of Stronsay is 3.5 knots.
	Around the S of Stronsay at Lamb Head, Burgh Head, and at Odness on the E coast is 1.8 knots. Tidal streams are negligible in Papa Sound.
Coastguard	Shetland

Camping at Sands of Rothiesholm, Stronsay | Chris Jex

Introduction

Stronsay (Island of Gain/profit or possibly Beach Island) has a number of extending fingers of fertile land which harbour unspoilt beaches and remote rocky headlands. The small isles and remote reefs are excellent places to observe grey and common seals, and a plethora of seabirds. The journey is best incorporated with at least one overnight camp on one of Stronsay's many superb white, sandy beaches.

Description

After disembarking from the roll-on roll-off ferry, a 50m walk with sea kayaks along the east side of the pier gives access down a set of narrow steps and onto the water. The journey described circumnavigates the island in a clockwise direction.

Opposite Whitehall village and the pier area lies the small, low island of Papa Stronsay. The island was bought in 1999 by the Transalpine Redemptionists, who follow the older practices of the Roman Catholic Church, including the use of Latin during prayer and services. A visit to the island can be organised with the monks who partake in monastic duties and farm the herd of Jersey cows to produce tasty cheese.

Heading south around Grice Ness leads the paddler past a small, chambered cairn on the headland and into Mill Bay. On the beach there is a rock known as the 'Mermaid's Chair'; legend says that any girl who sits here is meant to be able to foretell the future!

Further south Odin Bay is indented with a number of small beaches, a small quarry site and a number of short, freestanding rock outcrops. At Bluthers Geo an amazing flowstone lined cave is well worth exploring before heading around the corner and into the shelter of 'The Swimming Pool'. This is an inland seawater pool, which in the past used to be a popular spot for bathing. The rock walls between here and the Vat of Kirbuster provide excellent opportunities for rock climbers. The Vat of Kirbuster is one of Orkney's most picturesque and accessible archways. From the inland side there is an impressive view of the arch.

Heading south-east the steep indented coastline has a number of deep caves, small arches and unusual island stacks (including The Brough beyond Burgh Head). All three remote islands along the east coast are thought to have the remains of hermitages on them.

Vat of Kirbuster bay | Chris Jex

At Burgh Head an exciting shortcut within the rocky reef, just past the headland, is possible. There is no access around the back of The Brough due to a recent rock fall barring the way. A good rest spot, out of the easterly swell, may be found to the west of The Brough.

Heading south-east towards the broch and caves at the appropriately named Hells Mouth, the cliffs ease in height and offer a suitable get out on the beach, north of Lamb Head. Hells Mouth has a number of shallow reefs (like teeth) defending the entrance to the caves, which are meant to growl when there is a large easterly swell crashing into them.

On Lamb Head there are a number of chambered cairns. There is a spectacular view south towards Auskerry, allowing a quick scout of the coastline around the corner. Also present here and at Latan (east side of Rothiesholm Head) are a number of stone lined pits. The pits were used for burning kelp when the kelp industry was a major source of income for over 3,000 islanders (1722–1832). They sold the potash, iodine and potassium salts to traders from the south. A good campsite close to the beach may be found just north of Lamb Head.

It is important to plan to use the S/SW going tide on this first section of the journey. This will ease your passage around Lamb Head and into the shelter of the Bay of Houseby where a large number of seals may be present near The Pow. The southern most point of the island, Tor Ness, has a good beach to its east with an inland loch (named Lea Shun) behind it. The loch is home to a wide variety of wading, inland and sea birds.

A 4km paddle north will enable you to land on one of Stronsay's most idyllic beaches, the Sand of Rothiesholm. This glorious beach has shallow water, white sand and protective dunes making it a good choice for a campsite.

The high cliffs to the east of Rothiesholm Head, are host to a number of seabirds. The imposing headland, beneath which there may be fast currents and standing waves, is overlooked by three wind turbines. The receding cliff line further north enables the paddler to stop off at a sandy beach and explore the archaeological remains of a stalled burial chamber dating from 3,000 BC, close to the Hillock of Baywest.

Paddling NE and across St Catherine's Bay, a direct route through Linga Sound will lead the paddler to Linga Holm. Grey seals haul out here and congregate in large numbers during October to give birth to approx 2,000 pups each year. Large flocks of greylag geese may also be seen above the shoreline feeding on the coarse grasslands. A short paddle onward, past Little Linga and east into Huip Sound leads the paddler to the Holm of Huip, where grey seals, Arctic terns, black backed gulls and cormorants reside.

The final 4km south back into Papa Sound should include a detour and exploration of the sunken coal barge within the Bay of Franks. Within the sound there are numerous buoys which guide ferry traffic safely towards the pier. It is wise to stay to the landward side (west) of all buoyage if the ferry is due to be arriving or departing.

The short paddle back to the pier at Whitehall village allows the paddler to view the jagged skyline formed by the two-storey houses which are further testament to the wealth that the herring industry once brought to Stronsay's shores. A shop, pub, café and self-catering hostel are all situated within easy walking distance of the pier.

A number of new dwellings and a monastery are visible on the small island of Papa Stronsay. The island is privately owned by 'The Trans-alpine Redemptorist missionary priests and monks who follow the Roman Catholic religion. The island was first visited by St Columba over 1,400 years ago.

Tide and weather

All the island's major headlands are susceptible to tidal movement and rough seas if on the exposed windward shorelines. The east side of the island, although less prone to strong tidal movement, is open to the North Sea and ocean swell.

A portage across the road and narrow neck of land between the Bay of Holland beach car park and an access track leading to St Catherine's Bay is possible, if paddling around the south-west corner of the island is not a viable option.

There are a number of sheltered bays and sections of coastline around the island which offer poor weather alternatives if the full circumnavigation is not suitable.

Additional information

An additional clockwise journey around Papa Stronsay will add an extra 2-3km to the journey and provide an alternative finish to the circumnavigation. Also, a number of short open water crossings linking Stronsay to Sanday, Eday or Auskerry are possible, requiring appropriate experience and good tidal planning. In poor sea conditions, Stronsay has some excellent signposted walking routes around the spectacular coastlines and unspoilt beaches.

Admiralty Chart 2250, Imray Chart C68, and O.S. Explorer Map 465 cover this area.

Heading south to Whitehall village | Chris Jex

The herring industry

Heading east out of Whitehall village a steeply angled landing stage and number of abandoned buildings along the north shore give an indication of the island's prosperity during the boom years of the herring industry from 1816 to 1936.

During this busy period there were over 4,000 people employed in a number of trades related to the industry, including crewing the steam drifters, fish gutting, processing, salting, curing and barrel making. The season generally lasted for up to 3 months and in 1924 over 12,000 tons of herring was landed. The 15 curing stations were occupied by over 1,500 fish-wives who made use of the 40 pubs, 5 ice cream parlours and 10 general merchants that were all located within what was then the imposing and bustling village of Whitehall.

Broch of Gurness | Mark Rainsley

Rousay & Egilsay

No. 21 | Grade B | 33km | 7-8 hours | OS Sheet 6 | Tidal Port Dover

Start/Finish	Broch of Gurness Car Park (380 268)
HW	HW at Eynhallow Sound is 1 hour 40 minutes before HW Dover.
Tidal Times	The NW going tidal stream in Eynhallow Sound at Aikerness starts 30 minutes after HW Dover. The SE going tidal stream in Eynhallow Sound starts 5 hours 30 minutes before HW Dover.
	The NW going tidal stream in the Westray Firth starts 1 hour after HW Dover. The SE going tidal stream in the Westray Firth starts 5 hours before HW Dover.
	In Rousay Sound the N going tidal stream starts 10 minutes after HW Dover. The S going tidal stream starts 5 hours 50 minutes before HW Dover.
	In Wyre Sound the E going tidal stream starts 5 hours 55 minutes before HW Dover. The W going tidal stream starts 5 minutes after HW Dover.
Max Rate at Sp	In Eynhallow Sound reach 3.3 knots. Between Eynhallow and Rousay is 7 knots. In the Westray Firth is 3 knots. In the narrow channels of Rousay Sound, between Rousay, the Holm of Scockness and Egilsay is 6 knots.
Coastguard	Shetland

Cormorants, Rousay | Chris Jex

Introduction

The island of Rousay (Rolf's Island) is arguably one of the most interesting of all the smaller islands within Orkney, due to a number of well-preserved archaeological sites which can be easily accessed from the sea. There is an abundance of wildlife on the coastal fringes, with large cetacean sightings occuring often each year, especially around the deep-water areas west of Rousay. The circumnavigation can be completed in a day, or at a more leisurely pace over two days.

Description

The journey starts at either a small sandy beach next to the car park at the Broch of Gurness or at the car park adjacent to a public toilet and pier at the west end of the Sands of Evie.

The 2km crossing of Eynhallow Sound brings the paddler to the narrowing channel of water between Rousay and the small island of Eynhallow, where overfalls and the pull of the flowing water become more evident.

On the shore there is a well worn path running parallel to the Westness coast. The 'Heritage Walk' has been described as: "The most important archaeological mile in Scotland" and is why the island is described as "The Egypt of the north". The coastal walk or paddle enables you to see the remains of Bronze Age farmsteads, a chapel, numerous brochs and Midhowe Cairn, Orkney's largest Neolithic chambered cairn. Egress close to Midhowe Cairn (green roofed stone building) and the amazing broch to its west is highly recommended.

Highland Clearances

Rousay was the only island in Orkney heavily affected by the highland clearances during the mid 19th century. The rising area of hillside south of Wasbister Loch remains testament to the catastrophic decisions made by the landlord, George William Traill. Over 200 local crofters were evicted from their homes to make way for sheep, which were thought to be more prosperous to the landowner.

A scattering of abandoned cottages with small plots of 'Run-rig' marked land are all that remains.

Heading west the scenery quickly changes from low rocky shores to dramatic cliffs, caves and arches at Scabra Head where there are excellent examples of geological fault lines and bizarre strata formations. The next 2.5km of low rocky shoreline sports a number of shallow reefs, which are best given a wide berth during an ocean swell or an onshore wind.

The following 5.5km of paddling is a sea kayaker's paradise. The cliffs here are indented with hundreds of soft sandstone caves and archways formed by the harsh Atlantic storms. Many of the caves are a maze of interconnecting tunnels.

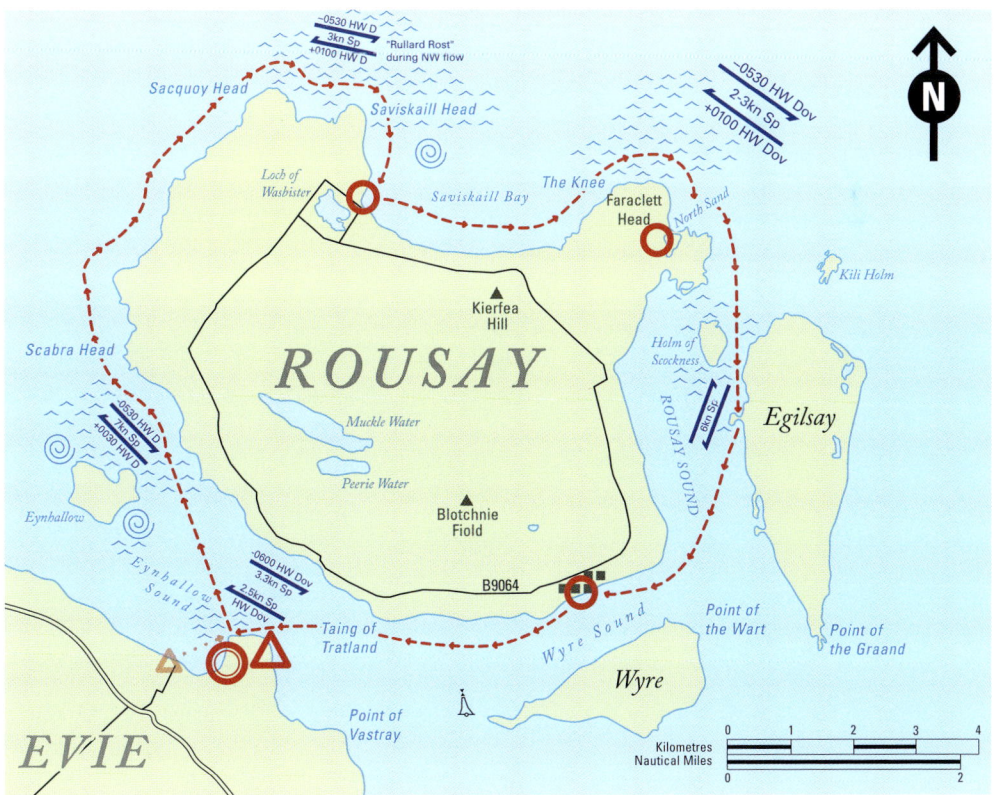

Exploring Midhowe Broch, Rousay | Alan Hughes

Bring Head and Hellia Spur are home to a wide variety of sea and inland birds which are attracted to the maritime heath and steep coastline crags. An impressive set of archways located at Sacquoy Head and Lobust have an amazing backdrop formed by the distant island of Westray and the Atlantic Ocean. Along this section of coastline it is worth searching out an impressive gloup located at Kilns of Brin Novan and the hidden Covenanters Cave, which was used in the 17th century by religious dissidents as a safe refuge.

North of Saviskaill Head there is an infamously rough sea area and tidal overfall known as 'Rullard Rost'. A small boulder beach to the east of Helliasour cave may provide egress before Saviskaill Head. The wide crescent of cliffs within Saviskaill Bay cuts a large bight out of Rousay's northern coastline. In the south-west corner of the bay there is an excellent camping spot and small sandy beach called Nousty Sand.

Cliffs and glaciated hills with steep grass terracing dominate the scenery along the north coast and around Faraclett Head. Tidal movement mixed with clapotis can create tricky rough water conditions, especially around the prominent headlands.

A secluded sandy beach called North Sand is tucked into the coast to the east of Faraclett Head. The beach offers the chance to explore the ruined broch, finding 'Groatie Buckies' or cowrie shells, and is an idyllic camping spot.

The Holm of Scockness, a small island in the middle of the Rousay Sound, is an excellent place to see otters. The shallow channels of water on each side of the island have strong tidal currents. A determined ferry glide may be required to get to the shoreline on Egilsay.

Scabra Head, Rousay | Chris Jex

The stony beach north of the pier on the island of Egilsay provides easy egress and the opportunity to visit the historical St Magnus Kirk. A walk along the quiet lanes on the small island of Egilsay offers a magical experience, the fields and roadside verges being alive with birds and ablaze with colourful wildflowers.

From the pier on Egilsay head south-west across Rousay Sound, past a low headland and towards the prominent pier. Facilities next to the pier include a public toilet and waiting room.

St Magnus

St Magnus Kirk with its unusual round tower marks the location where in 1117 Magnus was killed as a martyr. His death enabled his evil cousin Haakon full rule over the earldom of Orkney. A separate memorial and plaque 600m south-east of the Kirk marks the place where Magnus is reputed to have been killed.

The death of Magnus quickly gained him the title of St Magnus. His remains now lie in the St Magnus Cathedral in Kirkwall.

Continue along the low south-facing shoreline, past a ruined broch. From the Taing of Tratland head across Eynhallow Sound for 1.5km (possible ferry glide) to reach the Broch of Gurness and the journey's end.

St Magnus Church, Egilsay | Chris Jex

Tide and weather

Prior planning of tidal stream movement within Eynhallow, Rousay and Wyre Sound is advised. All major headlands have standing waves and overfalls.

The west through to north-east coastlines are prone to ocean swell and clapotis during strong tides and when onshore winds are present.

A large, slow-moving re-circulating eddy forms within Saviskaill Bay during both directions of tidal movement. The effect of this is most noticeable and more powerful near the headlands.

Additional information

It is important to ask permission from a landowner before camping because of the management of grazing livestock.

A regular ferry service runs between Tingwall (Orkney Mainland), Rousay, Egilsay and Wyre. This is worth considering if poor weather curtails the journey. The journey can be increased in distance by including a circumnavigation of Egilsay and Wyre.

Admiralty Chart 2249, Imray Chart C68 and O.S. Explorer Map 464 cover this area.

Red Head, Eday | Mark Rainsley

Eday & Faray

No. 22 | Grade B | 41km | 9 hours | OS Sheet 5 | Tidal Port Dover

Start/Finish	Ferry pier, Bay of Backaland (572 301)
HW	HW at Eday's ferry pier is 1 hour 40 minutes before HW Dover.
Tidal Times	On the E side of Eday (S of Eday Sound), the N going tidal stream starts 1-2 hrs after HW Dover. The S going tidal stream starts 4-5 hours before HW Dover.
	On the W side of the island, in the Westray Firth, the E going tidal stream, splits around the N of Faray and the S of Eday starting 5 hours 20 minutes before HW Dover. The NW going tidal stream starts 40 minutes after HW Dover.
	The N going tidal stream in the Sound of Faray, Weatherness Sound and Rapness Sound all start at 4 hours and 15 minutes after HW Dover. The S going tidal streams start 1 hour and 45 minutes before HW Dover.
	The S going tidal race in both Calf and Lashy Sound starts 5 hours 45 minutes before HW Dover. The N going tidal race starts 30 minutes after HW Dover.
	The SE going tidal stream through the Falls of Warness start at 5 hours before HW Dover. The NW going tidal stream starts at 1 hour after HW Dover.
Max Rate at Sp	In Lashy Sound is 5.2 knots.
	Around the SW corner of the island in the Falls of Warness is 7.2 knots.
	To the SW of Faray is 5.2 knots.
	In Rapness Sound and the Sound of Faray is 4 knots.
	In Calf Sound is 6 knots.
Coastguard	Shetland

Starry Geo, Faray | Chris Jex

Introduction

The island of Eday (Isthmus Isle) is situated in the centre of the North Isles group and within easy paddling distance of Westray, Sanday and Stronsay. The island has a diverse range of coastlines from beautiful golden sandy beaches to steep rocky headlands and imposing cliffs crowded with seabirds. The journey described includes a well worthwhile detour to visit the small island of Faray (Sheep Island) and the exposed cliffs on the Calf of Eday.

Description

The journey is described paddling clockwise and starting just after HW Dover. Opposite the ferry waiting room and toilets there is a steep ramp and a small set of steps. These offer access to the water within a small sheltered harbour.

The low lying shoreline around the south-east corner of Eday is a good warm up to the paddling, with farmland and quiet sandy shores which lead you past the Bay of Greentoft.

At the Falls of Warness a large volume of turbulent moving water is forced over a shallow seabed between the headland at War Ness and the island of Muckle Green Holm. It is prudent to be here about 1 hour after HW to avoid the overfalls and rough water. Once past the headland there is an interesting section of 25m high cliffs to the south of Ward Hill. An amazing contorted fault line runs along the cliff, with a number of rock arches above the HW line.

Paddling north to Seal Skerry a swathe of white sand awaits your arrival. The headland or the beach area close to the skerry makes a superb campsite. At Seal Skerry a quickening tidal stream

Calf of Eday | Chris Jex

flows over kelp and shallow rocks. Further North at Fers Ness a short open water crossing to the island of Faray will reward you with an assortment of geos, caves and short cliffs with regular sightings of seals, seabirds and porpoise.

A sandy beach on the west side of the island, north of Starry Geo, is an idyllic setting for a cliff top campsite, particularly on a summer's evening when the sun barely dips below the horizon. Camping on the island is possible but care must be taken due to the presence of livestock and nesting birds.

Faray

The long, thin island of Faray and Holm of Faray to the north were once home to eight farms supporting up to eighty-three people during the late 19th century. The people farmed and fished for a living in relative isolation. A small, well-built concrete jetty and large boat *'nousts'* at the south end of the island, reflect the importance of fishing to those who once lived here.

The last islanders departed in 1946 when the small schoolhouse finally closed. Many families moved to the nearby island of Westray. The island is now owned by Orkney Islands Council and has been chosen as one of three locations within Orkney for a number of wind turbine farms to be installed.

An optional 2km 'out and return' paddle to the uninhabited Rusk Holm will enable you explore the small island and stone built house with two seaweed kilns. You will not be alone, as you will have to share the memorable experience with the unique feral North Ronaldsay sheep which graze on seaweed along the shoreline.

From the Holm of Faray a 3 km paddle past Red Holm leads you towards a boulder lined shoreline beneath Little Noup Head. The high cliffs protect the high moorland which once provided an important income to islanders. They sold the rich dark peat to neighbouring islands and even exported it to a number of malt whisky distilleries on mainland Scotland.

In calm weather the glistening water around the base of Red Head is a sea kayaker's delight, with basking seals and a profusion of seabirds. Arriving here about 5-6 hours before HW Dover will ease your journey across Calf Sound towards the spectacular cliffs on the Calf of Eday.

The coastline around Grey Head and The Knees will reward the paddler with amazing scenery. The imposing cliffs, which provide a perfect sanctuary for nesting seabirds, are the highlight of this fantastic journey. A tall archway may be paddled through in calm conditions. An atmospheric camp high above the steep cliffs is accessed from the only landfall along the north coast of the Calf of Eday, above a rocky beach at Burry Geo.

The journey back along the cliffs lead south into Calf Sound. Tidal planning is required to ensure safe passage here as the standing waves and strong currents increase in speed as you are flushed around the U-bend created between the Calf of Eday and Eday.

On the west side of Calf Sound is a place known as Otterpool, where a large shingle and stone beach has been deposited. This area is seldom visited by walkers, partly because of an over-protective colony of Arctic terns! Otter spraint has been found here and otters are thought to frequent this aptly named area.

Further south a small but prominent automated light below Noup Hill stands sentinel. The imposing Carrick House was built in 1633 and has been home to a number of Lairds over the past four centuries. Visits to the historic house may be made by prior arrangement.

John Gow the pirate

In the 17th century John Gow, the famous pirate, decided to raid Carrick House on Eday. Being ill prepared for the fast moving waters within Calf Sound, his sailing ship *The Revenge* grounded on the Calf of Eday. Unfortunately for John Gow his old schoolmate James Fea, who owned Carrick House, successfully tricked and captured him with the use of alcohol!

John Gow was eventually handed over to the authorities and sent to London to be tried and hanged for his many crimes.

The old saltworks on the south-west shore on the Calf of Eday date back to the 18th century. Further east coast is one of Orkney's largest colonies of cormorants.

Once through Calf Sound, the route heads south along a rocky coastline passing a number of low cliffs and a small natural arch. Mill Bay has a beautiful sandy beach and is the closest egress point to the island's shop situated opposite Mill Loch.

The last 6km of low coastline is punctuated by the Bay of London and 'London Airport'. The word 'London' is thought to come from the norse word for 'small wood' which is thought to have then covered this area. A refurbished hostel is situated 500m north of the airport. At the Bay of Backaland fish farm nets break up the foreground and the view east towards Sanday's striking wind turbines, standing sentinel over the isles.

Tide and weather

Lashy Sound, the Falls of Warness, the channels around Faray and Calf Sound can all produce fast-flowing rough water and associated standing waves.

The island of Eday is exposed to the Atlantic Ocean to the west and north. Large sea swell and wind blown swell may continue for days after poor weather, or when there is a low pressure system to the west of Orkney.

Starting the journey at HW Dover (or slightly later) and stopping off en route will enable you to be at Red Head at about 6 hours before HW Dover when the north going tidal stream starts to weaken within Calf Sound. After a visit to the cliffs on the Calf of Eday, the south going tidal stream will assist you through Calf Sound and along the east coast of Eday.

Additional information

Ferry access to the island of Eday is via the North Isles service run by Orkney Ferries. The service operates between Kirkwall, Sanday, Stronsay and Eday on a daily basis. A short crossing to any of the other inhabited islands is easily undertaken with tidal planning.

If you choose to wild camp please, where possible, request permission from the landowner before setting up your tent. Both the islands of Faray and Calf of Eday are privately owned and visitors should respect the buildings, livestock and wildlife.

Admiralty Chart 2250, Imray Chart C68, and O.S. Explorer Map 464 & 465 cover this area.

Cata Sand, Sanday | Chris Jex

Sanday

No. 23 | Grade B | 65km | 14 hours | OS Sheet 5 | Tidal Port Dover

Start/Finish	△○ Loth Pier (603 339)
HW	HW Loth is 40 minutes before HW Dover.
	HW at Kettletoft Pier is 15 minutes before HW Dover.
Tidal Times	To the N of the island, in the North Ronaldsay Firth, the E going tidal stream begins 6 hours before HW Dover. The W going stream starts at HW Dover.
	To the S of the island within Sanday Sound the NE going stream begins 5 hours before HW Dover. The NE stream eases 3 hours before HW Dover.
	To the S of Spur Ness the E going stream starts 6 hours after HW Dover. The SW going tidal stream starts 50 minutes before HW Dover.
	Within Lashy Sound the S going stream starts 5 hours and 45 minutes after HW Dover. The N going stream starts 30 minutes before HW Dover.
	At Start Point, during the S going stream a tidal race begins 5 hours 20 minutes afer HW Dover.
	A weak but continuous NE going tidal stream exists between Tres Ness and Start Point.
Max Rate at Sp	In North Ronaldsay Firth is 4 knots.
	In Spurness Sound is 3.5 knots.
	In Lashy Sound is 6 knots.
Coastguard	Shetland

Introduction

Sanday (Sand Isle) is the third largest island within Orkney. The rich soils of the island provide an abundance of wildlife and plant habitats. Exploring them rarely involves an uphill walk anywhere as the island only reaches a maximum of 65m above sea level.

When the sun is shining and the wind calm, the beaches and azure sea create a relaxed atmosphere akin to being on a tropical hideaway … except for the lack of palm trees and sunbathers on the pristine white sands!

Description

A toilet and waiting room close to the Loth ferry terminal mark the access point onto the water and the start of the journey. Ensuring the tide at Spur Ness is heading east, paddle around the low headland and through the short overfall beneath the new wind turbines. Look out for otters along this shoreline.

The first deep bay is the Bay of Stove. If heading into the sandy bay, be aware that the drying sands extend south for at least 1km at LW.

The low lying and remote peninsulas of Hacks Ness and Quoys Ness quickly pass and lead towards the steep grass and sandy slopes beneath The Wart, the island's highpoint. The bay of Backaskaill has a ruined church and cemetery dating from the 16th century and a glorious arc of white sand. At Kettletoft, a harbour and slipway offer easy access to a couple of excellent pubs and hotels.

The open water paddle past the Holm of Elsness provides an excellent opportunity to see the twenty-six cairns and eleven larger mounds scattered around the end of the Els Ness peninsula. Remains found at the site have been dated back to 3,000 BC. The best preserved archaeological site on Sanday is the Quoyness chambered cairn on the east side of Els Ness. Easy access can be gained from the shoreline and a visit is highly recommended. The remains of a broch and a chambered cairn can be explored 3km further east on the Tres Ness peninsula.

Further north a thin spit of sand connects Tres Ness and the farm buildings to the rest of Sanday. The impressive dunes tower over Cata Sands creating a stark skyline. From the top of the dunes amongst the swathe of marram and lyme grasses you'll get an excellent view of the island and the curving beach which leads to Start Point, 8.5km away. The long stretch of sand dunes, which mark the edge of the Bay of Newark, conceal a nine hole golf course. The sandy soil behind the dunes supports an amazing variety of grasses, wild flowers, birds and rare insects.

The wide arc of the Bay of Lopness is punctuated by a World War I shipwreck mid way along its shallow shoreline. The German B98 was sunk in 1919 and eventually towed into shallow waters for salvage. The boilers are visible at LW.

Once around the headland at Lop Ness, Start Point lighthouse is clearly visible, standing tall with vertical black and white stripes. The light, built in 1806, was the first to be automated and have a revolving light installed (1962). The small flat tidal island which the lighthouse stands guard over is only accessible at LW. The chambered cairn to the south of the island was once used by the lighthouse keepers for storing potatoes! At dusk keep a look out for both sooty and Manx shearwaters as they head out of their underground burrows to feed under the cover of darkness.

An area of rough water and standing waves may be present south-east of Tobacco Rock where a tidal overfall heading south builds momentum about 5 hours before HW Dover. The north and east-facing coastlines comprise of steep pebble and sandy beaches heaped up with storm tossed rocks and kelp.

The UK's largest unexcavated funerary complex lies at Tofts Ness. There are over 300 cairns, dykes and ditches which are thought to date back to the Neolithic and Bronze Age. At LW, within the Bay of Otterwick, there are signs of fossilised tree stumps (willow) submerged in the sand and mud. Carbon dating estimates that the stumps date back to 4500 BC.

On the west shoreline, close to Whitemill Point, is an area marked as 'Ortie' on the OS map. Here a long double row of cottages was built for up to sixty fishing and kelp workers during the boom and bust years of the 19th century. The majority now lie empty and ruined.

The shallow rocks and reefs around Whitemill Point and The Riv cause the sea's surface to change character and in poor weather may produce a large ocean swell and confused tidal water. A beacon marks the furthest submerged reef, home to a large number of grey and common seals.

The west coast of Sanday contains a number of rocky cliffs, deep sandy bays and breath-taking views towards the imposing cliffs of the Calf of Eday and the Red Head. Heading south it is wise to have the tidal stream going in the same direction so as to avoid fighting the tidal current for 16km back to the sanctuary of Loth pier.

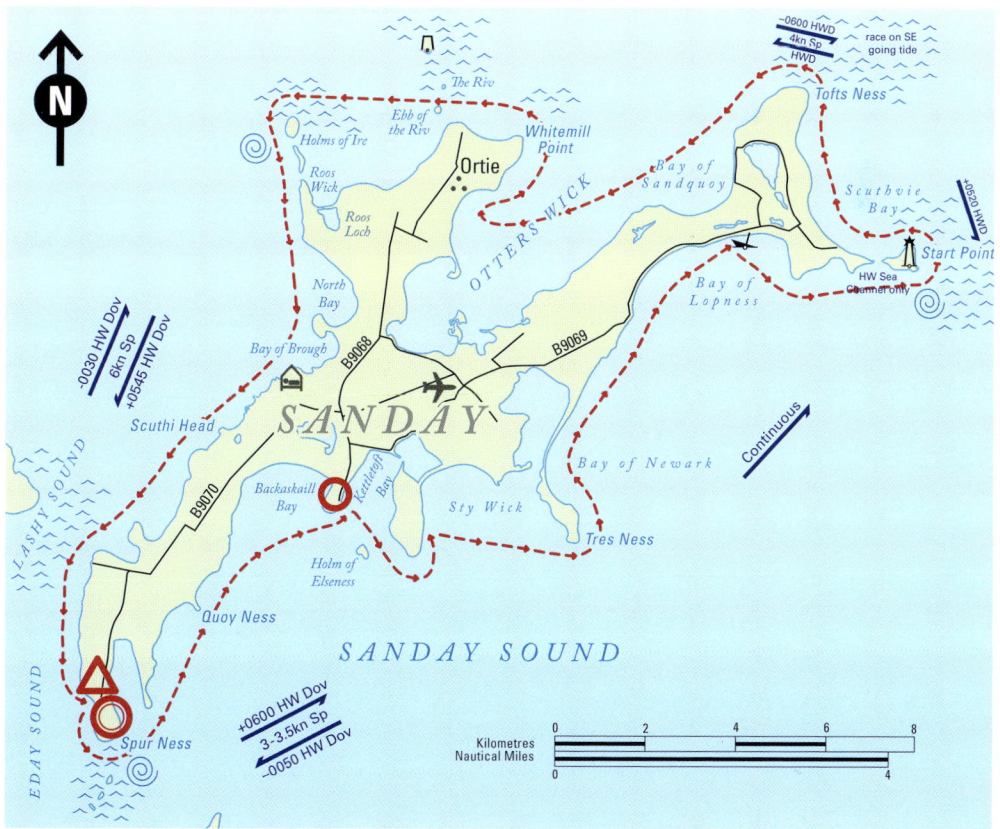

> ### Viking burial boats and shipwrecks
>
> Erosion along the coastline at Quoy Banks in 1991 unearthed a 7m long Viking burial ship. Within the clay and rock lined wooden ship were three skeletons of varying ages. Their possessions included a number of highly prized weapons, jewellery, working utensils and a carved whalebone plaque similar to those excavated in Norway.
>
> The protruding islands which make up the Holms of Ire have claimed a large number of shipwrecks. Most notable was the *Utrecht*, a Danish frigate which, in February 1807, was on its way to Curacao in the West Indies to defend the island from the invading British. Fortunately for the British, the well-equipped warship was wrecked. It capsized, losing a large number of its crew in the freezing waters. The captain and 366 survivors surrendered to the local laird. Small sections of copper plating, nails and a cannon remain on the shallow seabed amongst thick forests of kelp and seaweed.

South of the Bay of Brough is the Noust of Ayre. An easy landing in the bay gains access to the self-catering bunkhouse, hostel and campsite known as 'Ayres Rock'. The remaining rugged coastline, along the east coast, is in stark contrast to the rest of the coastline around Sanday. Jutting headlands, archways, caves and contorted rock architecture punctuate the cliffs for 3 km after the Bay of Brough.

Entering the narrows of Lashy Sound can be an exciting business at certain states of the tide. This is due to the speed of the water and mountainous white-capped waves which break and boil in the open shallow sea channel between Sanday and Eday. The final 3km of rocky coastline leads back to Loth Pier. Within Eday Sound, at certain states of tide, there may be a slow moving eddy heading north along the Sanday shoreline.

Tide and weather

Prior practice of launching and landing in dumping surf (which may be present on all beaches around Sanday) is advisable ... as is undertaking the journey in calm, or at most, moderate conditions. Ocean swell from the north-west can remain for days after poor weather.

Additional information

Camping on a deserted beach sounds idyllic. However, if it is wet or windy try to find a campsite away from the sand. Sand will get into everything, no matter how hard you try to avoid it!

There are two main shops on Sanday (Lady village and north of Bea Loch) both supplying a wealth of goods to satisfy any hungry or thirsty paddler. An excellent café and pizzeria, 500m inland from Roos Wick bay (59 degrees North), is well worth planning into your adventure once onto terra-firma.

The 4km open water crossing to North Ronaldsay (if linking the two journeys together) requires careful tidal planning and a watchful eye on the weather.

Admiralty Chart 2250, Imray Chart C68, and O.S. Explorer Map 465 cover this area.

Noup Head lighthouse and cliffs | Doug Cooper

Westray & Papa Westray

No. 24 | Grade C | 65km | 14 hours | OS Sheet 5 | Tidal Port Dover

Start/Finish	△○ Rapness Pier (510 405)
HW	HW Rapness is 1 hour 55 minutess before HW Dover. HW Pierowall is 1 hour 40 minutes before HW Dover.
Tidal Times	At Noup Head The general E going tidal flow is divided into two tidal streams. The ENE tidal stream heads towards Bow Head, and the SE tidal stream heads into the Westray Firth towards Inga Ness. Both tidal streams start 6 hours and ten minutes after HW Dover. In the Westray Firth between Wart Holm and Inga Ness the NW going tidal stream starts at 1 hour after HW Dover. Close inshore around Mull Head on Papa Westray the E going Tidal Stream starts 4 hours 15 minutes after HW Dover. The W going Tidal Stream starts 1 hour 45 minutes before HW Dover. The S going tidal stream in Papa Sound starts 6 hours after HW Dover. The N going tidal stream starts at HW Dover.
Max Rate at Sp	In Westray Firth (to the S of the island) is 3 knots. In Papa Sound is 3 knots in the narrows. Around Noup Head is up to 2 knots.

Pierowall Bay, fishing boat life rings | Chris Jex

	Off Bow Head 4 knots, and off Mull Head on Papa Westray it is up to 6 knots (The Bore Rost).
Coastguard	Shetland

Introduction

Westray (West Isle) is the most north-westerly island within the Orkney archipelago and has the prestigious title of 'The Queen of the Isles'. The island has a mixture of cultivated farmland, wild uplands, well-preserved historic sights, remote beaches and wave lashed cliffs. The neighbouring island of Papa Westray is home to the rare Scottish primrose, birdlife and has a wealth of interesting cliffs and archaeological sites. The two to three day journey passes some of the most spectacular and remote locations to be found in Orkney.

Description

Access onto the water is from a rocky beach north-west of the Rapness Pier. The ferry terminal has a waiting room, toilet and ample car parking area.

The journey south to the Point of Huro through the Rapness Sound passes a number of secluded sandy beaches. A short paddle out to Wart Holm provides an excellent vantage point to see the swirling waters and standing waves further south. From here either head north-west across the large open bay towards Kirk Taing, or paddle north around the coastline passing the Bay of Tafts.

Once past the unspoilt sandy beach at Mae Sands and the headland at Berst Ness, a small archway and remains of a broch signal the start of the more committing sections of coastline. Above the dramatic cliffs, a coastal path and moorland area provide an excellent walk for those less keen to paddle. The valley between Fitty and Gallo Hill is reputed to have staged a bloody battle between Westraymen and raiders from Lewis in the Outer Hebrides. Both sides fought

so hard that all were slain except one highlander. The name 'Highland-man's Hamar' is still used for a large outcrop of rock marking the spot where he fought. A number of large mounds close by are thought to be the mass graves of those slain in battle.

From Inga Ness follow the cliffs towards Bis Geos. The cliffs along the west facing coast have an amazing number of caves, waterfalls, archways and are exposed to the Atlantic swells. A short break at the small innaccessable beach below Bis Geos prepares the paddler for the next 'never to be forgotten' section of coastline.

The next 3km of cliffs, headlands, deep geos and spectacular views out west is one of the most memorable and special sections of paddling within Orkney. Paddling here in calm conditions will allow you to explore close in under the cliffs and adventure into the geos and caves that indent this section of coastline leading to the Lighthouse at Noup Head.

Below North Hill a narrow platform of rock cuts the cliffs at half height giving access to the Gentleman's Cave. The cave was used as a hideout by two lairds after the Jacobite rebellion. East of the distinct rock promontory known as Lawrence's Piece, a deep geo cuts into the land.

At the end of Noup Head an immense overhanging headwall stands beneath the lighthouse. The lighthouse, built in 1898, was the first to be built on the west coast of Orkney and can be seen up to 20 nautical miles offshore.

The white streaked cliffs and RSPB bird reserve at Noup Head are home to a large number of seabirds. During the nesting season they form the second largest breeding site in the UK. The sights, sounds and smell beneath the sea cliffs are truly memorable, the splatter of guano on your kayak not easily forgotten!

After 2.5 km of paddling along the north facing coast, the Bay of Noup offers respite from the sea and a secluded sandy beach. Further east, the pebbled beach at Grobust, fossils can be found on the angular rock slabs. The partially uncovered remains of a Skara Brae like village settlement lie unexcavated in the sand dunes.

The swell along the coastline and on the beautiful beach north of the golf course and Noltland Castle can build up quickly. If you camp here and wake to the roar and thunder of rolling waves, it may be worth hitching a lift and relocating your kayak to the shelter of the Bay of Pierowall, about 1km over land to the south-east.

Rock arches, pillars, blowholes and rocky reefs adorn the coastline between The Nev and Bow Head. The wave scoured rock platform before Bow Head was thought to have been the landing place of the first invading Vikings. Smerry Geo has two flat-topped rocks, supposedly where the Vikings had their first meal after landing on Westray!

The Survivors of the Spanish Armada

In 1588 a small boatload of survivors from a ship of the Spanish Armada landed on Westray. The 'Dons', as the survivors were known, settled on the island, married local girls and took on Orkney surnames. Even today a number of islanders can trace their ancestry back to the Spanish sailors.

Lady Kirk, Pierowall, Westray | Chris Jex

It is now possible to include a clockwise journey around Papa Westray before heading back west into Pierowall Bay. If time is short, head south through Papa Sound to the Bay of Pierowall and the main village.

After rounding Mull Head on Papa Westray, the first rock feature along the east coast is a spectacular archway and blowhole. The caves along Fowl Crag provide interesting exploration. At Leapers Geo it is possible to get out onto the rock shelf and scramble up the stepped rocks towards the twin stiles to visit the newly built bronze statue and monument to the last great auk in the UK (unfortunately shot in 1813). On the other side of the stone wall is a well known area for finding *Primula scotica* or the Scottish primrose. This dwarf sized version of the primrose is a rare species with a deep purple petal with a yellow centre and only grows in a few locations dotted around the Northern Isles.

At Cairn Head on the Holm of Papa, a square obelisk marks the location of a Neolithic chambered cairn. The short walk up to the cairn is rewarded with a stunning 360° panorama and the prospect of sighting storm petrels. Entry to the well-preserved 35m long underground chamber is via a metal trapdoor located half way along the grassy mound.

A short walk from the small pier on the east side of Papa Westray leads you past a small cooperative shop and hostel accommodation to a small museum next to Holland Farm.

At the south end of the island there is a beautiful sand beach within the Bay of Moclett. Inquisitive seals, stunning machair and wild flower meadows complete the ensemble and make for an excellent campsite.

On the west coastline of Papa Westray lies The Knap of Howar settlement. The dwellings were used from about 3600 BC, making them one of the oldest known houses within Northern

Europe. A knocking stone (used for grinding) and the intact 1.6m thick walls, shelves, walls, bed areas and cupboards are all in place, giving us a glimpse of life over 5 millennia ago.

Head west across open water and (at times) standing waves to the Bay of Pierowall. The village of Pierowall has a large pier, a restored water mill, a number of churches, village shops, a hotel and pub and the local school. Archaeological artefacts dating back to the 8th century, including axes, swords, beads and spears, have been unearthed from Viking war and boat graves. Noltland Castle (to the west) is worth a visit.

At the south end of the bay is The Barn hostel and campsite, easily accessed from the water. Fish and chips from Jack's Chippy or the Pierowall Hotel should be on the dinner menu of every hungry sea kayaker.

Open bays and low headlands lead to Castle O'Burrian, a loose rock stack with the remains of a hermitage and wall. The top of the stack is home to the largest puffin colony in Orkney.

The caves and steep rock walls of Stanger Head mark the final section of inaccessible coastline, culminating in the triangular shaped rock stack at Weather Ness. From here easy paddling (once through the tidal race) brings you back to the pier at Rapness.

The World's shortest flight

The airfield on Papa Westray, which lies only 2.5km away from the airfield on the neighbouring island of Westray, is famous for having the 'Shortest flight in the World'. The flight takes just under 2 minutes. The ten seater 'Islander' aeroplane barely gains height after take-off, before starting its descent. The record is 58 seconds from take off to landing!

Tide and weather

Tidal overfalls may be found at Point of Huro, Inga Ness, Noup Head, Bow Head and within Papa and Weatherness Sounds. North going eddy's form on both E and W coastlines of Papa Westray at the N end of the island for up to 9 hours.

Ocean swell along the west and north coast of Westray and east of Papa Westray should be planned for throughout the year except after unusually long periods of calm settled weather.

Beaches facing north or west may be difficult to land on in a moderate ocean swell.

Additional information

If choosing to camp at the Bay of Noup, please ask permission from Noup farm.

There is a daily ferry to Westray from Kirkwall and a weekly ferry service to Papa Westray. A passenger ferry from Pierowall in Westray to Papa Westray runs up to six times a day.

A short walk north-west from the pier is the Bird Observatory, a B&B, a self-catering hostel, café and local shop.

Admiralty Charts 2249 and 2250, 2250, Imray Chart C68, and O.S. Explorer Map 464 cover this area.

Arrival at North Ronaldsay, in the fog | Mark Rainsley

North Ronaldsay

25

No. 25 | Grade C | 18km | 4 hours | OS Sheet 5 | Tidal Port Dover	
Start/Finish	South Bay Pier (750 522)
HW	at North Ronaldsay is 1 hour 40 minutes before HW Dover.
Tidal Times	At the S and N ends of the island, the E going tidal stream starts 4-5 hours before HW Dover. To the S of the island, in the North Ronaldsay Firth, the NW going tidal stream starts at HW Dover. The SE going tidal stream starts 6 hours before HW Dover. To the N of the island, the S going tidal stream starts 1 hour after HW Dover veering SW, then NW, 3 hours after HW Dover.
Tidal Rates	at Dennis Head reach 5 Knots. off the headland at Twinyess reach 4 knots.
Coastguard	Shetland

Introduction

North Ronaldsay (Ringan's Isle) is the most northerly of the Orkney Islands. On a clear day, Fair Isle can be seen rising steeply out of the sea, 43km to the north-east. The unspoilt, laid back, nature of this peaceful island and its helpful and resourceful community make it a real gem in the crown of Orkney and an ideal place to escape the crowds.

145

North Ronaldsay lighthouse and sheep | Chris Jex

Description

The journey starts and finishes at the ferry terminal and pier on the island situated next to South Bay. A small flight of steps on the east side of the pier leads to the water. The direction of circumnavigation will generally be dependent on wind and/or tidal flow, but is described clockwise.

The coastline on the exposed west of the island has a number of low rocky outcrops, boulder beaches and a continuous dry stone dyke which guards the inner sanctum of the island. This dyke is designed to keep the island's unique population of North Ronaldsay sheep off the land, restricting them to the coastal fringe around the island for the majority of the year. The sheep's coarse wool is used to knit an array of expensive designer fashions and the rich dark red meat is highly prized and in demand in many top restaurants around the world.

A number of shallow geos break up the journey and allow paddlers to take a break if needed. The headlands along the west and north coast often produce large breaking waves. It is worth being cautious and keeping your distance from the shore when in the vicinity of any shallow reefs or headlands, especially west of The Lurn, Hoe Skerries and Green Skerry.

Once past Green Skerry, at the north end of the island, the reef to the north-west is aptly named Seal Skerry. The seals here, and at other haul outs around the island, seem to be inquisitive and relatively relaxed when humans are in the vicinity. At close range the reef also is home to a large number of cormorants that are often seen preening and drying their wings.

As you head around the Point of Sinsoss and past the new lighthouse the shallow water quickly speeds up and standing waves appear. The speed and power created by the tidal water and rumbling overfalls around this exposed headland can be humbling, even on a neap tide!

Once around Dennis Head you will find a small rocky pier jutting out just south of Dennis Loch. This is an excellent place to get out and stretch your legs. A short walk to the new lighthouse, café, and self catering accommodation will enable you to visit the felt making factory and island interpretation centre and, if timed appropriately, take a tour of the lighthouse guided by the keeper. The panoramic view from the top, after ascending the endless spiral steps, is definitely worth the effort.

The sanctuary of Linklet Bay along the east side of the island has a beautiful sandy beach. Straggly-coated sheep forage amongst the washed-up kelp, and a small colony of seals bask on the sand. The grassy area back from the beach is home to the North Ronaldsay Golf Course, a windswept area of hardy grass kept short by the sheep. Finding the holes and a fairway is not as straightforward as you may think!

Rounding Bride's Ness and the Point of Burrian, there is a notorious area of shallow water out to the east known as Reef Dyke. The reef is only 3m below LW and can amplify swell, especially if the wind is blowing from the south-east. At the Point of Burrian the exposed remains of a small iron age walled broch and settlement is visible. Off the point there is a tidal overfall which forms during a south-east going tide. Once into the safety of South Bay, with its crystal clear water and golden sands, a pleasant paddle along the shoreline will lead you back to the pier.

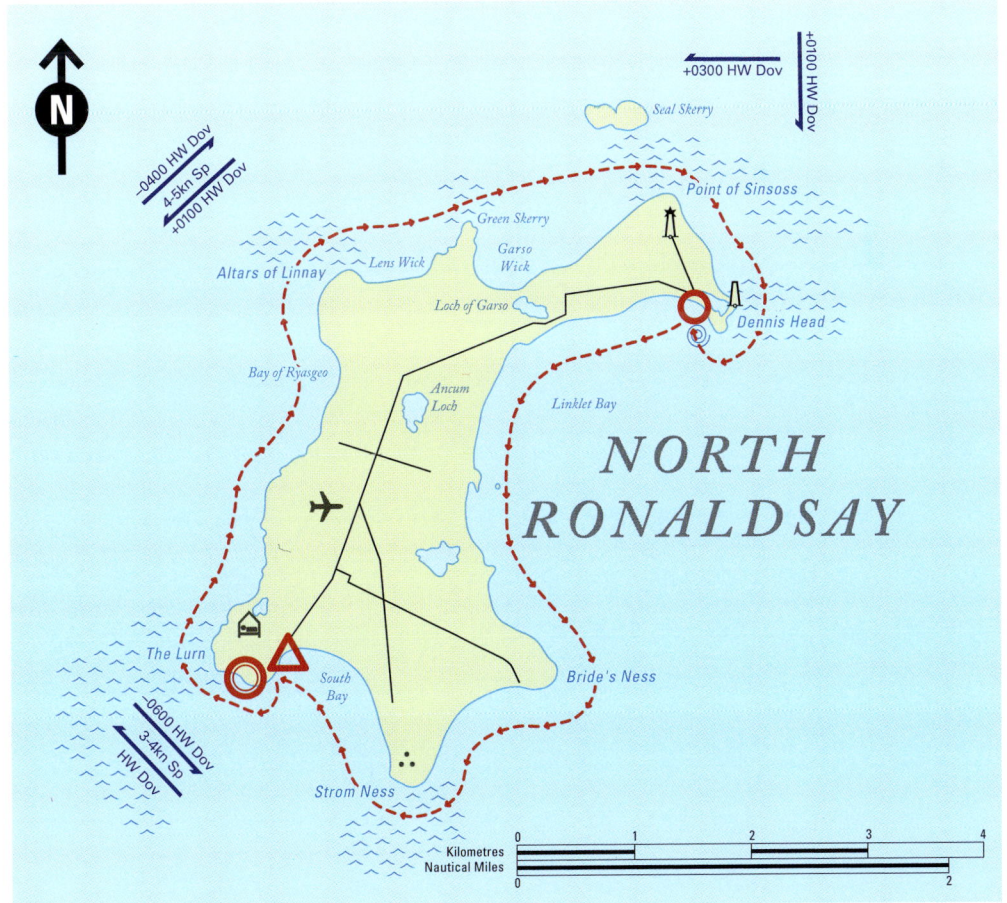

Tide and weather

The journey is exposed on all shores and there is little shelter once on the water. A close watch should be kept on increasing winds and changeable weather patterns as the weather on the island can be very localised. Summer fog after an east or south easterly wind is common. Calm weather before and during the journey will decrease the chance of a significant ocean swell or rough seas.

Departing approximately 6 hours before HW Dover and paddling clockwise will enable you to have the tide behind you at the start the journey. The south going stream around the north of the island starts 1-2 hours after HW Dover, by which time you should have rounded Dennis Head and be heading south.

Tidal streams generally run north and south on the E side of the island around, and over Reef Dyke. The north going flow starts 1 hour 45 minutes before HW Dover for 9 and half hours and the south going flow starts 4 hours 45 minutes before HW Dover lasting for 3 hours.

There is a weak clockwise eddy which forms in Linklet Bay during the E going tidal stream around the top of the island. This forms the 'Dennis Rost' off the NE extremity of the island.

Additional information

There is a weekly ferry service (Saturdays only) and regular daily flights from Kirkwall. From May until September (subject to weather) there is a Tuesday cargo sailing and a Sunday excursion sailing which may be from, or via Papa Westray (check Orkney Ferries timetable).

A short walk north-west from the pier is the Bird Observatory, a B&B, a self-catering hostel, café and local shop.

North Ronaldsay will be the last stopping off point for paddlers intending to complete the crossing to Fair Isle. This spectacular island is situated 43km away about halfway between Orkney and Shetland. Experienced paddlers wishing to attempt the crossing will of course be aware of prior sea conditions and any tidal movement during the 7-8 hour journey. Good Luck!

Admiralty Chart 2250, Imray Chart C68 and, O.S. Explorer Map 465 covers this area.

The Shetland Isles

An Introduction

The most northerly part of the British Isles, Shetland is a group of islands stretching around 180km north to south and about 60km east to west, mostly above the 60° north line of latitude. The capital Lerwick is about 290km north of Aberdeen in Scotland and a similar distance west of Bergen in Norway. There are approximately one hundred islands in total, of which fifteen are inhabited. Most of the population of around 23,000 live on the largest island, Mainland. Four islands, East and West Burra, Trondra, and Muckle Roe are linked to Mainland by bridges. The larger islands to the north and east, Yell, Unst, Fetlar, Whalsay, and Bressay are served by regular car ferries, as are the Out Skerries and Papa Stour. The more remote islands of Foula and Fair Isle have passenger ferries and air links.

Both Shetland and Orkney were part of Denmark until just over 500 years ago, when they passed to Scotland as part of the dowry of a Danish princess. Sadly she died before the marriage to the future Scottish king could take place, but both island groups have been Scottish ever since. Unlike in the Western Isles, Gaelic was never spoken in Orkney or Shetland. The dialect in both island groups derives from Norn, the old Norse language, with later Scottish additions. Most place names have their origins in Norn. A number of historic buildings, such as Scalloway Castle and Muness Castle in Unst, date from the period immediately after the transfer, when the kings of Scotland sent their favourites to establish Scottish rule.

The geology of Shetland is complex and fascinating, giving rise as it does to hundreds of miles of magnificent cliff scenery, riddled with caves, arches, stacks and passages. There are also some beautiful beaches, never overcrowded and frequently deserted.

This seashore is home to a large population of grey and common seals, otters, and huge numbers of seabirds. Many of the seabirds are only present in the summer nesting season, spending their winters at sea or in warmer climates. Their numbers are augmented by winter visitors from the Arctic, and by passage migrants in spring and autumn. Many of these migrants are rare in Britain, and Fair Isle and Fetlar in particular have become Meccas for birdwatchers. Shetland is home to a diverse range of whales and dolphins, from small elusive porpoises to orcas (killer whales) and humpback whales.

Shetland is often characterised as treeless. Although this is not quite true the typical Shetland view is of open windswept heath or moorland, populated by curlews, lapwings, plovers, and carpeted in wild flowers in spring and early summer.

The economy of the islands has traditionally been based on fishing and crofting. It used to be said that an Orkneyman was a farmer with a boat, but that a Shetlander was a fisherman with a croft. Shetland, and Fair Isle in particular, were also famous for their distinctive knitwear. Today, despite many recent troubles, fishing remains a major component of the Shetland economy, but very few Shetlanders are full-time farmers or crofters, and even fewer are employed in the knitwear industry. Since the 1970s the oil industry has been a major component of the local economy, and the Sullom Voe Terminal, and more recently the Shetland Gas Plant are important employers. Fish farming has grown to be a visible feature of almost every voe and inlet around the coast, and is Shetland's largest employer. Tourism is also important, and increasing numbers are choosing to visit some of the most beautiful, dramatic and unspoiled coastlines in Europe.

The climate in the isles is characterised as western maritime. It is much milder than the latitude would lead you to expect because of the influence of the North Atlantic Drift, a powerful ocean current that is part of the larger Gulf Stream system which carries warmer water towards Europe. Winters are wet, windy, and often stormy. Snow is less common than in the north of Scotland and tends not to last. Spring and early summer can be cool and changeable, and sea fog is common especially in the east and south. The best chance of a settled spell of weather is from May to July. High pressure over the British Isles does not guarantee good weather in Shetland; high pressure over southern Scandinavia is a better indicator.

Because the islands are so close to the Arctic Circle it never gets really dark around midsummer. The sun will dip below the horizon for an hour or so and the resulting twilight is known as the *'simmer dim'*. It is quite possible to find your way around, and even to read a book by this light. In complete contrast there is very little daylight in late December, and when the weather is overcast the streetlights will stay on all day. However if the weather is clear and frosty in winter the aurora borealis or northern lights is a frequent companion.

The west side of the islands is much affected by Atlantic swell, while the east side is a typical North Sea environment. The tidal flow around Shetland is shaped by the interaction between the Atlantic Ocean to the west and the North Sea to the east. This dynamic creates complex tidal patterns, with flows influenced by the large-scale circulation of water from both bodies and the intricate local topography. As the tide rises (flood tide), water typically moves around Shetland in a clockwise direction. This means that water flows from the south, sweeping up the west coast, then around the northern tip of the islands, and down the east coast. During the falling tide (ebb), the flow reverses. The water tends to move in an anticlockwise direction, draining from the east side, circulating northwards, and flowing down the west coast. The strongest tidal flows are in the sounds between the islands and around the northern and southern headlands. Elsewhere tidal streams are normally not severe. The rise and fall is typically 2m on springs. High Water Lerwick is within ten minutes of Dover, so Dover tide tables can be used as a reasonable approximation. All the secondary port corrections are negative with respect to Lerwick, with high water on the west side between one and two hours earlier. The Clyde Cruising Club's *Sailing Directions for Shetland* and the *Admiralty Tidal Stream Atlas for Orkney and Shetland* are recommended sources of tidal information.

The Maritime Rescue Co-ordination Centre covering the Northern Isles is Shetland Coastguard in Lerwick, tel. 01595 692976. Carrying a handheld VHF radio is recommended, although coverage can be patchy, particular close to cliffs which can block line-of-sight transmission. However, there are often fishing boats and other vessels around who can relay messages. Mobile phone coverage, like VHF can be limited in rural locations and areas of high cliff.

There are a number of official campsites in Shetland and where relevant these are referred to in the text. Elsewhere camping is generally not a problem in uncultivated areas. If there is a house within sight of your chosen pitch it is polite to ask permission. This is unlikely to be refused, and will often be accompanied by generous hospitality and sound advice on local conditions.

Bannamin beach, Burra | Mark Rainsley

Burra & South Havra

No. 26	**Grade B**	**20km**	**6 hours**	**OS Sheet 4**	**Tidal Port Lerwick**
Start/Finish	Bridge End Outdoor Centre (373 332)
HW	Local HW is 1 hour 20 minutes before HW Lerwick.
Tides	There are no significant tidal streams in this area.
Coastguard	Shetland

Introduction

West Burra, East Burra and Trondra are three long narrow islands lying roughly NNE to SSW off the west side of the Shetland mainland, just south of Scalloway; they are linked to the mainland and to each other by bridges. Bridge End Outdoor Centre is located next to the old bridge linking East and West Burra. There is direct access to the sheltered water of South Voe via a slipway and pontoon, which are available to the public. There is a launching fee of £1 per kayak as of 2025, and payment is via an honesty box. Alternative and free access is at the beach at Papil to the south, although parking is more limited. The island of South Havra to the south is sometimes known as 'Shetland's St Kilda'. It was inhabited until 1923 when the remaining inhabitants were evacuated to Scalloway or Burra.

Little Havra | Geoff Burke

Description

This trip starts from the Bridge End Outdoor Centre, and initially takes us south via the Holm of Houss and the deserted croft of Symbister on East Burra. Here there is a shingle spit and a large area of shallow water to be negotiated. From May to August this spit is home to a colony of Arctic terns, and care should be taken to avoid disturbing them.

Continuing south along the coast the scenery gradually becomes more interesting until rounding Scaalie Point you come into a small bay. There are several caves here and a fine natural arch. The best of the caves is the most westerly, where a very obvious and clear entrance leads into a shallow cave with a pebble beach. As you approach the beach you become aware of another exit to the right, narrower and more open to southerly or westerly swell. On the east side of the bay are the Stacks of Houssness, a jumble of contorted shapes sticking out of the water like rotten teeth, home to large numbers of shags. This area can become difficult in a westerly swell (particularly when the tide is ebbing against the swell) when a break can extend some distance to the south of the stacks. In these conditions it is best to give the area a wide berth to the west and south but come around and explore the stacks from the east.

South Havra is the island dominating the view to the south from here. It has a small square structure prominent on its highest point. The best point to aim for is the north coast a little to the right of this. The crossing is just under a mile and you may see porpoises in the sound. Arriving at South Havra come into the small bay about midway along the north coast, where you will find an interesting blind arch and a number of caves and stacks. Following round onto the east coast the

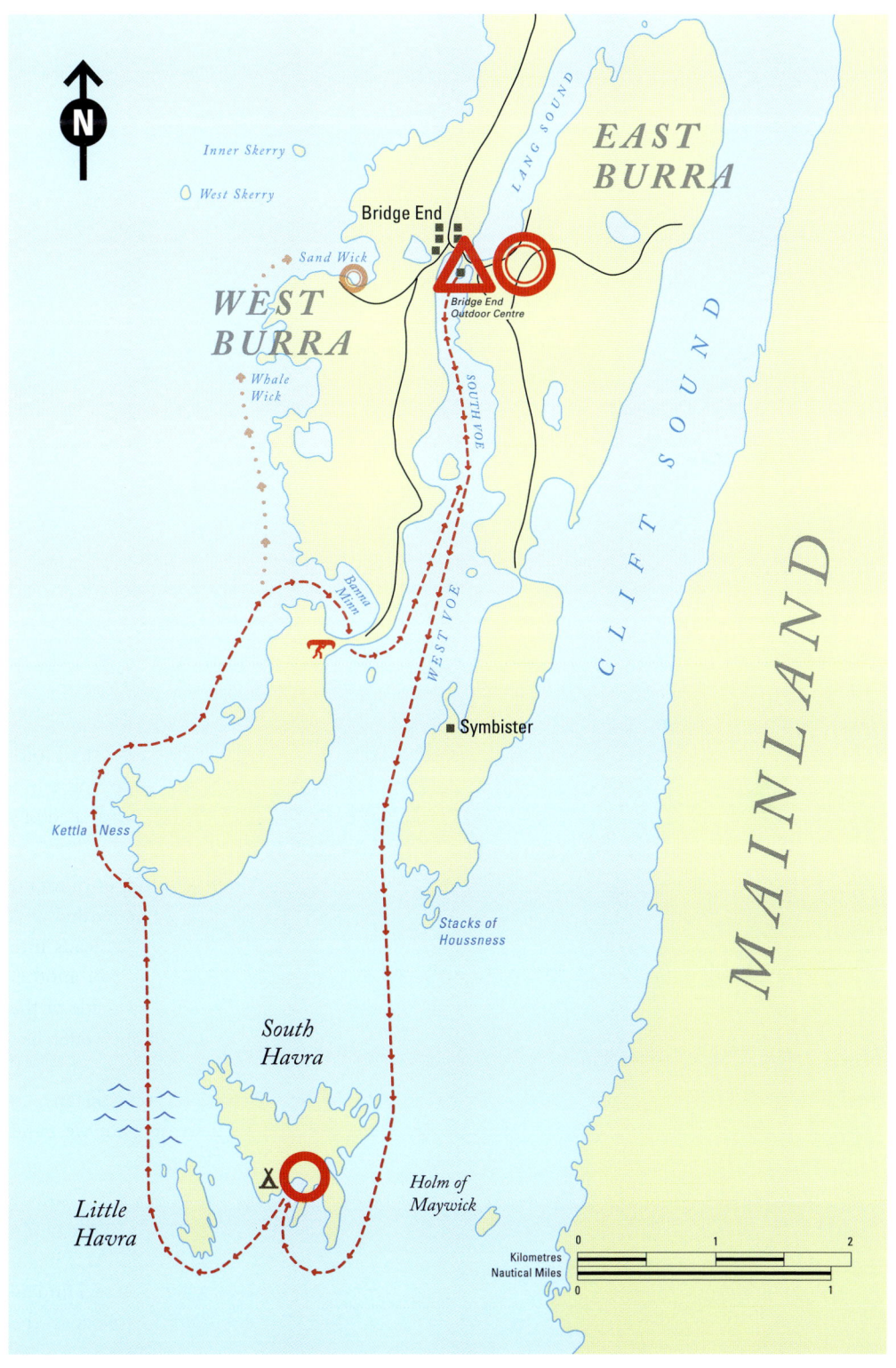

South Havra | Rachel Shucksmith

route passes a small kittiwake colony and comes to a deep inlet near the southeast corner, with a pebble beach at the inner end overlooked by a small sheepfold. This is the beach generally used by local boats visiting the island, and is the best one to use in westerly conditions. Otherwise continue round the south end of the island and turn into the sound between South Havra and the small island to the west. There is a group of ruined houses on a headland to the north. Around this headland the next inlet is West Ham, where you can land on a small sandy beach below the houses to explore the island.

South Havra is a fertile little island, which supported a small but significant population until 1923. There was even a school with eight pupils at one time. All the houses were in a small compact settlement near the cliff edge. This precarious situation led to the practice of tethering young children so they would not fall over the cliffs. The reason for crowding the houses so close together in such an exposed position was to free up as much as possible of the good land for agricultural use. However there is no peat on the island so the inhabitants had to cast their fuel on the mainland and bring it across by boat. Similarly there are no streams on South Havra, all the water coming from a couple of wells, so the click mills commonly used in other parts of Shetland for grinding corn were not possible here. Accordingly in the 19th century the inhabitants built a windmill and this is the prominent structure on the skyline that dominates the island.

As in most of Shetland subsistence agriculture was supplemented by fishing. For much of the 19th century this was carried out with small open boats called sixareens, rowed by a crew of six. These boats were normally hauled up over the beach when not in use. With the coming of the herring boom at the end of that century came the steam drifters, which needed a safe harbour

West Ham, South Havra | Geoff Burke

and there was none on South Havra. All these factors, together with the increasing aspirations brought on by modern communications, probably contributed to the final decision to evacuate. One of the old croft houses in the settlement has been renovated and is used by crofters from Burra who keep sheep on the island.

Setting off again you could include a circuit of the West Isle (Little Havra on the OS map). There is a cave with a collapsed roof at the south end, a blowhole, and a profusion of wild flowers in season. The sea to the west and north of the West Isle is often confused with shallows and a number of offshore rocks, much affected by westerly swell. The headland of Kettla Ness on West Burra is now about a mile due north. From here it is possible to explore the many caves, arches and stacks on the west coast of West Burra. The large stack in the north-facing bay just after rounding The Heugg has an arch through it. Look for the large bulk of Fugla Stack a little further on. The inside channel here is normally passable but dries to a kelp bed at low tide and sheep can occasionally be seen crossing over. An alternative to paddling round West Burra is to come in to the large sheltered bay at Bannaminn. The entrance is less than a hundred metres wide and fairly clear but subject to swell. The best place to land in the bay is at the farthest right end of the beach, with a short carry over the narrow neck to West Voe. From here it is about 3km back to the outdoor centre.

VARIATIONS

If you have time to continue north along the west coast of West Burra the area around Whale Wick is worth exploring. There are a couple of tortuous linked caves at the south end of the bay

Bridge End outdoor centre | Geoff Burke

and a reasonably straightforward landing on a shingle beach at the north end. The large stack which guards the north entrance to Whale Wick is split by a fine arch. Landing is possible in Sandwick at a small, sandy beach on the south side. A short carry to a rough road followed by a short walk takes you back to the outdoor centre. It is possible to carry on round the north end of West Burra returning to the outdoor centre via Lang Sound. It is also possible to land on the beach at Sands of Meal, or alongside the pier at Hamnavoe.

Sands of Meal is a popular tourist beach and there is a good path leading to a car park and toilets at the main road. It also offers reasonable surf in a south-westerly swell, plus some good breaks on the skerries offshore.

Tide and weather

Tide is not a major consideration here in good weather, but a south-westerly wind against an ebbing tide can cause a break at Houss Ness. Westerly or south-westerly swell can make conditions difficult on the west side of West Burra and particularly around the northwest of South Havra.

Additional information

Accommodation at Bridge End Outdoor Centre is available for groups. There is an area for camping immediately to the south of the centre with basic facilities and a hook-up area for campervans and caravans. There is a shop by the pier in Hamnavoe.

OS Explorer Map 466 and Admiralty Chart 3283 also cover this area.

© Langa and Hildasay | Rachel Shucksmith

Skeld to Scalloway

No. 27	**Grade B** | **20km** | **5 hours** | **OS Sheet 4** | **Tidal Port Lerwick**
Start	△ Skeld Boating Club (448 313)
Finish	◯ Scalloway Boating Club (400 394)
HW	Local HW is 1 hour 20 minutes before HW Lerwick.
Tides	There are no significant tidal streams in this area.
Coastguard	Shetland

Introduction

This is a varied trip, starting with a fine section of coast around the Reawick peninsula, followed by a short open crossing, then a tour through the Scalloway Islands, a popular area for boating and sailing. There are several salmon farms, and Scalloway is a working harbour used by fishing boats and other commercial traffic.

Description

The best starting point for this trip is the Boating Club at Easter Skeld. There is a small caravan park and campsite here, with public toilets and a slipway. The suggested route initially heads south

157

© Skelda Voe | Katie Brigden

out of Skelda Voe then southeast around the Reawick peninsula to the headland at Roe Ness. The Aa Skerries on the way are home to a colony of grey seals. There are a number of caves and passages in this section, including one very deep cave with two entrances just west of the Bay of Deepdale. There is a good landing at Deepdale on a sheltered beach before rounding Roe Ness.

From Roe Ness it is possible to cross directly east towards the chain of islets and skerries known as the Sandas. A more interesting option is to paddle north along the Reawick cliffs first. This shortens the open crossing a little and the cliff scenery is well worth the diversion. The crossing will now be a little over 2km, and there is a good chance of sighting porpoises on the way. It is possible to land on a boulder beach on the north side of Sanda Stour, the largest and most southerly of the group. A deep cleft entered from the south side of Sanda Stour almost divides the island in two.

Crossing now to the northwest corner of Hildasay the route takes us down the east side of the island to the obvious landing point in a small bay sheltered by a little pier. Hildasay is the largest and most interesting of the Scalloway Islands. Although inhabited in the 19th century it has been abandoned for many years. At one time granite was quarried on Hildasay and carried to waiting ships, which could lie alongside in deep water on the north-east corner. The abandoned quarry can be seen just north of West Loch, the larger of the two lochs on the island. The stone used to be transported by a small railway, the line of which can still just be made out. It was used as ballast in sailing ships going to Australia and the Far East, and several public buildings in Sydney are said to be faced with Hildasay granite. The two freshwater lochs, one with a small

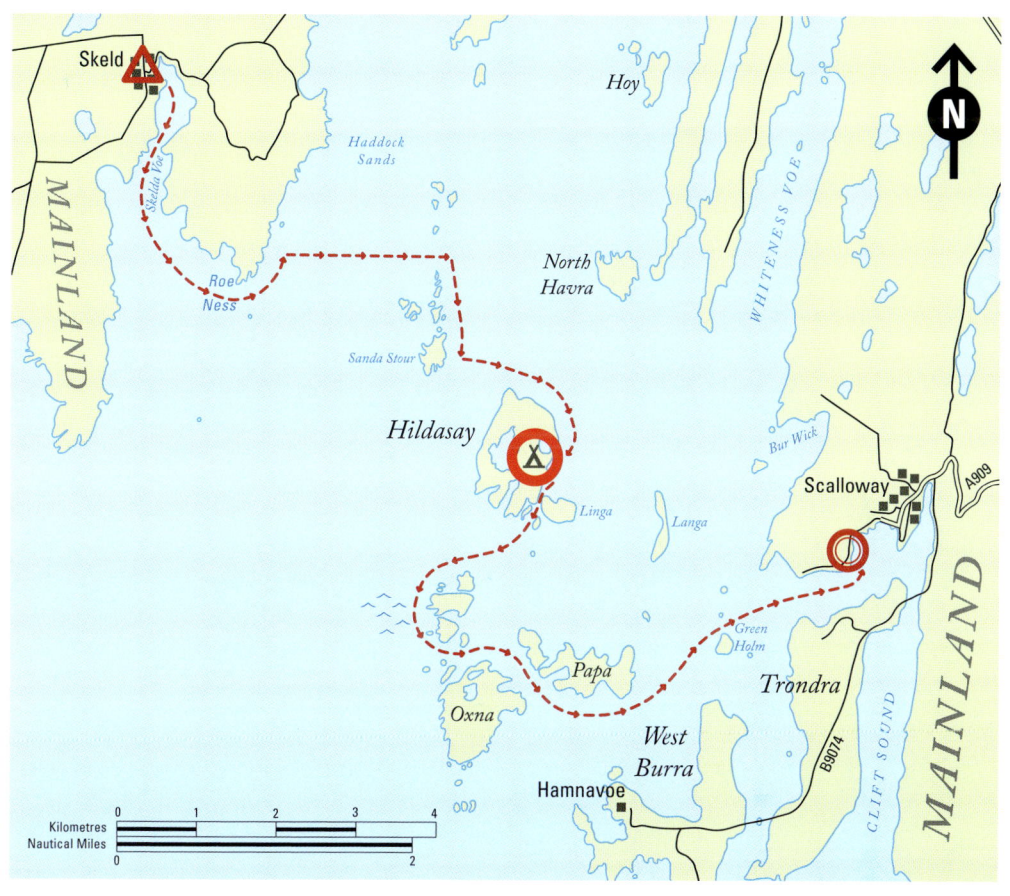

island in it, take up a surprisingly large part of the interior. Red-throated divers can usually be spotted on these lochs. Toward the north end of the island is an old crofthouse, restored in Norwegian style with a turf roof and used as a summerhouse.

From Hildasay it is possible to make your way by a number of different routes through the rest of the Scalloway Islands. The suggested route takes you through the sound between Oxna and Papa, the next two islands in size after Hildasay. Both of these were formerly inhabited and Oxna, like Hildasay, has a restored house used as a summerhouse. If you have time to explore these islands the natural landing place on Papa is at North Voe, and the ruins of the former inhabitants' houses are at the back of the beach here. Landing is also possible on the east side on a pebble beach a little south of the Hogg of Papa. On Oxna the natural landing place is at Sandy Voe on the north-east, just below the restored two-storey cottage, but there is an easy beach landing in Hogg Sound on the north-west. In westerly weather there is often a considerable swell on the west side of Oxna and especially around the Steggies, a group of rocks a few hundred metres to the south. The passage to the north of Bulta Skerry on the north side of Oxna can look daunting in these conditions but is fairly straightforward.

House on Hildasay | Katie Brigden

27 Skeld to Scalloway

The final stage from Papa into Scalloway takes us north of the Green Holm, a prominent (and very green!) islet. There are a number of skerries to watch for. The main shipping channel into Scalloway here passes between the Green Holm and the Merry Holm. This seems highly unlikely on the map, but makes much more sense when seen from the water.

Coming into Scalloway, it is advisable to stay close to the north shore to avoid the shipping channel, and follow round past the prominent buildings of UHI Shetland (although frequently referred to by its historic name 'the fisheries college' by locals). The landing place is a slipway adjacent to the Boating Club premises, just before the marina.

Tide and weather

This is a relatively sheltered trip, with no serious tidal considerations and few weather problems in anything other than a strong southerly. In south-westerly swell conditions it may be advisable to stay on the east side of Oxna.

Additional information

Scalloway is a working harbour, and the suggested route will keep you clear of the buoyed channel but look out for fish farm traffic and other fast moving powerboats. Scalloway is also Shetland's second town and former capital, and has much to see, including a ruined castle dating back to the 16th century, an excellent small museum, and a memorial to the wartime Shetland Bus. UHI Shetland is home to an excellent fish restaurant.

OS Explorer Map 466 and Admiralty Chart 3283 also cover this area.

Raewick beach | Katie Brigden

Reawick to Walls, & Vaila

No. 28 | Grade B | 30km | 8 hours | OS Sheet 3 & 4 | Tidal Port Lerwick

Start	△ Reawick (330 446)
Finish	○ Walls Boating Club (244 494)
HW	Local HW is 1 hour 50 minutes before HW Lerwick.
Tidal Times	The SE going stream starts about 3 hours before HW Lerwick and the NW going stream starts about 3 hours after HW Lerwick.
Max Rate at Sp	West of Vaila is 1.5 knots.
Coastguard	Shetland

Introduction

This is a magnificent stretch of coastline, often overlooked in favour of the 'blockbusters' like Papa Stour and Esha Ness. The highlight is the fine stretch of cliffs either side of the dramatic bay of Westerwick. The island of Vaila is worth a trip in itself.

Giltarump and the Nev | Geoff Burke

Description

The best start point is the beach at Reawick. Alternatively you could start from alongside the boating club at Easter Skeld, as described in Route 27. There is a car park here and public toilets, but this would mean missing a really fine section of coast south of Reawick.

From Reawick follow the coast south to Roe Ness exploring as you go. The cliffs here are impressive and there are a number of stacks and small caves, with one fairly large cave to find. After rounding Roe Ness there is a possible landing at Deepdale, the first beach you come to. The coastline from here to Aa Skerry is particularly fine with a number of passages and hidden caves, including one close to Deepdale which is very deep though narrow. Aa Skerry is usually populated by a small colony of grey seals. From here the route crosses Skelda Voe and follows the coast south to the headland at Skelda Ness. The view to the south is dominated by the distant bulk of Fitful Head. As you round Skelda Ness a spectacular view opens up along the coast, with Foula on the western horizon. In the first bay at Silwick is a pair of stacks, marked Clett on the map, with several arches and passages between them. From here to the huge stack of the Rump (Giltarump on the OS Map, from the words 'galti' meaning a hog and 'runk' meaning bulky) is only about 2km, but there is so much of interest it is unlikely to take much less than two hours. The stacks and caves are endless. The Bay of Westerwick is particularly dramatic, and on the mainland opposite the Rump are a couple of really exceptional caves.

The next section of coast also has much of interest but is overshadowed by the Westerwick section and the island of Vaila ahead. Heading into Walls the best landing is by the Boating Club at the head of the sound. Road access is by taking a left turn just past the public hall in Walls and almost immediately a slip road to the right. The commercial pier on the west side of the voe is less inviting. Another possible landing is at the far west of Lera Voe where a conspicuous round tower on the shore indicates the mainland landfall for the private ferry to Vaila. This is also the best starting point for a trip round Vaila. To reach it by road drive through Walls and follow signs for Burrastow. The tower is on the shore about 1km before Burrastow House.

VARIATIONS

Other access points on this section are at Westerwick, a short carry from the road end over a field to a small pebble beach beside an old boathouse, and Culswick, a bit more of a carry and not recommended. Landings are also possible at Deepdale on Roe Ness and at Silwick, but without road access. If visiting Vaila it is possible to land at the pier on the north-east corner or on the shingle beach in front of Vaila House, the large prominent building on the north-west corner.

The Nev | Doug Cooper

The island is private but visitors are not discouraged. Continuing round, the west and south-west of the island is often rough as the tide runs close to shore here. The main interest on the island is the beautiful bay of the Muckle Bight on the southeast bounded by the Gaada Stacks on the east. A landing is usually possible in the north-west corner of this bay.

Tide and weather

The main thing to be aware of here is the westerly swell. The tide sets along the coast flooding to the south-east and ebbing to the north-west. Streams are generally weak, but somewhat stronger around Skelda Ness and the south-west of Vaila between Strom Ness and Reitta Ness. Both of these places can be difficult if the tide is ebbing against a westerly swell. This area tends to be sheltered in a north-easterly.

Additional information

OS Explorer Map 467 and Admiralty Chart 3283 also cover this area.

Approaching Foula | Mark Rainsley

Foula

No. 29 | Grade C | 26km | 6 hours | OS Sheet 4 | Tidal Port Lerwick

Start	△ Dale of Walls (174 523)
Finish	◯ Ham (974 387)
HW	Local HW is 1 hour 35 minutes before HW Lerwick.
Tidal Times	Off Strem Ness the SE going stream starts 2 hours before HW Lerwick, and the NW going stream starts 3 hours after HW Lerwick.
Max Rate at Sp	Is typically 2 knots offshore.
Coastguard	Shetland

Introduction

Foula is arguably the most remote inhabited island in Britain. Its only serious rival for that title is Fair Isle which is further from the nearest other land; but Fair Isle has inhabited islands to north and south, while there is nothing west of Foula but the open Atlantic. The crossing from mainland Shetland is shorter than the Fair Isle channel, but potentially very rewarding.

© Gaada stack, Foula | Mark Rainsley

Description

The nearest mainland point to Foula with road access is the beach at Dale of Walls. To get there follow the road through the village of Walls, past places with names like Burraland and Greenland, until eventually the road winds down into this Brigadoon-like valley; then turn left on a rough track leading to a similarly rough car park overlooking a shingle beach. Looking straight out to the south-west the view is dominated by the high peaked outline of Foula about 24km away.

Tides in this area are not very reliable but generally flood from north-west to south-east and ebb in the opposite direction, becoming circular in open water. To the east of Foula the tide tends to run strongly north and south over an area of shallows and rocks. It was on these shallows, the Shaalds o' Foula, that the *Titanic's* sister-ship the *Oceanic* was sunk in the First World War. There is a fascinating account of diving on this wreck contained in the book *The Other Titanic* by Simon Martin. The suggested route makes landfall just south of Stremness on the north-east corner of the island, thus avoiding the Shaalds, but it is still a good idea to aim to arrive at slack water. After making landfall the route follows the coast south to land at the slipway by the ferry pier at Ham.

ALTERNATIVE ROUTE

If the trip to Foula seems a bit ambitious there is an excellent coastal trip available from Sandness to Walls, taking in Dale of Walls, and with superb views of Foula along the way. Leaving from the beach at Melby in Sandness this route initially turns west around Ness of Melby and the off-lying skerries, then goes along a section of coast known as the Clumpers, which is exposed to westerly swells and liable to break in moderate conditions. Next comes the Bay of Deepdale, with its high cliffs and dumping beach. It is difficult to land on, and accessible from the land only by following the gorge of the Burn of Deepdale, which reaches the sea at the southern end of the beach. The next 3km is a maze of stacks and arches, with much to explore, until you enter the Voe of Dale. Here you can break for lunch on the shingle beach and enjoy the view of Foula.

Continuing south, the great headland of Watsness is the closest mainland point to Foula and has a couple of large skerries and a particularly fine cave. The next few kilometres past Footabrough are less interesting, until the headland which marks the entrance to Wester Sound between Walls and Vaila. It is worth spending a little time exploring the stacks and caves here before finishing, usually either in front of Burrastow House or at the head of Lera Voe (see route 28).

Tide and weather

The crossing to Foula should only be considered in good weather with favourable sea conditions. The tides run largely directly across the route. The best plan is to allow about 5 hours for the crossing and aim to make landfall close to HW slack, about 2 hours 30 minutes after HW Dover. This means the tide will be pushing you south towards the Shaalds for the whole crossing.

Additional information

At 370m the cliffs on the west side of Foula are the highest in Britain after St Kilda, but, unlike St Kilda, Foula is still inhabited by around thirty hardy souls. The famous 1930s film *The Edge of the World*, which was based on the evacuation of St Kilda, was actually filmed on Foula.

OS Explorer Map 467 and Admiralty Charts 3283 and 3281 cover this area.

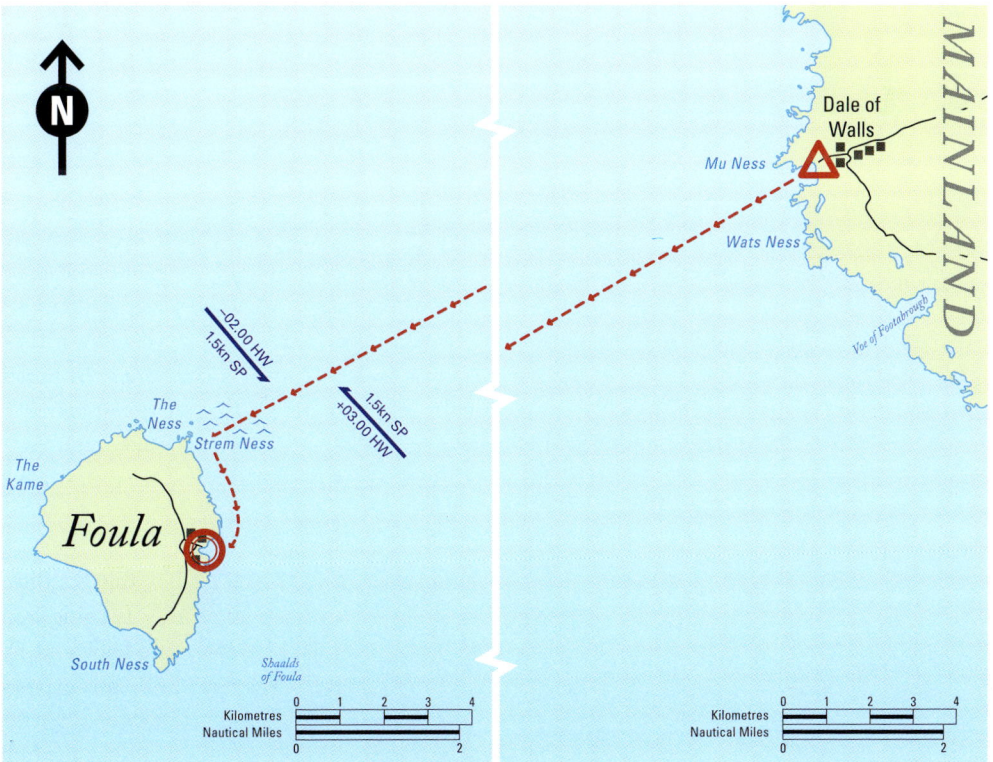

Bonxie (Great Skua) | Richard Shucksmith

The Bonxie

Foula may be home to only around thirty people but its cliffs and high moors are inhabited by vast numbers of seabirds, notably gannets, puffins, and guillemots. Perhaps its most famous resident is the great skua or 'bonxie', as it is known to every Shetlander. They are closely related to the brown skuas and Antarctic skuas of the southern hemisphere, and of course to their more elegant northern cousins the Arctic skuas, but they are not numerous in global terms. A significant proportion of the total world population is found in Shetland, with the island of Foula of particular importance. However, bans on fisheries discards, which supported the great skua population and more recently bird flu (summers 2022 and 2023) have led to nesting bird declines of over 70%. In the summer of 2022 over 1,400 great skuas were found dead in Foula alone. They are big strong birds best known for their aggressive behaviour both towards other birds and towards humans who are unwise enough to stray into their nesting area. They are known as pirate birds because they live by stealing food from other seabirds, most notably gannets which they persecute endlessly. Their usual technique is to pick on a gannet returning to its nest and drive it down onto the sea, where they will force its head under water until it regurgitates its stomach contents, giving the bonxies a free meal which was destined for the gannet's young. The bonxie is equally aggressive in defence of its own young, and anyone who strays into a bonxie nesting site can expect to see a large brown bird heading straight for them at speed. Generally they fly just over the head, but there's no guarantee, and the sight alone is enough to scare most people off.

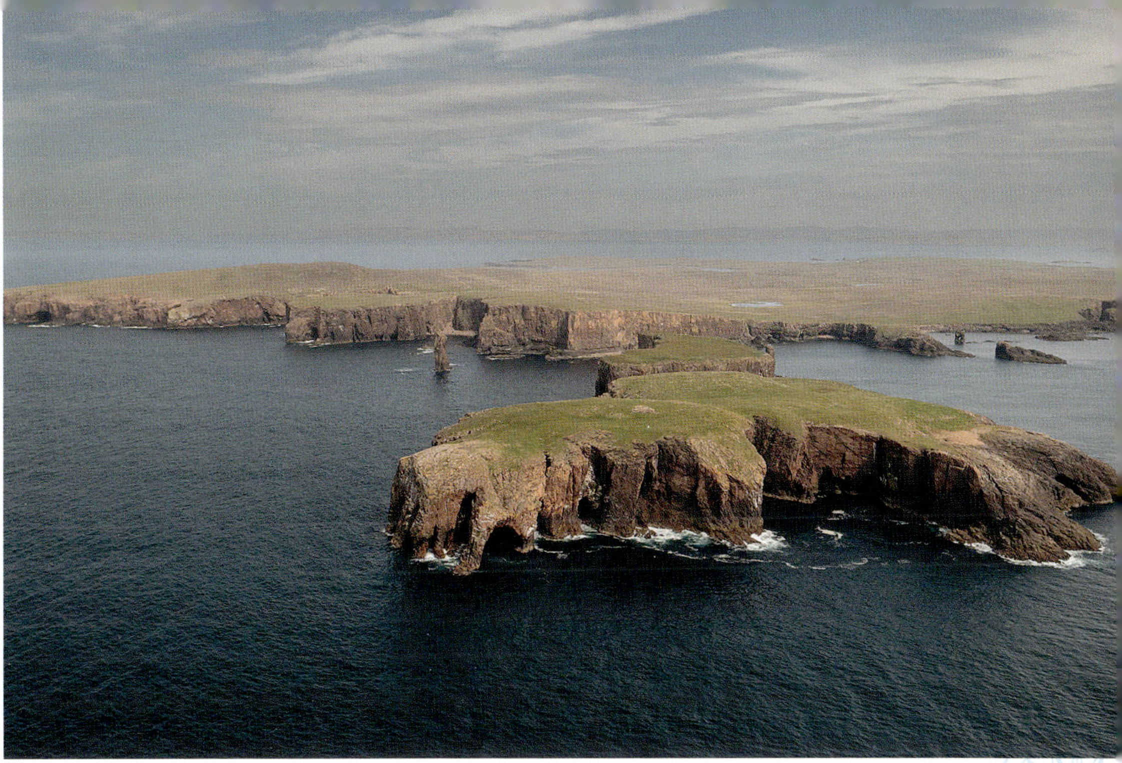

Papa Stour

No. 30	Grade C | 23km | 6 hours | OS Sheet 3 | Tidal Port Lerwick
Start/Finish	△○ Melby (187 579)
HW	Local HW is 2 hours 5 minutes before HW Lerwick.
Tidal Times	In the Sound of Papa the W going stream starts approximately 4 hours before HW Lerwick, and the E going stream starts approximately 3 hours 30 minutes after HW Lerwick. Tide times off the NW corner of the island are similar.
Max Rate at Sp	In the Sound of Papa is 6 knots. Off the headland of Boardie is 4 knots.
Coastguard	Shetland

Introduction

In my opinion the circumnavigation of Papa Stour is one of the best day trips to be found anywhere. The sea cliffs on the west side are rightly renowned and the Hol o' Boardie, a 300m long tunnel through the north-western headland, is believed to be the fourth longest sea cave in the world.

~ *The jewel in the crown* ~

Lyra Skerry, Papa Stour | Nick McCaffrey.

Description

The trip round Papa Stour can be done from a base on the island itself, and this greatly eases the tidal calculations. The natural starting point on the Mainland is at Melby in Sandness. Travelling out from Lerwick towards Walls, ignore signs for the Papa Stour ferry, which now leaves from West Burrafirth, and continue on to the end of the road in Sandness at the car park by a slipway and a sandy beach. This was the original Papa Stour ferry terminal and there are toilets and a storeroom as well as the slipway.

Leaving Melby, the route is round the headland to the left, then to the northwest, avoiding the rocks shown on the map as the Grava Skerries. Landfall should be made at the more westerly and smaller of the two visible beaches on the Papa shore near Scarvi Taing. This is the most southerly part of the island and in westerly conditions the size of the break on the shallow bar here is a good guide to conditions to the west.

The first major point of interest is just around this corner at Clingri Geo where there is a collapsed cave with some remarkable erosion patterns in the rock. There are a number of large caves and stacks in the area of Mo Geo, and a good landing just around the corner on the east side of Hamna Voe. Crossing Hamna Voe and passing inside the low-lying Swarta Skerry, the next target is the Galti Stacks. The next 5km stretch of coast has the most spectacular. sequence of caves, arches and skerries to be seen anywhere. After Breigeo Head is North Lungi Geo, a deep inlet with a steep pebble beach where it is usually possible to land. The next geo is the entrance to the best known of Papa's caves, Christie's Hole, or more correctly Kirstan Hol. The entrance is through a large clear arch, guarded by a tall stack. You are now in a long collapsed cave. At the start of the cave proper the main passage splits into three, all of which lead to another huge chamber, the roof of which collapsed in 1983. Unfortunately a further collapse in the winter of 2022/2023 has dramatically changed the character of this cave, with the roof rubble blocking the back of the cave. It is possible that over subsequent winters the sea will remove loose material, restoring some of its former glory.

The next major highlights are the two enormous stacks of the Lyra Skerry and the Fogla Skerry off Aesha Head. The Lyra Skerry is split by a wide passage running north to south, and a much narrower, longer passage running east to west, forming a dramatic 'crossroads' in the middle. The Fogla Skerry is riddled with passages and chambers, including a huge cavern with several entrances. Care should be taken here as the tide runs strongly around both skerries and through the passages, especially the main passage in the Lyra Skerry. Another factor is that conditions can often be very different on the north side of the skerries.

Heading now past the dramatic vertical stack of the Snolda towards the huge block of Boardie, the isolated lighthouse on the Ve Skerries should be visible on the horizon about 5 miles to the north-west. On the main island around here there used to be a huge arch known as the 'Horn o'

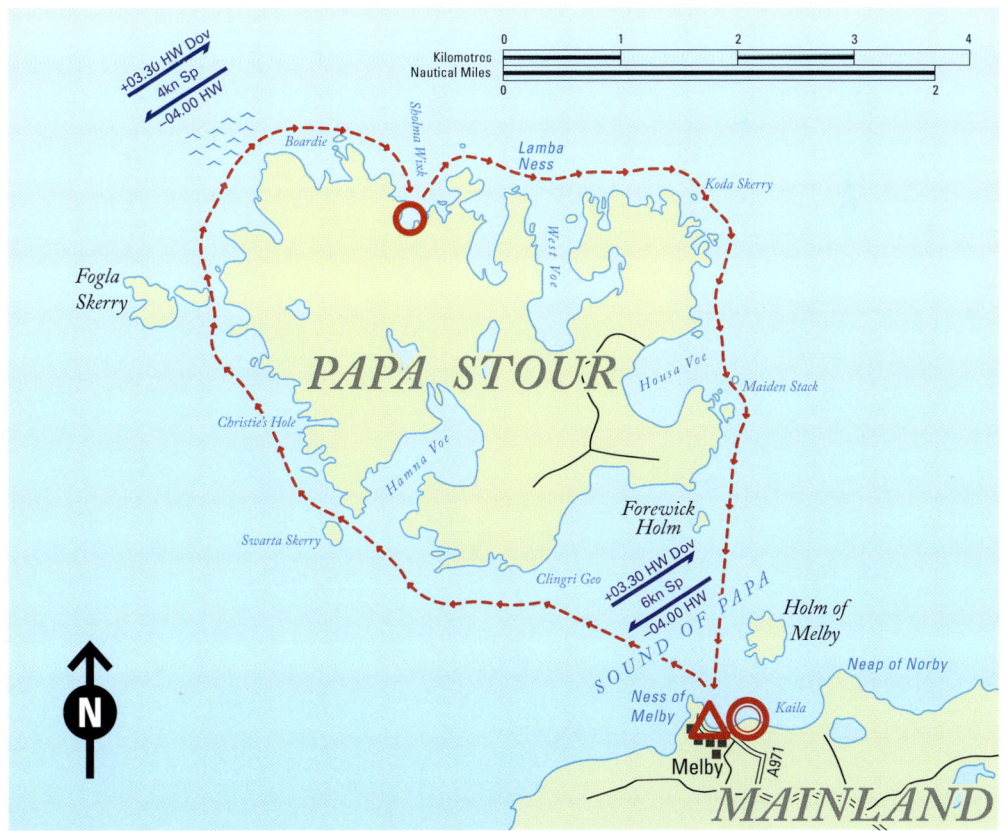

Fulmar | Mark Rainsley

Papa', big enough for a sailing ship to pass under it, but it collapsed in a storm in January 1953. The headland at Boardie is split by a 300m long tunnel, the Hol o' Boardie. The entrance from the west side is clear and easily found, but a northerly swell can close the exit. The passage is around 3m wide and similar in height. It twists first left then right, so it is completely dark in the middle section. A torch is essential.

The north and east coasts of Papa, though not as dramatic as the west, nevertheless have much of interest. There is a good landing at Sholma Wick in all except a northerly swell, and nearby Lamba Ness is split by three small parallel tunnels. There is also a large cave in the geo on the west side of Willie's Taing, at the northeast corner. From here down to the entrance to Housa Voe is another fine stretch of coastline well worth exploring in detail. Look for the hidden beach reached through an arch.

Housa Voe is the large inlet on the east coast of the island. Most of the twenty or thirty inhabitants live around here, and the modern ferry terminal is on the north shore. Crossing the entrance to Housa Voe look for the small white structure housing a light on the shore about the middle of the bay. This is the leading light for the ferry and other craft entering Housa Voe. It will change from green to white to red as you cross from north to south, with the white sector representing the safe passage into the bay for the ferry.

Just south of the Maiden Stack is Breis Holm, which is joined to the main island at low tide. It is pierced by an impressive tunnel and there is a fine natural arch on its south side.

Cave, Papa Stour | Geoff Burke

The Maiden Stack

On the south side of Housa Voe are a number of stacks, the tallest of which is known as the Maiden Stack and it has an interesting story. It seems that in Viking times the daughter of the local headman fell in love with a young man who was considered unsuitable for her. To stop this liaison her father confined her to a small cell on top of the Stack, but undeterred the young man climbed the stack one night and freed her. They then escaped and were married. According to the story they were eventually reconciled with the girl's father. The story may be apocryphal but it is just possible to make out the remains of a stone wall on top of the stack on the south side. This may, more prosaically, have been a small nunnery.

Returning to the mainland across Papa Sound the direct route passes to the east of Forewick Holm and west of Holm of Melby. The prominent two-storey Melby House makes a good target to head for. This is just behind the beach at Melby. However this part of the Sound is also where the tides are strongest. If you are crossing at any time other than slack water, and particularly if the wind is westerly, it is a good idea to take a more easterly course into St Magnus Bay and come around the east side of Holm of Melby. Porpoises and dolphins are often sighted in this area.

Tide and weather

Papa Sound can be a tricky crossing with strong tides, up to 6 knots at springs. Crossings should be timed for slack water. According to what appears to be the most reliable source, the Clyde

Archway, Papa Stour | Mark Rainsley

Cruising Club's Sailing Directions, the east-going stream starts approximately 3 hours 30 minutes after HW Dover, and the west-going about 4 hours before HW Dover. There is a short period of slack before both these times.

There are also strong tides through the big skerries on the west side and around the headland at Boardie. If you cross Papa Sound on the slack before the east-going tide and go round clockwise as described, the tide should be assisting at Boardie. Westerly swells can make the whole area from Hamna Voe to Boardie difficult. Southerly and south-easterly winds can also cause problems in the Sound. If crossing outside of slack it should be noted that back eddies can form within the Sound of Papa.

Additional information

If you are planning to stay on the island you should be aware that there are no shops, so all provisions must be brought in. It is possible to camp in many places on the island but it is always a good idea to ask at the nearest house, if there is one close by.

Papa Stour means 'the big island of the priests', and it is likely that it was the site of a very early Christian church. It is certain that it was an important place in Viking times, and an interpretive panel at the Biggings indicates the site of an important excavation in the 1970s.

OS Explorer Map 467 and Admiralty Chart 3281 cover this area.

First World War Gun on Vementry | Geoff Burke

Vementry

No. 31 | Grade A | 13km | 5 hours | OS Sheet 3 | Tidal Port Lerwick

Start/Finish	Brindister (283 578)
HW	Local HW is 2 hours 15 minutes before HW Lerwick.
Tides	There are no significant tidal streams on this route.
Coastguard	Shetland

Introduction

Vementry is an interesting and often overlooked island in St Magnus Bay; it is also the name of the farm at the nearest point to it on the mainland. Cribba Sound here narrows down to around 20m, and there are several mussel farms.

Description

For the closest point to the island drive west from Lerwick and follow the signs for Aith. Just as you enter the village take a left fork signposted Vementry and follow it to the end of the road at a large farmhouse. A short private road leads down on the right through a gate to a mussel farm shore base and slipway. The operators do not object to kayaks launching here but cars should be left outside the gate, and not taken down the track without permission.

An alternative starting point is to follow signs for the Papa Stour ferry, but shortly before reaching the terminal at West Burrafirth take a right turn signposted Brindister and follow it to the end at another mussel farm base. Here there is public access at a small beach just outside the mussel farm shore base but cars should not be parked within the shorebase/pier area and, while parking on the road side is possible, care should be taken not to restrict access.

Starting from Brindister the suggested route initially follows the coast north past the small island of Linga to Shaabers Head. From here it crosses north-east to the other small island of Gruna, and on into Suthra Voe on Vementry. From Suthra Voe we continue round Heill Head. The next section to Swarbacks Head is open to any westerly swell in St Magnus Bay, and often lumpy. There is a fine passage between Swarbacks Head, at the northernmost point of Vementry, and the imposing Swarbacks Skerry.

Turning into Northra Voe, it is worth landing in the small bay on the west side and climbing Swarbacks Head. This headland, which dominates the western approach to Swarbacks Minn, is itself dominated by two intact rusting naval guns from the First World War, together with the remains of the barracks of the soldiers who manned them. Swarbacks Minn was then home to the 10th Cruiser Squadron, guarding the northern approaches to Britain, and the guns were there to defend the anchorage against attack from the sea. They were never fired in anger.

On the other side of Northra Voe is the Muckle Ward, at 90m the highest point on the island. On the top of it there is one of the best examples in Shetland of a neolithic chambered cairn. These cairns, which are believed to be ancient burial sites dating back to about 4,000 BC, are found all over northern Scotland. The Vementry cairn, like most of those in Shetland, is heel-shaped, a style which is almost unique to Shetland.

It is possible to extend the trip here by crossing the short distance (less than 1km) to Muckle Roe. The next section of coast from Northra Voe to Cow Head and Holms of Uyeasound is the most interesting part of the Vementry coastline, with a number of narrow but surprisingly deep caves. This area is generally quite sheltered and easy to explore. After rounding Cow Head, Vementry House comes into view on the mainland. The promontory of land extending north-west from the house almost reaches the island itself, leaving only a narrow passage into the southern half of Cribba Sound. If you now head south-west towards Voe of Clousta, where there is a confusing meeting of four voes, then west past a pair of small rocks known as the Icelanders, the entrance to Brindister Voe will appear on the left.

ALTERNATIVE ROUTE

The coastline from Vementry to Melby offers a pleasant extension to the trip. Access is possible at Snarraness – drive to the end of the road past the West Burrafirth ferry terminal, launch or land on the west side of the isthmus – and at Bousta, an idyllic spot which can be difficult to spot from the sea. To launch from Bousta, drive to Sandness and take a right fork just by the public hall. At the end of the road you will come to a sheltered beach in a small bay, with a slipway for access and a flat grassy field behind it. Camping should be possible here. Ask at any of the houses round about.

Tide and weather

The south and east of Vementry are generally sheltered with no particular problems, but the north-west, from Heill Head to Swarbacks Skerry, is exposed to any west or north-west swell in St Magnus Bay. There is some tide around Swarbacks Skerry, flooding east and ebbing west.

Additional information

OS Explorer Map 467 and Admiralty Chart 3281 cover this area.

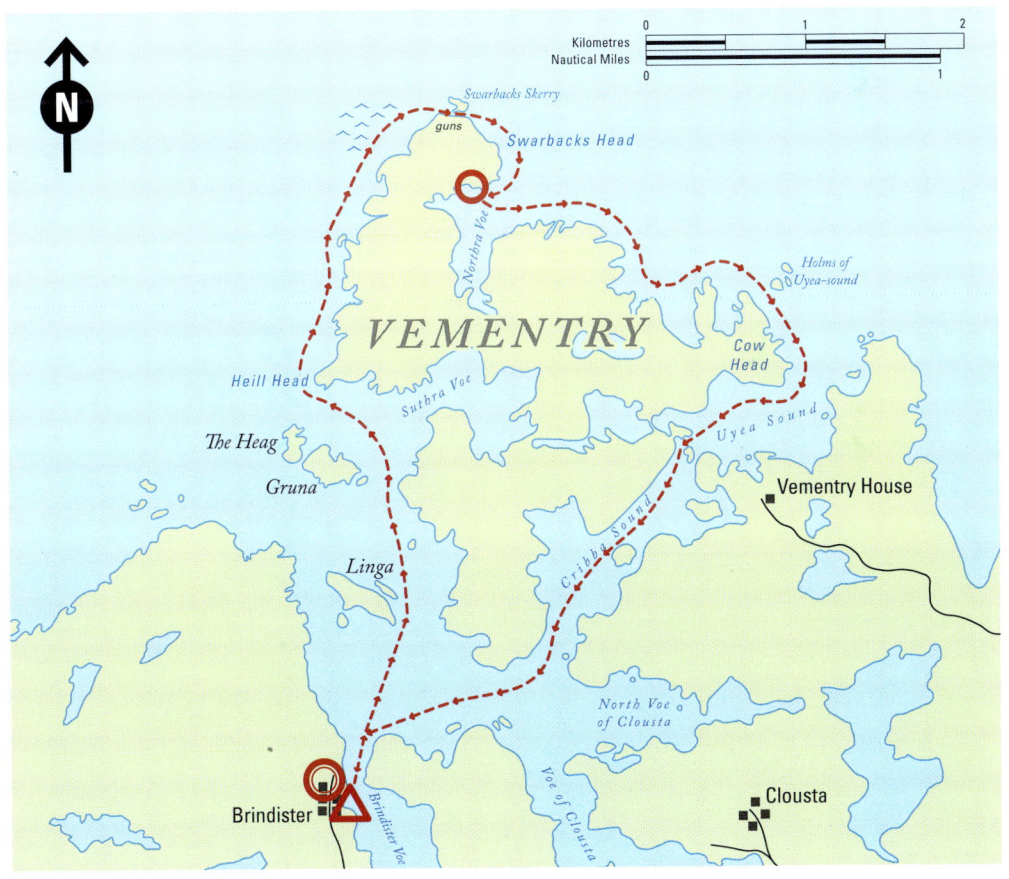

Shetland fish farm | Rachel Shucksmith

Vementry

Fish Farming

Aquaculture started in Shetland in the late 1970s and early 1980s, and since then has come from nowhere to being a major part of the Shetland economy, and farms are now to be seen in most voes and sounds. Most common are the salmon farms, typically consisting of round black plastic cages in groups of ten to fourteen. Often there will be a feeding barge moored alongside, housing the automatic feeders and providing a base for the farm workers. Mussel farming is also common in Shetland, with Shetland producing nearly 75% of all farmed mussels in Scotland. On the surface these appear as long parallel strings of floating barrels. The mussels grow on ropes hanging underneath.

As a general rule it is best to keep a reasonable distance away from any of these.

North Hams, Muckle Roe | Doug Cooper

Muckle Roe

No. 32 | **Grade B** | **25km** | **7 hours** | **OS Sheet 3** | **Tidal Port Lerwick**

Start/Finish	▲◯ Muckle Roe marina (348 663)
HW	Local HW is 2 hours 20 minutes before HW Lerwick.
Tides	There are no significant tidal streams on this route.
Coastguard	Shetland

Introduction

Second only to Papa Stour this is a superb day trip, with little in the way of tidal problems. The eastern half of the island is settled with good agricultural land, while the western half is part of the Shetland National Scenic Area with some of the finest cliff scenery in Shetland. The name Muckle Roe, meaning 'big red island', derives from these distinctive red granite cliffs.

Description

The best start point for the circumnavigation is the marina on the Mainland side of Roe Sound. From Brae follow the signs for Muckle Roe, then on the crest of a hill just before the road drops down to the bridge at Muckle Roe turn off on an unmarked road to the right. If you can see the bridge you've missed it! Follow this road down to the marina car park.

© Lichen covered rocks, Muckle Roe | Doug Cooper

Muckle Roe

If you are doing the circumnavigation in a clockwise direction ('sungaets' in Shetland dialect) set off under the bridge which links the island of Muckle Roe to the mainland, and head south. This section of coast is pleasantly rural, backed by a road and a scatter of houses and crofts. Gradually it becomes more rugged around the south coast until you reach two fine red sand beaches at Little Ayre and Muckle Ayre. Just after the Burki Skerries there are two sheltered beaches at the foot of the cliffs. Next, and just before the lighthouse, is the Hole of Hellier, a fine collapsed cave with two entrances. It is well worth looking for the less obvious eastern entrance.

The next section of coast is dominated by the famous red cliffs, with numerous stacks and skerries, the most dramatic of which, the Spindle, has an arch through which the westerly swells surge. Shortly after the Spindle a narrow opening on the north wall of a fairly unassuming cave leads to a tortuous passage through one of the many headlands. Coming round the most westerly point of the island at Strom Ness, the route takes you into a wide northwest-facing bay, called the South Ham. At the far side is a bluff pierced by three small tunnels. Immediately behind is a sheltered sandy beach and one of the best lunch stops to be found anywhere. This is the North Ham. Just behind the beach is a lush green park with a fresh water loch, and the remains of a number of old settlements. If you decide to take a little time to explore, have a look for the ruins of a couple of old click mills on the stream that enters the loch from the north side.

Setting off again, the headland on the north side of the bay is split by several clefts, the most easterly of which leads to a passage through to a beautiful sheltered geo. From here to the northern tip of the island at Lothan Ness, less than 2km away, is a dramatic sequence of caves and stacks, well worth exploring. Several of the caves are deep and complex, with links between them. The highest point of the cliffs here is called Erne Stack, indicating that it is a former haunt of the sea eagle. As of 2025 sea eagles are still absent in Shetland, except for the occasional vagrant, despite successful introduction of this species in the Sound of Mull in the 1970s, and the subsequent re-establishment across much of Scotland.

Rounding Lothan Ness you will pass the isolated rock of The Lothan on your left, and the last 3km down Roe Sound to the marina is a pleasant wind-down.

Tide and weather

There are no real problems with tide around Muckle Roe, except for some tidal flow under the bridge in Roe Sound and around the lighthouse. The west side of the island is open to west or north-west swell.

Additional information

There is a very pleasant short walk on a good track from the end of the road through Muckle Roe to the North Ham. Walk past the last house and look for a path striking up the gentle slope to the right. This leads to a wide track through a heather-clad valley and eventually to the lush grasslands behind the North Ham. From here it is possible to cross to the South Ham and return by a more westerly and higher route.

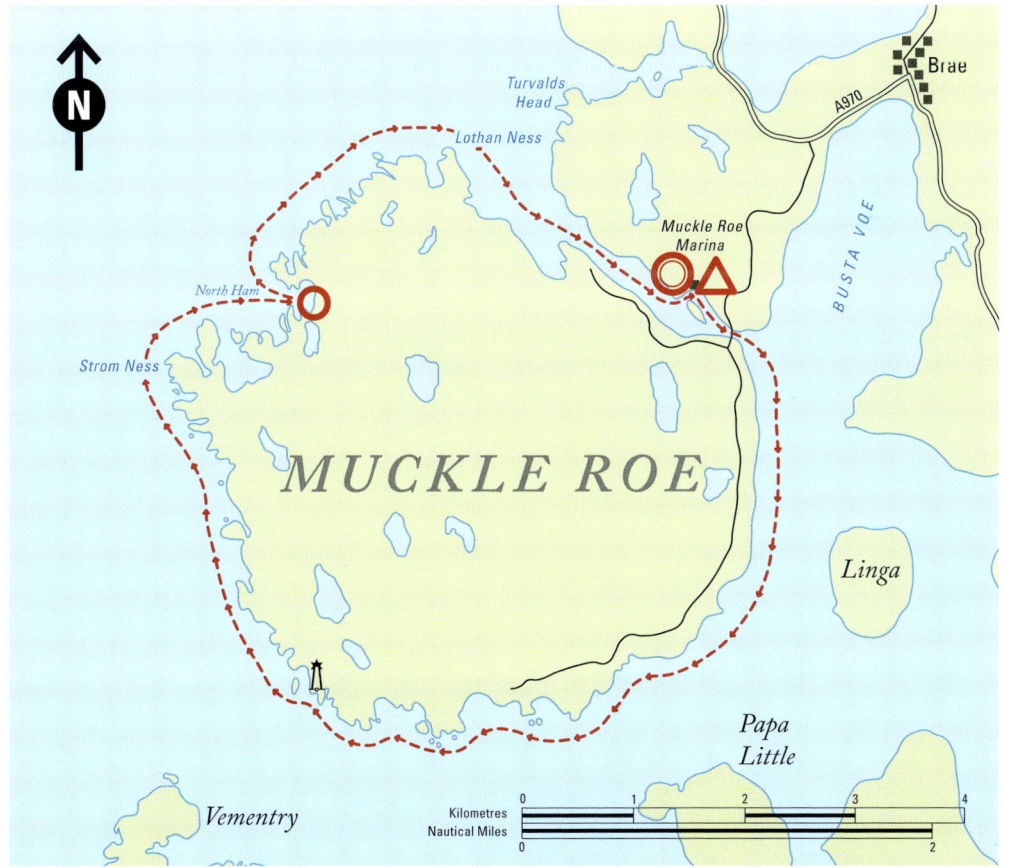

Click mills on Papa Stour | Tom Smith

Explorer Map 469 and Admiralty Chart 3281 cover this area.

Click mills

Along most streams near settlements in Shetland you can see the ruins of small buildings built over the stream. Often there is evidence of a mill lade and a sluice gate as well. On a good stream there can be as many as four or five of these click mills in a line. They were used for grinding locally grown crops like corn and bere. This type of mill originated in Norway and the mechanism was simple in the extreme. A horizontal wooden wheel would drive a horizontal millstone above via a vertical shaft, with no gearing of any kind. Invariably now all the wood has gone, including the roof of the building. The millstones are also normally missing, frequently turning up as garden ornaments. In the 19th century the click mills were superseded by larger and more efficient vertical wheel mills; sited in a few central locations.

The Drongs, Hillswickness | Doug Cooper

Hillswick Ness

No. 33 | Grade B | 18km | 5 hours | OS Sheet 3 | Tidal Port Lerwick

Start	△ Hillswick (282 770)
Finish	○ Tangwick (230 776)
HW	HW Hillswick is 2 hours 20 minutes before HW Lerwick.
Tides	There are no significant tidal problems on this route.
Coastguard	Shetland

Introduction

The headland of Hillswick Ness is part of the Shetland National Scenic Area. Two routes are described here starting from the village of Hillswick. The main route takes us round Hillswick Ness and out to the dramatic sea stacks known as The Drongs, then along the south side of the Eshaness peninsula. An alternative trip heads south along the west coast of Northmavine, taking in some fine caves and the pretty isles of Gunnister and Nibon.

Zoar beach | Geoff Burke

Description

Both trips start from the steep pebble beach in front of The Booth in Hillswick. This building has an interesting history, a former Hanseatic trading station turned public house (the first in Shetland) and now a private gallery and seal sanctuary. Public toilets and good parking are available.

The east side of Hillswick Ness has a number of caves and passages, initially on a small scale but gradually building up to the 60m cliffs near the lighthouse. Coming round to the west side, the sea is littered with stacks and skerries, all the way to the sheltered sandy beach at Pund of Grevasand. From here the route is out past the Isle of Westerhouse to the weird shapes of The Drongs, the huge stacks which will have caught your eye as soon as you rounded the main headland. These are impressive from any angle and the sea here is invariably in motion even on the quietest day.

Now the route takes us directly north towards the Heads of Grocken to explore the dramatic coastline from here through the wide bay of Brae Wick. There are a number of huge stacks and several hidden passages and tunnels. There are also a couple of good landings on sheltered beaches on the east side of Brae Wick, with a fine view back out to The Drongs. Finally, rounding Scarf Skerry, the trip ends on a shingle beach with road access just west of the Tangwick Museum.

VARIATION

From The Drongs it is possible to return to Hillswick Ness and follow the coast north to land on the beach at Sandwick. From here it is about 200m across a field to a gate onto the road near The Booth.

ALTERNATIVE ROUTE

The other possible trip from Hillswick leads south towards Mavis Grind or Muckle Roe. From Hillswick the route crosses Ura Firth towards Hamar Voe and goes south. There are several caves along this section, the best ones being near Red Head at the north side of Gunnister Voe. The isles of Gunnister and Nibon are also worth exploring, particularly the south side of Nibon Isle, where a fine natural arch and a deep geo lead to a hidden pebble beach. There is road access close to a good landing point on the mainland opposite Nibon Isle.

Continuing south the coastline is interesting all the way, including one particularly impressive natural arch and several deep caves. After about 3km the coast turns east at the entrance to Mangaster Voe. On the right now is the island of Egilsay which is split virtually in half by a deep cleft, just negotiable at high tide, or a short portage at low water.

From here the options are to head in through a very narrow gap to a sheltered landing near the main road at Mavis Grind, or continue on into Roe Sound and the Muckle Roe marina.

Tide and weather

There are no particular problems with tide in this area, but St Magnus Bay is prone to westerly swells, and the area around The Drongs is seldom still. With the wind in the north most of this trip is well sheltered, however Braewick Bay tends to funnel the wind quite strongly.

Natural arch Breiwick bay looking towards the Drongs | Doug Cooper

Additional information

If possible allow a little time to visit the museum at Tangwick, which is one of a number of small local museums in Shetland, and one of the most interesting.

There is a campsite with an excellent café overlooking the bay at Braewick.

Explorer Map 469 and Admiralty Chart 3281 cover this area.

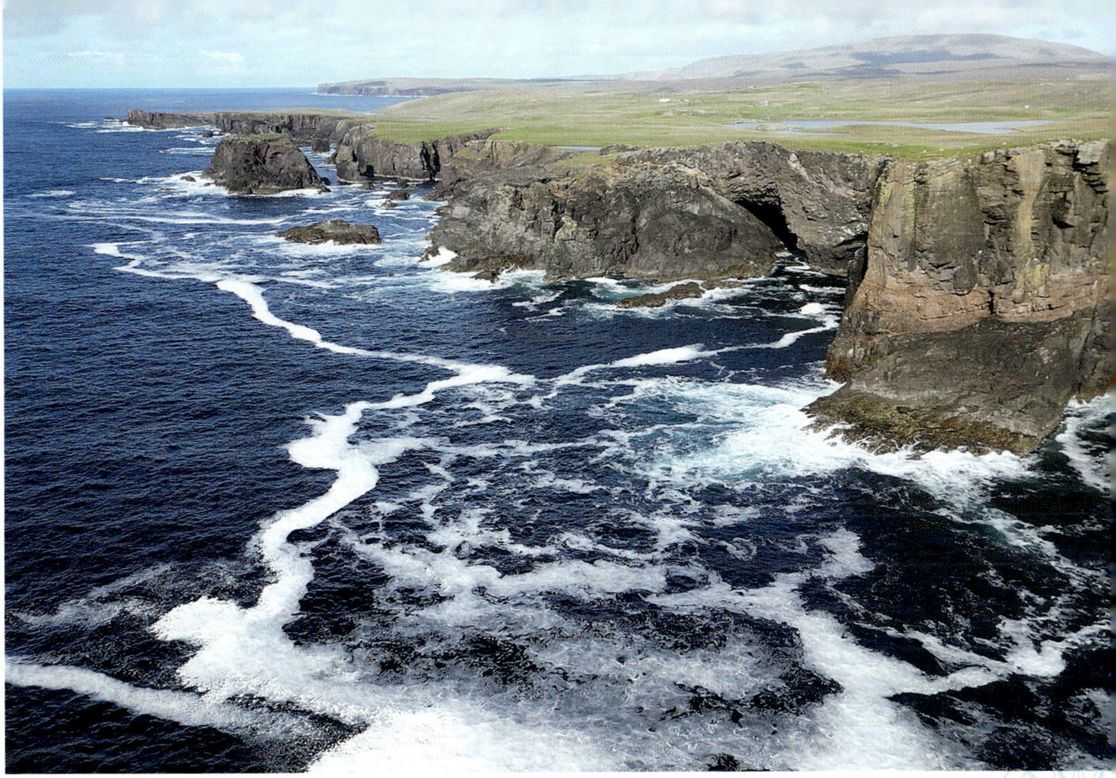

Eshaness

No. 34	Grade C | 33km | 8 hours | OS Sheet 3 | Tidal Port Lerwick
Start	△ Tangwick (230 776)
Finish	○ Heylor (292 810)
HW	Local HW is 2 hours before HW Lerwick.
Tides	There are no significant tidal problems on this route.
Coastguard	Shetland

Introduction

This is a large, impressive headland in the north-west of the mainland, offering some spectacular paddling on a fine day, and a dramatic view on a rough day. The view north from the lighthouse is one of the most recognisable in Shetland.

Description

The best launch point is just beyond the small museum at Tangwick. The road continues a short distance through a gate to a pebble beach. From here the view is dominated by Dore Holm, a large stack about a kilometre off the headland at Stenness, with a towering natural arch. Head for

Dore Holm | Geoff Burke

this first, go through the main arch then round to the south side of the Holm where you will see a less dramatic but more challenging passage leading back through to the north side. Crossing back to Stenness, the view is dominated by the two high islands to the west: the Isle of Stenness and the Skerry of Eshaness. These are home to significant numbers of seabirds, and well worth a diversion. The steep pebble beach by the old fishing station at Stenness is the last reliable landing before the Eshaness cliffs … that is unless the westerly swell makes it unusable, in which case another trip might be indicated!

After negotiating the slabs at Bruddans there follows a kilometre or so of 50m plus unbroken cliffs until the deep inlet of Calders Geo opens up north of the lighthouse. Entering Calders Geo look for a modest looking cave entrance on the left. If you go in, you will find yourself in one of the largest and most atmospheric caves in Shetland, with an alternative exit to the north. The next section of coast is a spectacular mix of caves and stacks. Most remarkable is the Holes of Scraada. Just north of the biggest stack, the Moo Stack, look for another modest looking cave entrance at the head of a small geo. This leads to a clear high passage around 3m wide. After about 100m and a slight dogleg it emerges into a large collapsed cave with a beach at the back. Landing is usually straightforward and the cliff top can be reached by an easy scramble. There is a ruined broch on an island in the nearby loch, and several click mills on the burn which runs from the loch into Scraada.

Emerging from Scraada, the next section of coast is a maze of caves and passages, sheltered by numerous stacks close to shore. This suddenly changes when you reach the dramatic cleft of the Grind of the Navir, effectively the end of the cliffs. The sea on the north-facing section of the headland is relatively shallow and prone to breaking in unexpected places in a swell.

It is possible to finish the trip at the sheltered inlet of Hamnavoe, where there is road access to a commercial pier at the southwest corner. From here it is a short walk back to Tangwick, unless of course you had the foresight to leave a car here.

As an alternative to landing at Hamnavoe, if you are continuing the trip to Ronas Voe, it is usually possible to land at Whal Wick, a little further on. The section of coast from here to The Faither, the headland that marks the outer end of Ronas Voe, is wild and exposed with many dramatic features. The Warie Gill is a huge cauldron, entered via a large natural arch, where the Burn of Tingon falls 20 or 30m straight into the sea. Look also for South Gill and for Geo of Ockran where there is another natural arch and an impressive waterfall. From here the trip could be extended by a diversion out to the two large stacks 2km to the northwest, Muckle Ossa and Little Ossa. Just before The Faither, one of Shetland's longest subterranean passages can be found at Gorsendi Geo. A small innocuous cave entrance opens up into a wide cave, at the back

© Calders Geo cave, Eshaness | Charlotte Black

of the cave a sharp left hand turn leads to a tunnel several hundred meters long transecting the headland, rivaling the Hol o' Boardie in Papa Stour.

Ronas Voe is a trip in itself and is described in the next chapter.

Tide and weather

Tides are not a major consideration in this trip, but any westerly or northerly swell will create problems. If there is any doubt go up to the lighthouse first and look along the cliffs to the north.

Additional information

The storm beach at Stenness is another possible start point for the Eshaness cliffs. Access from the road end is down a fairly steep grassy slope. Stenness was a haaf fishing station (see the discussion in the Fethaland chapter) and the ruins are still visible.

Explorer Map 469 and Admiralty Chart 3281 cover this area.

Cliffs and caves of Ronas Voe | Doug Cooper

Ronas Voe & Uyea

No. 35 | Grade C | 32km | 8 hours | OS Sheet 3 | Tidal Port Lerwick

Start	△ Heylor (292 810)
Finish	◯ Sandvoe (364 908)
HW	HW Ronas Voe is 2 hours before HW Lerwick.
Tidal Times	Off the island of Uyea the SW going stream starts about 5 hours 30 minutes before HW Lerwick and the NE going stream starts at about 1 hour after HW Lerwick.
Max Rate at Sp	At Uyea is 1 knot offshore but more over the shallows close to the isle.
Coastguard	Shetland

Introduction

Ronas Voe is said to be the only true fjord in Shetland, with spectacular and varied cliff scenery, mainly on the south side. It provides good shelter from westerly swells, making it accessible when other west side paddling areas are not. The journey also gives access to the beautiful and (from the land) almost inaccessible red sand beach at the Lang Ayre. This is a memorable trip that explores the remote and beautiful far north-west of the Shetland mainland.

Beach landing, Ronas Voe | Doug Cooper

Description

The best launch point to explore Ronas Voe is The Blade, a small sandy beach beside a gravel spit which houses an Arctic tern colony in summer. To reach The Blade follow the signs for Heylor from the junction at Urafirth on the Hillswick road, then when the gravel spit comes into view look for a small, unmarked road leading down to the beach before it.

Heading out to the north-west it is worth exploring every corner of the south side cliffs as there are many hidden surprises. The cliffs here climb to over 90m with endless stacks, passages and arches, though not many actual caves. Several of the passages and arches are only passable at low tide, while one or two are only negotiable at high tide. Around Quida Ness there are several beaches, usually popular with grey seals, offering the chance of an early break. From Quida Ness the route crosses the outer part of Ronas Voe towards the prominent headland of Whal Horn and continues up to Ketligill Head, which guards the south end of the Lang Ayre. A landing should be possible on the broad beach between Whal Horn and Ketligill. Off Ketligill there is a group of stacks called The Roodrans which are worth exploring, and there is an obvious passage through Ketligill which dries at low tide.

Next comes the Lang Ayre, a wide sweep of a beach almost inaccessible from the land. This is a magical place with a stream flowing into the southern end and numerous impressive stacks offshore. The most notable of these is The Cleiver, which from a distance looks a bit like an old-fashioned tin-opener. However the beach is steep and dumps heavily in any westerly or north-westerly swell, so a landing may not be feasible. Turls Head, at the north end, is split by

Stacks, Ronas Voe | Doug Cooper

at least three passages ranging from easy to quite tortuous. Offshore is another, even more impressive, group of rocky islets, the Gruna Stacks. The north-west corner of the mainland is now about 8km away, along a beautiful and seldom visited coastline. Look for the small south-facing beach at the north end of Lang Clodie Wick, and the small waterfall almost hidden in a cave at its eastern end.

At the north-west corner of the mainland the island of Uyea is linked to the mainland by a sandspit. The portage is easy and the alternative route round the island is challenging, with strong tides and numerous off-lying rocks. From the sand spit it is worth climbing the path to the fields above to see the deserted crofting township of Uyea, and in springtime some of the finest wild flower meadows in Shetland.

The view ahead now is dominated by the Ramna Stacks to the north-east, but our route continues along the north coast of the mainland via a maze of caves, arches and passages, and many more offshore stacks, to the narrow steep-sided inlet of Sandvoe. The journey ends at the head of Sandvoe on a small beach backed by an equally small cemetery. The public road is just beyond.

ALTERNATIVE ROUTE

From Ketligill Head there is the option to return to The Blade via the north shore of Ronas Voe, which is less dramatic than the south but well worth exploring. The journey includes a number of small passages, a beautiful sheltered south-facing beach, and at least one cave which, from

a narrow and easily missed entrance, opens out into a surprisingly big chamber with passages leading off. This shorter trip makes for an ideal and relatively straightforward introduction to Shetland's classic cliff scenery.

Tide and weather

Tide is not a problem in Ronas Voe. The only factor it affects is determining which of the many arches and passages will be negotiable. The south side is well sheltered from westerlies, but the outer part of the Voe and the Lang Ayre are not. Northwesterlies can set up a swell right into Ronas Voe, and easterlies tend to funnel out quite strongly. The coast from Ketligill Head to Uyea is open to westerly and north-westerly swell, while northerly or north-easterly swell can cause problems along the north coast. Tide is again not a major consideration except around the outside of Uyea, and this is easily avoided by portaging over the sand spit.

Additional Information

Uyea here is pronounced something like 'uh-ya', unlike the island of the same name in Unst, which is pronounced 'yoo-ee'.

OS Explorer Map 469 and Amiralty Chart 3281 cover this area.

Seals, Uyea | Richard Shucksmith

Swell

All waves at sea are ultimately caused by the wind, but they can travel over huge distances, decaying slowly as they travel further and further away from the wind system that generated them. This is known as swell. Around the coast of Britain the prevailing winds are westerly and south-westerly from the Atlantic, so swell is most often felt as westerly swell on the exposed west coasts. However, it can come from any direction if there is sufficient 'fetch', ie. if the distance from the far shore is great enough. It is important to realise that even in calm conditions the swell can be significant. Offshore the swell is generally benign in the absence of local wind, but inshore it is a different story. Swell hitting a cliff line out of deep water will bounce back and the reflected waves will interfere with the incoming swell, creating turbulence and clapotis (the Shetland dialect word for clapotis is 'affrug'), often extending well out to sea. In shallowing water the wave will generally begin to 'feel the bottom' when the depth of water is about half the wavelength. The face of the wave will start to steepen and eventually break as the bottom of the wave slows down and the top begins to overtake it. This is what generates surf, and turbulence and unexpected breaks on rocky shores.

Haaf fishing station, Fethaland | Geoff Burke

Fethaland & the Ramna Stacks

No. 36 | Grade B | 20km | 5 hours | OS Sheet 1 | Tidal Port Lerwick

Start	△ Sandvoe (364 908)
Finish	◯ Burravoe (367 886)
HW	HW Fethaland is 1 hour 50 minutes before HW Lerwick.
Tidal Times	The E going tidal stream at Point of Fethaland starts about 4 hours before HW Lerwick, with the W going stream starting about 2 hours after HW Lerwick.
Max Rate at Sp	In the north end of Yell Sound are generally about 2 knots, but are higher between Point of Fethaland and Gruney.
Coastguard	Shetland

Introduction

The Fethaland peninsula is the most northerly part of mainland Shetland, shaped like a closed hand with the forefinger extended and pointing north towards the Ramna Stacks 2km away. The

Ramna Stacks is an RSPB reserve, and home to large numbers of common seabirds. The whole of the Fethaland peninsula is part of the Shetland National Scenic Area.

Description

For the start of this trip take the road through North Roe, leaving a car near the former North Roe shop for the shuttle; then take the side road to Sandvoe. Just before the road climbs to the last houses there is a small cemetery on the right of the road with a car parking area on the left. The launch point is the beach just beyond the cemetery. Our route first takes us north out of Sandvoe to Garmus Taing. The small north-facing bay between here and Fethaland itself is worth exploring. A small stream runs into the head of it with the remains of at least three small click mills visible. The route now heads north again past a narrow neck with a beach of large boulders to the Point of Fethaland. The tide here runs strongly between the Point and the Ramna Stacks offshore, but the final headland is a narrow finger and the passage inside the rock of the Inner Booth is usually passable. The crossing to the Ramna Stacks should be planned for slack water. There is much to see here, including a fine natural arch on Fladda. Landings are difficult but the best chance is on the east side of Gruney, the largest and most southerly of the group. If you do manage to land be aware that the rare Leach's petrel nests in burrows in the grass here. Please be very careful moving around and avoid camping or lighting fires.

Returning to the Point of Fethaland the route now follows the eastern, or Yell Sound, side to a small bay with a beach at its north corner in front of the ruins of an old 'haaf' fishing station. This is on a narrow neck of land with the boulder beach mentioned earlier on the other side. It is well worth spending some time exploring this relic of Shetland's history.

Haaf fishing

In Shetland dialect inshore fishing is known as 'the eela' and distant water fishing is 'the haaf'. In the second half of the 19th century the haaf fishing was pursued by crews of six in small open boats called sixareens or sixerns, powered by oars and simple square-sails. The fishing involved using several miles of baited long lines. The crews would normally spend the summer months at a fishing station as near as possible to the fishing grounds. The stations usually had a pebble beach to launch and land from. The practice was to spend a day or two fishing at sea, and then return to the shore station with their catch, generally of cod and ling. There the fish would be split, cleaned and salted, then spread out to dry on the beach. It was a hard and dangerous occupation. The crews were always at risk of being caught out by a sudden storm and reliant entirely on their own strength and skill for their survival.

Ramna Stack | Geoff Burke

The coast from here south to the bay at Burravoe, a distance of 5 or 6km, is much underrated, with many caves and arches. The Kame of Isbister, about half way down, is the site of an old settlement, thought to be an early Christian monastery. Just after passing the two small islands of the North and South Holms of Burravoe, we turn into the bay of Burravoe and land on the beach beside the pier in the south-west corner.

Tide and weather

There are moderate tides around the northern tip of Fethaland. It is generally possible to stay close in to the rocks inside the Inner Booth and avoid most of it, but the crossing to the Ramna Stacks is best planned for slack tide. About 5 hours before HW Lerwick is best, then the first of the flood should carry you into the north end of Yell Sound on the return.

Additional information

There is a particularly good walk from North Roe to Fethaland. Instead of turning left to Sandvoe, continue straight on to the road end at Isbister. Leave your car in the lay-by and continue through the gate on a good path to the left of the group of buildings. Guided walks are available here.

The north part of Yell Sound is part of the approaches to the Sullom Voe oil terminal. Tankers generally pick up the pilot off the Ramna Stacks before proceeding in.

OS Explorer Map 469 and Admiralty Chart 3281 also cover this area.

The Horse of Burravoe | Geoff Burke

South Yell

No. 37 | Grade C | 33km | 7 hours | OS Sheet 2 | Tidal Port Lerwick

Start	△ Toft (436 763)
Finish	⭕ Mid Yell (517 908)
HW	HW Burravoe is 25 minutes before HW Lerwick.
Tidal Times	In the south end of Yell Sound the S going stream starts about 5 hours 30 minutes before HW Lerwick and the N going stream 1 hour after HW Lerwick. SW of Hascosay the S going stream starts about 4 hours 30 minutes before HW Lerwick and the N going stream 1 hour 30 minutes after HW Lerwick.
Max Rate at Sp	Around The Rumble is 7 knots. SW of Hascosay is 2 knots.
Coastguard	Shetland

Introduction

Shetland's second island is often characterized as dull ... an impression readily gained by simply driving through between ferry terminals on the way to Unst or Fetlar. However most of the coastline is anything but dull, and Yell offers much of interest to the kayaker. South-east Yell has one of the finest coastal features in Shetland, the Horse of Burravoe.

Archway, south east Yell | Geoff Burke

37 South Yell

Description

The best way to reach Yell from the Shetland Mainland is to launch from the beach alongside the ferry terminal at Toft. There are strong tides in the south end of Yell Sound, especially around the north end of Samphrey and the isolated rock of The Rumble, which marks the eastern entrance to the Port of Sullom Voe. Cross at low water slack if possible and pick up the Yell shore near the ruined broch at Holm of Copister, passing through the Sound of Orfasay and on to Burravoe, where there is road and slipway access. There is also an excellent small museum housed in the Old Haa, the former laird's house.

The route continues around the headland at Heoga Ness and one of the most impressive coastal features in Shetland, the Horse of Burravoe, is just ahead. It is worth taking some time to investigate the various passages, caves and stacks. The coastline from here north to Mid Yell Voe is continuously interesting with several large unmarked caves. There is a good sheltered landing on the north-facing beach at Wick of Gossabrough with road access. On the north side of the bay near Otterswick is the 'White Wife', a replica of the figurehead of a German sailing ship wrecked here a century or so ago, and raised as a memorial by the local people. On the north side of the small storm beach at Ayre of Birrier look for a narrow passage through the headland and a deep narrow cave near the exit.

Approaching Mid Yell, camping should be possible at the head of Wick of Vatsetter, where there is road access. Alternatively continue on to finish on the beach on the east side of Linkshouse Pier.

Archway, Horse of Burravoe | Doug Cooper

VARIATIONS

The trip can be shortened and the crossing of Yell Sound avoided by starting at Burravoe. Burravoe marina has toilet facilities, parking and hook-up points for camper vans and is signposted from the crossroads.

Tide and weather

The main consideration here is the tide in the south end of Yell Sound, which can reach up to 7 knots around Samphrey and the Rumble, an isolated rock halfway between Samphrey and Orfasay. On a south-going tide a west-going eddy sets up to the east of Orfasay. This can be avoided by keeping close to the Yell shore through the Sound of Orfasay, then crossing Hamna Voe directly to Burra Ness, before continuing to Burravoe. The south-east headland at Heoga Ness and the coast north to Mid Yell are exposed to the south-east. South Sound, between Yell and Hascosay, is subject to the same tide conditions as Colgrave Sound between Yell and Fetlar.

Additional information

The south end of Yell Sound as far as a line from Samphrey to Orfasay is part of the Sullom Voe harbour area. Tankers and other large vessels generally use the north entrance to Yell Sound. Fishing boat traffic is common in the south end, and the Yell ferries run regularly between Tofts Voe and Ulsta in Yell.

OS Explorer Maps 470 and 468, and Admiralty Chart 3282, also cover this area.

Wick of Breckon, North Yell | Richard Shucksmith

North Yell

| No. 38 | Grade C | 35km | 8 hours | OS Sheet 1 | Tidal Port Lerwick |

Start	Gutcher (548 993)
Finish	Westsandwick (446 890)
HW	HW in Yell Sound is 1 hour 30 minutes before HW Lerwick.
Tidal Times	The S going stream in Bluemull Sound starts at approximately 4 hours 30 minutes before HW Lerwick, and the N going stream 1 hour 30 minutes after HW Lerwick. In the north end of Yell Sound the S going stream starts about 5 hours 30 minutes before HW Lerwick and the N going stream 1 hour after HW Lerwick.
Max Rate at Sp	Off Cullivoe is 7 knots. In the north entrance to Yell Sound is typically 2 knots.
Coastguard	Shetland

Introduction

This is a demanding trip in one of the less visited parts of Shetland. That said, the rewards are great as there is much to see. Bluemull Sound, the stretch of water between Yell and Unst, has some of the strongest tides in Shetland, particularly around Ness of Cullivoe where it reaches 7 knots on springs. The north and west coasts of Yell have some spectacular and remote cliff scenery with few landings, and those exposed to north-west swell.

205

Gloup Holm, north coast of Yell | Tom Smith

Description

The trip starts with an easy launch from the beach alongside the ferry terminal at Gutcher, then leads north with the ebb tide. Beware of possible turbulence especially between Grimsetter and Ness of Cullivoe. The exit from Bluemull Sound onto the north coast is abrupt, as you pass between Papil Ness and the Blue Mull on the Unst side. As elsewhere in Shetland the name Papil indicates an early religious site (the Irish monks who first brought Christianity to Shetland were known as 'papar') and there are many signs of ancient settlement here, together with an abandoned medieval church. Legend has it that it was from here that Leif Erikson set off to discover America.

Main points of interest on the north-east coast are the numerous narrow passages around Migga Ness and Ness of Houlland, and a fine beach at Sands of Breckon. Turning into Gloup Voe a landing is possible at Whallerie, where there is also road access. From here it is a short walk to the prominent memorial overlooking the voe. This commemorates a fishing disaster from the end of the 19th century, when ten boats were lost in a sudden storm with fifty-eight men, almost the entire male population of the area.

Setting off again from Gloup Voe, the route leads west towards a scatter of rocks off the headland of Rivvalee. Gloup Holm just offshore has dramatic stacks and at least one large cave. There are numerous arches and passages around Aastack and Birrier, and a possible storm beach landing at Geo of Vigon. An easy scramble at the head of this geo leads up to some wild open moorland and spectacular views over the north end of Yell Sound. A short walk south along the coast leads to the remains of an Iron Age promontory fort and blockhouse at Burgi Geos. After this there are no reliable landings until the beach at Westsandwick, where there is road access. This is a serious section of around 18km of rugged uninhabited coastline with moderate tide.

Sands of Breckon | Becky Giesler

VARIATIONS

An alternative finish is in Whale Firth, either below The Herra, with an awkward carry up to the road end, or at the head of the firth where the main road is close by.

From Westsandwick it is possible to continue on down to the ferry terminal at Ulsta. Tides are again strong here, particularly just north of Ulsta and around the headland at Ness of Sound. A more interesting option is to cross the north end of Yell Sound from Westsandwick to Burravoe in North Roe on the mainland, via the two small islands of Holm of Westsandwick and Muckle Holm, both of which have small arches. Tides are again significant here but not as strong as the southern end of Yell Sound.

Tide and weather

Tidal considerations are key to this trip. The maximum spring rate in Bluemull Sound is 7 knots, and there is turbulence and a strong tide race off Ness of Cullivoe. Tidal streams in the north end of Yell Sound are less severe, around 2 knots. The best strategy is to aim to be paddling north through Bluemull Sound with the last of the north-going tide. The tide should then be assisting when you come to Yell Sound. This trip is not advised with a northerly wind or any northerly or north-westerly swell.

Additional information

OS Explorer Map 470 and Admiralty Chart 3282 also cover this area.

Fetlar

No. 39 | Grade C | 54km | 14 hours | OS Sheet 1 | Tidal Port Lerwick

Start/Finish	△○ Mid Yell (517 908)
HW	Local HW is 40 minutes before HW Lerwick.
Tidal Times	The S going tidal stream in Colgrave Sound begins about 4 hours 30 minutes before HW Lerwick, and the N going stream begins 1 hour 30 minutes after HW Lerwick.
Max Rate at Sp	East of Hascosay is 3 knots.
Coastguard	Shetland

Introduction

Fetlar is known as the 'garden of Shetland'. It is a large, traditionally fertile island – the name Fetlar means 'fat land'. The population now is less than a hundred but it has in the past been closer to a thousand.

It is quite possible to paddle round Fetlar in two days (or even one if you are 'on a mission'!) but the suggestion here is for a three-day trip starting and finishing on the neighbouring island of Yell, and taking in the uninhabited island of Hascosay.

Tystie (black guillemot) | Richard Shucksmith.

Black guillemots

The black guillemot, or 'tystie' as it is known in Shetland, is one of our most popular birds. It is very recognisable, being jet black all over except for a prominent white wing patch and a delicate black beak and red legs. They are found in practically every voe and inlet around the Shetland coast, usually in ones or twos, occasionally small groups, but seldom in large flocks. Unlike most of the other common seabirds they are present all year round, but in winter their plumage becomes white with shades of grey. If you see a 'tystie' in what appears to be winter plumage in August, it does not mean that winter has come early. Newly fledged young birds look very like the winter adults.

SUGGESTED ITINERIES

DAY 1: Mid Yell to Wick of Gruting, 18km, 5 hours.
DAY 2: Gruting to Lambhoga, 20km, 5 hours.
DAY 3: Lambhoga to Mid Yell, 16km, 4 hours.

Description

Fetlar is most easily reached by crossing the north end of Colgrave Sound from Mid Yell to Brough passing north of the small, uninhabited island of Hascosay. The tide runs strongly to east and west of Hascosay. Landfall on Fetlar should be around Ness of Snabrough just south of the ferry terminal at Oddsta, which is very close to the north-west corner of the island at Hamars Ness.

Camping is possible at several points along the north coast, particularly around Urie Ness and in Wick of Gruting, but is less easy on the east and south.

The cliffs between Tressa Ness in the north and Wick of Gruting (known as the East Neap) are particularly impressive, rising to over 120m with many stacks and arches. The entrance to the broad bay at Wick of Gruting is marked by the dramatic Stack of Birrier. Beyond Wick of Gruting the passage between Strandburgh Ness and the Outer Brough in the north-east is quite dramatic. There are few landings on the east side until the shingle beach below the houses at Funzie (pronounce 'finny'). Just inland from here are the Mires of Funzie, an area of freshwater pools which in summer are home to one of Britain's rarest birds, the red-necked phalarope. The RSPB have erected a hide here, which makes it easy to see them and many other birds including whimbrel.

The route now continues around the Snap onto the south coast and the beach at Wick of Aith. The camping böd at Aithbank on Fetlar was once home to one of the island's most gifted storytellers, Jamsie Laurenson. It is currently shut (2025) but it is hoped it will reopen under community management, and provide basic accommodation under cover. At Houbie there is a shop and an interpretation centre near the pier. This is well worth a visit before carrying on to the magnificent beach at Wick of Tresta. Camping is quite possible here provided the Scottish Outdoor Access Code is followed. Another option for camping on the south coast is at Moo Wick on the end of the headland of Lambhoga.

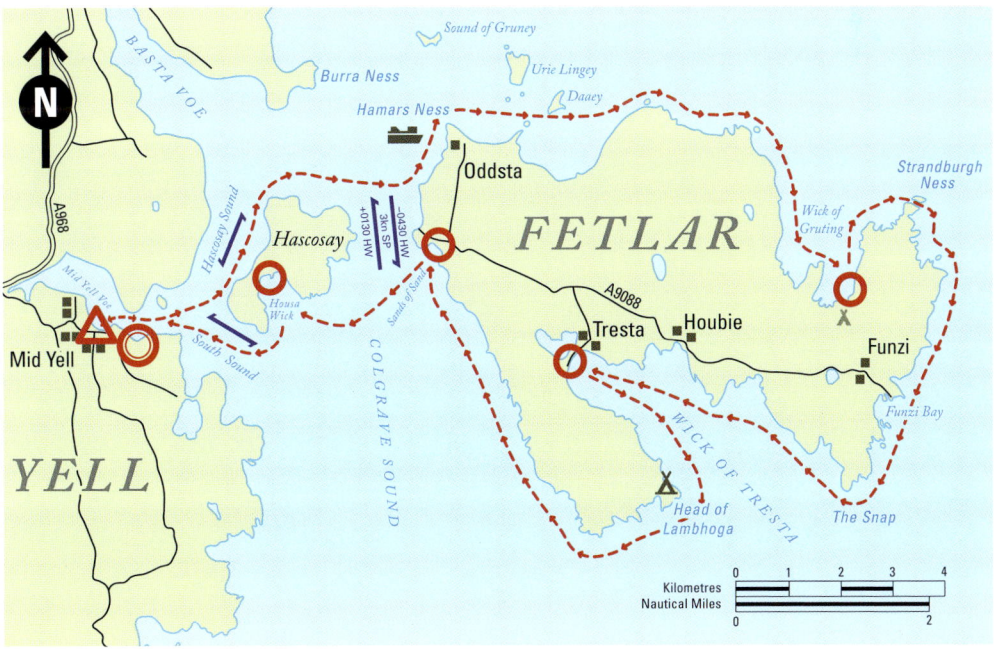

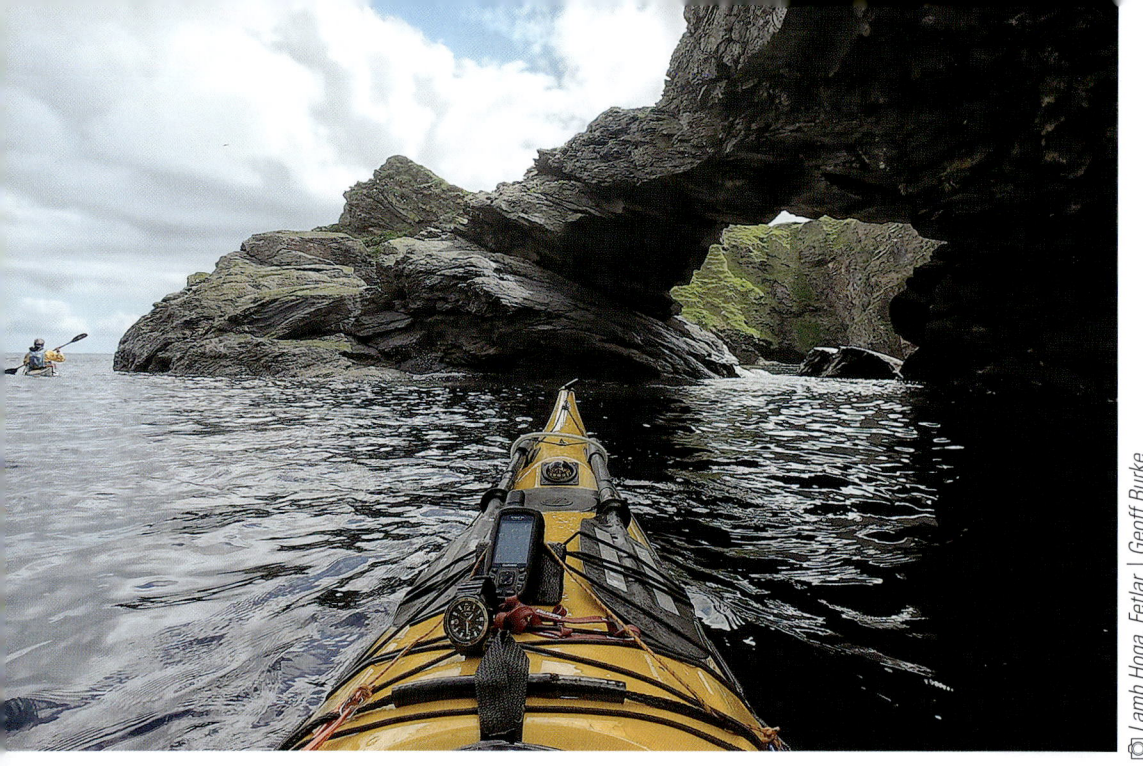

Lamb Hoga, Fetlar | Geoff Burke

The long peninsula of Lambhoga is entirely uninhabited but has much of interest, including the remains of a number of old settlements and extensive peat workings. The next sign of more recent human habitation comes at the intriguingly named Sands of Sand, just south of the headland at Ness of Brough. The beach is backed by fields and the abandoned Brough Lodge, the former laird's house. There are in fact two 'big houses' on Fetlar. The other one at Leagarth near Houbie is still in use, and has in the past doubled as a community hall. The return crossing to Mid Yell now takes us across Colgrave Sound, passing this time to the south of Hascosay. If time permits, a landing at Housa Wick allows the chance to explore this flat windswept island. It is uninhabited now though, like most of the smaller Shetland isles, it once supported a few families. This is one of the best areas in Shetland for sightings of otters. The trip ends back on the beach at Mid Yell.

Tide and weather

The main tidal considerations here are in the sounds to the west and east of Hascosay where rates can reach more than 3 knots. There is also some tide on the east side of Fetlar. The south-east corner around the Snap is exposed to the south-east and can be rough, with hidden rocks.

Additional information

Fetlar is served by roll-on roll-off ferry from Gutcher in Yell, the same terminal as the ferries for Unst. However, the ferries to Fetlar are much less frequent.

OS Explorer map 470 and Admiralty Chart 3282 cover this area.

Gannetry, Hermaness, Unst | Richard Shucksmith

< Unst

40

Unst

No. 40	**Grade C** | **94km** | **19 hours** | **OS Sheet 1** | **Tidal Port Lerwick**
Start/Finish	△○ Uyeasound (592 010)
HW	HW Baltasound is 55 minutes before Lerwick.
Tidal Times	In Bluemull Sound the S going stream starts about 4 hours 30 minutes before HW Lerwick, and the N going stream about 1 hour 30 minutes after HW Lerwick. At Hermaness the E going stream starts about 3 hours before HW Lerwick and the W going stream starts 2 hours after HW Lerwick. At Skaw the S going stream starts approximately 3 hours 30 minutes before HW Lerwick and the N going stream starts 2 hours 30 minutes after HW Lerwick.
Max Rate at Sp	In Bluemull Sound is 7 knots. At Muckle Flugga is 5 knots. At Skaw and Lamba Ness is 5 knots.
Coastguard	Shetland

Introduction

Unst is the most northerly of the Shetland Islands, and the off-lying isle of Muckle Flugga, with its Stevenson-built lighthouse, is famous as the most northerly land in the British Isles.

213

Muckle Flugga, Unst | Richard Shucksmith

Technically this distinction should be reserved for an isolated rock called the Out Stack about 500m north-east of the lighthouse … it just depends how determined you are.

Three days are allowed here to go round the whole of Unst. However there is road access to all the overnight stops, so each section could be treated as a day trip.

SUGGESTED ITINERARIES:

DAY 1: Uyeasound to Burrafirth, 32km, 8 hours.

DAY 2: Burrafirth to Haroldswick, 35km, 6 hours.

DAY 3: Haroldswick to Uyeasound, 27km, 5 hours.

Description

Uyeasound makes a good base for a visit to Unst. It is possible to stay at the hostel at Gardiesfauld, or camp in its grounds, and there is good access to the sea close by.

DAY 1

This is a big day and the west coast of Unst from the ferry terminal north to Hermaness is a serious and committing paddle. Launch from the beach at Uyeasound, just west of the small harbour and toilet block. The section through Bluemull Sound has some of Shetland's strongest tides, 7 knots at springs. North of the Blue Mull there is some very attractive coastline around Lunda Wick and Collaster. North of Collaster the coast becomes more exposed to the north-west, with only the storm beach at Wood Wick as a possible landing. The deep cleft of Longa Geo on

Hagdale Ness and the two small islands of the South Holms are well worth exploring. After Wood Wick the cliffs climb steadily to the 170m heights of the Neap and Saito with their huge gannet colonies. The last section on the west side of Hermaness itself is particularly impressive, being riddled with caves, arches and stacks. At Hermaness, if the tides are right, it is possible to cross to Muckle Flugga before heading into the shelter of Burrafirth, but it makes more sense to keep that for the second day and the Burrafirth to Haroldswick section.

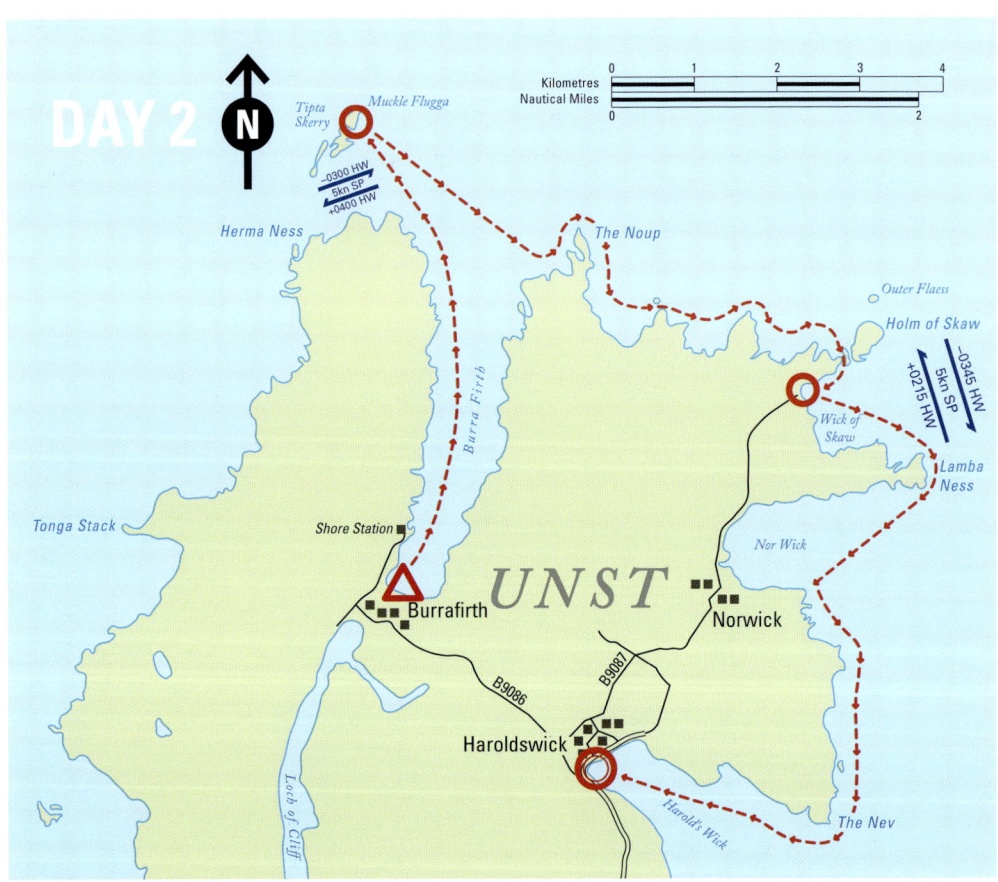

DAY 2

If the object of your visit to Unst is just to reach Muckle Flugga, then the best place to start from is the former Lighthouse Shore Station at Burrafirth. There is limited car parking and access to the old slipway in a sheltered inlet on the west side of Burrafirth. To reach it by road you will need to drive north towards Haroldswick, then follow signs for Burrafirth and Hermaness. On the way you will cross the Links of Burrafirth. Camping is possible in this area. The best site is at the north-west corner of Loch of Cliff, reached by turning left instead of right after crossing the Links.

Muckle Flugga, Unst | Geoff Burke

It would be a mistake just to paddle directly to Muckle Flugga and back. It is well worth taking the time to explore both sides of Burrafirth. The north-east corner, directly below the radar domes of the former early warning station on Saxa Vord, is particularly worth investigating. The cliffs here are 200m high and there are numerous arches and caves including a large, easily negotiated tunnel at Hols Hellier.

Muckle Flugga is the most prominent of a string of rocks lying about a kilometre off the northern tip of Hermaness. Tides are strong here and it is as well to plan the crossing for slack water, and preferably neap tides. There are no dangers other than the tide and the visible rocks. In summer the skies are likely to be filled with seabirds; gannets from the huge colonies on the west side of Hermaness, skuas constantly harrying them for the fish they have caught, and puffins, guillemots, kittiwakes, fulmars and terns going about their business among it all.

If you are continuing to Haroldswick the route is now across to the cliffs of Saxa Vord, now home to a space launch site, and on round to the north coast. The headland of Skaw has a reputation for a tidal 'roost' (tide race with big overfalls) almost as celebrated as the one at Sumburgh, but like Sumburgh it is easily avoided. There are several possible routes through the rocks inside the Inner Holm of Skaw. At the north end of the bay of Wick of Skaw there is a beautiful sandy beach, the most northerly in Britain, and accessible by road. Skaw beach provides the first of several landing/finishing points along the east coast, particularly if tidal conditions are not favorable at Lamba Ness. Lamba Ness is also affected by the the Skaw Roost, but here there is no avoiding route, so timing is critical. If you aim to be here about an hour after HW Lerwick you should catch the last of the south-going stream. Continuing down the east coast,

Balta Isle, Unst | Becky Giesler

landings are possible at Norwick, another beautiful beach, and at Haroldswick near the Unst Boat Haven – well worth a visit if it is open – or continue on into Baltasound. Baltasound is a fine natural harbour sheltered on the east by the island of Balta, or Balti Isle as it is usually called locally. If you are camping, there is a fine beach on the west coast of Balti Isle, about two thirds of the way down with flat ground behind.

DAY 3

The south of Unst is generally less dramatic and more sheltered than the north and west. The trip can start from Haroldswick or Baltasound. If you are starting from Baltasound follow the road along the north side of the sound to the Boating Club slipway just west of the commercial pier. Baltasound was a major fishing port in the days of the herring boom in the early part of the 20th century. The east side of Balti Isle is the most dramatic and interesting part of this section of coast, and if conditions permit should not be missed. Balti Isle can also be paddled as a short day/evening trip, starting at the slipway in Baltisound. The next island south, Huney, is almost joined to the main island of Unst by a sandspit which is just covered at low tide. As you cross the wide bay from Colvadale to Muness the shore is a steady succession of abandoned and ruined crofts, a testimony to the depopulation which plagued this beautiful island before the coming of the RAF station at Saxa Vord. Now the RAF has gone and other sectors such as tourism and aquaculture are supporting the local population.

The beautiful white sand beach at Sandwick is a rewarding stop, and a short stroll northwards to the old chapel and burial ground at Framgord is an interesting diversion. Round the headland

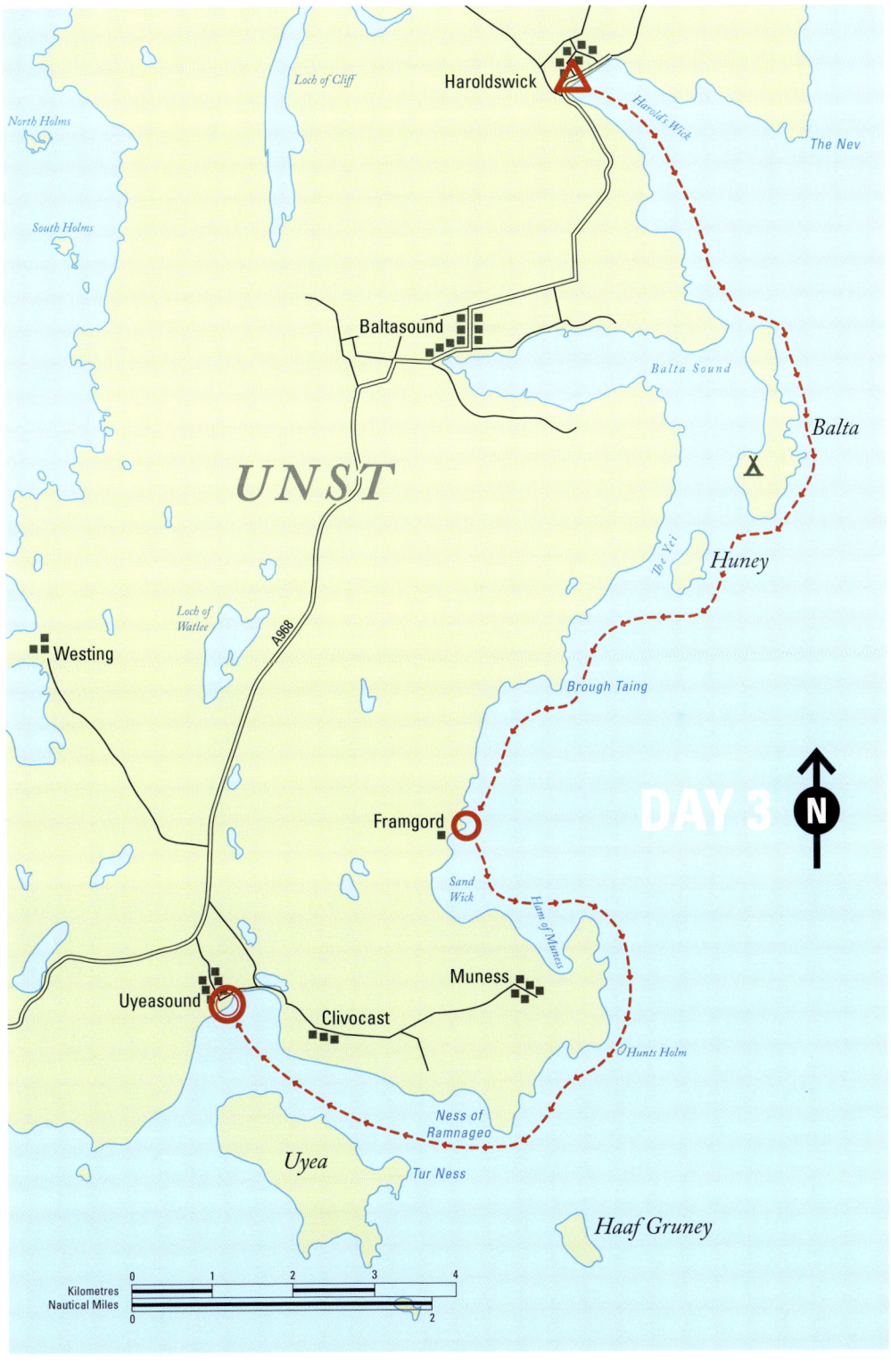

of Muness the south coast offers a couple of offshore isles. Haaf Gruney is a former National Nature Reserve, and the larger island of Uyea boasts an impressive but sadly disintegrating old house, former summer residence of Sir Basil Neven-Spence. Continue on round to land on the beach west of the jetty in Uyeasound.

VARIATIONS

Another possible start point on Day 1 is the pebble beach at Westing, just north of Lunda Wick. This has the effect of shortening the day by about 10km and avoiding the tides in Bluemull Sound. To get to the beach from either the ferry terminal at Belmont or from Gardiesfauld, drive north towards Baltasound and take the first proper road on the left after the Uyeasound junction. Follow this road, ignoring turnoffs, until it ends at the back of the beach at Westing. If you only have one day in Unst you might want to combine this shorter trip with a diversion to Muckle Flugga.

Tide and weather

The west and north coasts of Unst are as exposed as anywhere in Shetland and should be avoided in conditions of westerly or northerly swell. Tides are strong in Bluemull Sound, around Muckle Flugga, and on the northeast at Skaw and Lamba Ness. Passage north through Bluemull Sound is best timed to take advantage of the last of the ebb tide, around 3 to 4 hours after HW Lerwick. This should make it possible to be coming round Hermaness as the east-going stream starts there about 5 hours later. At Skaw the north-going stream starts just over 2 hours after HW Lerwick. It is important to be round both Skaw and Lamba Ness before this.

Additional information

Unst has a fair claim to be the most interesting of the North Isles of Shetland. Because of its geographical position it has many of Britain's 'most northerlies'. The Unst Boat Haven in Haroldswick is well worth a visit, especially if you are interested in the history of boats and fishing. Muness Castle is a contemporary of the more famous castle at Scalloway, from the period in the 16th century when Shetland and Orkney had only recently passed from Norwegian to Scottish sovereignty.

There is much of interest also for walkers, including a pleasant stroll through one of the smaller National Nature Reserves at Keen of Hamar, just east of Baltasound. The Keen of Hamar is home to a variety of unique plants which have adapted to the rare serpentine rock habitat. It is also home to a Edmondston's chickweed, which is only found on Unst. The more demanding walk to the cliffs of Hermaness is recommended, with views to Muckle Flugga and over the expansive gannet colonies.

OS Explorer Map 470 and Admiralty Chart 3282 cover this area.

Out Skerries lighthouse, Bound Skerry | Rachel Shucksmith

Out Skerries

No. 41 | Grade C | 46km | 10 hours | OS Sheet 3 | Tidal Port Lerwick

Start	△ Vidlin marina (480 655)
Finish	○ Out Skerries Pier (688 716)
HW	Local HW is 25 minutes before HW Lerwick.
Tidal Times	In the north end of Lunning Sound and also east of Skaw in Whalsay, the S going stream starts about 3 hours before HW Lerwick, and the N going stream starts about 3 hours after HW Lerwick.
Max Rate at Sp	In the north end of Lunning Sound is 2 knots. Off Skaw is 4 knots.
Coastguard	Shetland

Introduction

The Out Skerries are a small group of rocky islands about 10km to the north-east of Whalsay. The name is a corruption of Aus Skerries, meaning 'east skerries', and complements the Ve Skerries, or 'west skerries' off Papa Stour. The two larger islands of Housay and Bruray are linked by a bridge and form a natural harbour facing south-east and sheltered by the third island of Grunay.

221

Arch at the South Mouth harbour entrance, Skerries | Hamish Leslie

Grunay is no longer permanently inhabited, but Housay and Bruray support a population of about thirty-five people. The economy is one of fishing based on a small, natural harbour, and two other sheltered sea inlets at North Mouth and West Voe. In good weather the islands are idyllic. The people are among the most hospitable anywhere.

Day 1: Vidlin to Out Skerries 25km, 6 hours

Day 2: Circumnavigation of Skerries 21km, 4 hours

Description

DAY 1

There are several possible starting points for the trip to the Out Skerries. The easiest is the marina in Vidlin, just a short distance from the ferry terminal which serves the islands. From the marina the route leads north and east around the blunt mass of the Lunning peninsula and across the north end of Lunning Sound. Tidal streams are strong in the southern part of the sound, but should not cause any problems here. The best option is to head directly from Lunning Head to Challister Ness on Whalsay, a distance of about 6km almost due east, then continue on to Skaw, the north-east point of Whalsay. The tidal streams are strong here around the Inner and Outer Holms. From the Outer Holm there is another open stretch of 5km, again almost due east, to the first of a group of low-lying skerries called the Benelips. The highest of these, Filla, gives its name to one of the Shetland Islands Council ferries originally used for the Skerries route. Beware of strong tides and extensive shallows here. Paddling north through the Benelips, it is a short distance to Mio Ness, the south-western tip of Housay. The route then continues along the south coast of Housay to the South Mouth of the harbour.

There are several possible landing places on Skerries. If returning by ferry there is a slip next to the ferry terminal. If camping, a few options exist. Camping should be possible on Grunay, which is uninhabited now, or in the small bay opposite, near the end of the airstrip (now mainly unused).

DAY 2

A circumnavigation of Skerries is a relatively short but recommended extension to this paddle. The low-lying coastline has a small number of caves and arches, most noticeably at Flat Lamba stack on the east side and at the south mouth of the harbour between Housay and Grunay. The islands of Grunay and Bound Skerry are worth landing on and exploring, and can be easily incorporated into a circumnavigation of these isles. It is possible to walk up to the lighthouse on Bound Skerry, and has a relatively easy landing point at the jetty and concrete path up to the lighthouse. It should be noted that a tide race forms through Benelip Sound, which can be mainly avoided staying close to Housay.

Variations

It is of course possible to paddle back the same way to Vidlin, but the return trip could be combined with a visit to Whalsay. The return to Vidlin could be made by ferry. Booking is essential on the Skerries ferry as the number of passengers is limited. The ferry does not run every day, and some sailings will not take place unless there are advance bookings. As with all Shetland ferries there should be no problem about carrying kayaks on board.

Tide and weather

This trip should ideally be planned so as to be passing Skaw, on the north-east corner of Whalsay, at slack water, about 4 hours before HW Lerwick, and not at all if the wind is significant from the south-east, or there is a big south-easterly swell.

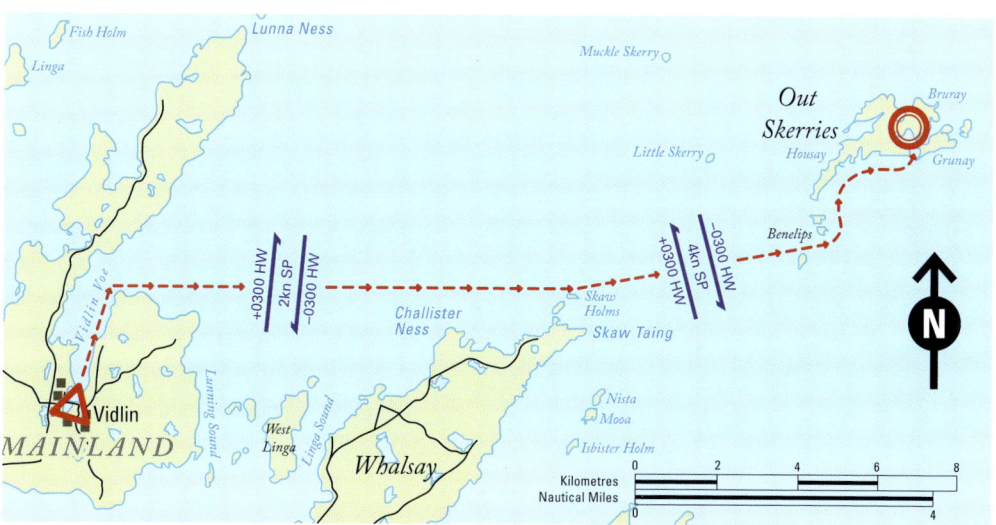

Killer Whales (Orcas) | Richard Shucksmith

Cetaceans

Whales, dolphins, and porpoises, known together as cetaceans, thrive in Scottish seas, particularly the north and west of Scotland. In Shetland the proximity to the continental shelf edge, only 30 miles to the west of Shetland creates a perfect home for a wide variety of species. Fifteen different species of cetaceans have been spotted along the Shetland coast, including some species associated with deeper water, such as the fin whale. Common species include harbour porpoises, orcas, minke whales, white-sided dolphins, Risso's dolphins, and humpback whales. Some of these, like the harbour porpoise (known locally as neesiks) and orca (also known as killer whales), are seen year-round, while others, like the fin whale, are rare visitors.

If circumnavigating, staying close inshore most of the tidal flow around the isle can be avoided, but wind against tide at south-west, northly and easterly points of the Out Skerries can lead to larger sea conditions.

Additional information

There is much to explore around these islands. The Skerries lighthouse is on Bound Skerry, the most easterly of the group. The area around the entrance to the South Mouth is riddled with passages among the stacks and skerries.

OS Explorer map 468 and Admiralty Chart 3282 cover this area.

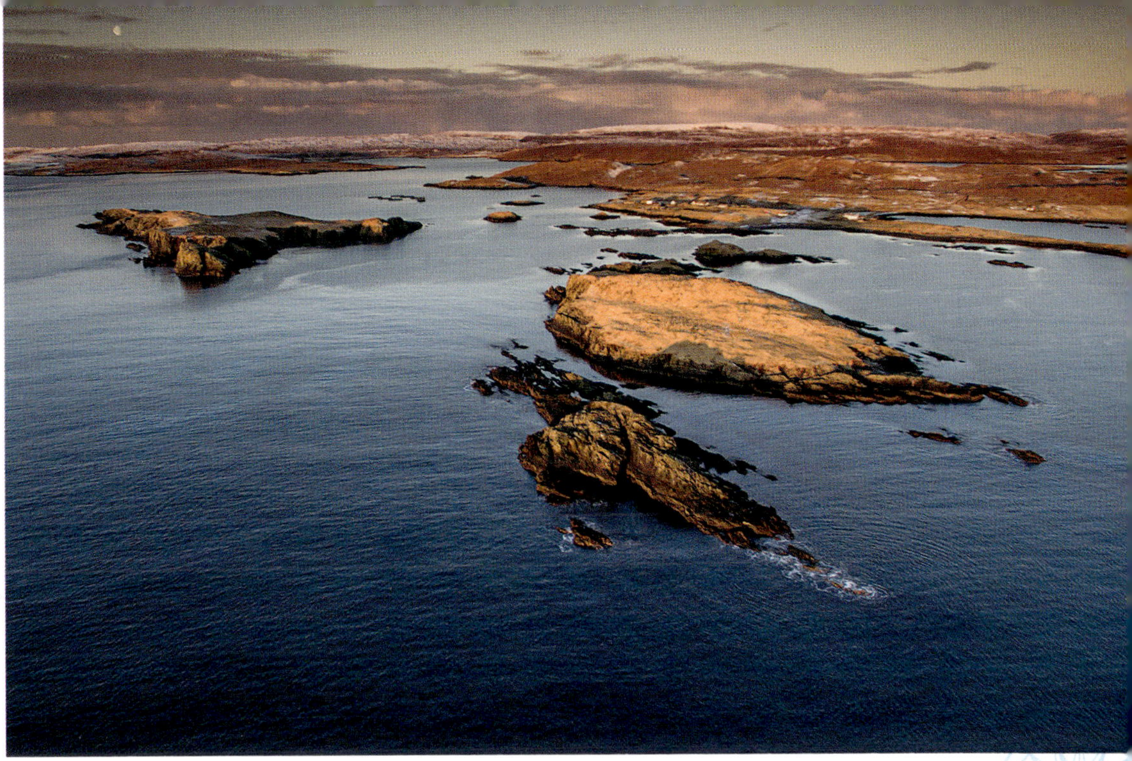

Nesting

No. 42	Grade B | 22km | 6 hours | OS Sheet 3 | Tidal Port Lerwick
Start	△ Vassa Voe (462 533)
Finish	◯ Billister (478 605)
HW	Local HW is 10 minutes before HW Lerwick.
Tidal Times	The S going stream on this coast starts about 4 hours 30 minutes before HW Lerwick, and the N going stream starts about 1 hour 30 minutes after HW Lerwick.
Max Rate at Sp	Off Stava Ness is 1.5 knots Otherwise tidal streams are generally weak.
Coastguard	Shetland

Introduction

The two peninsulas of North Nesting and South Nesting are on the east coast of the mainland north of Lerwick, and are separated from each other by South Nesting Bay. This is perhaps the most attractive stretch of coastline on the east coast of the mainland north of Lerwick. The Isles of Gletness are particularly attractive, and there are fine views to Whalsay and the north from North Nesting.

South Isle, Gletness | Doug Cooper

Description

The best starting point is at Vassa Voe in South Nesting. There are suitable parking areas on both sides of the loop road in front of the old school building. The route first leads south out of Cat Firth, then round the headland of Railsbrough to the Isles of Gletness. These are well worth exploring, especially the South Isle where there is a good landing in a small cove on the north-east side, and a fine natural arch on the eastern tip.

From here the diversion to the Hoo Stack, about 2km off the Moul of Eswick, is well worth considering. Alternatively follow the long narrow headland of Gletness which points to the Aswick Skerries and the South Bay of Eswick, where there is some interesting cliff scenery and a couple of small caves. The headland at Moul of Eswick comes next, and it can be rough in easterly or south-easterly conditions.

Turning into South Nesting Bay, alternative landing points are possible at south and north ends of the bay, at the beach at the West Voe of Skellister, but with a bit of a carry up to the road, or at Housabister, at the north end of the bay.

Coming round North Nesting, Hog Island has a narrow passage, a small arch and an impressive collapsed cave. A rockfall in 2023 has blocked a possible second north exit to this cave, but subsequent winter storms may clear this rock debris. The rest of the North Nesting peninsula is a pleasant paddle with a good view of the neighbouring island of Whalsay. Finally, turning into Dury Voe, watch for the almost hidden entrance to the little harbour at Billister about 3km along the south shore. This was the original crossing point for boats going to Whalsay, and still gives the shortest crossing to the island.

Tide and weather

There is some tide here, mainly around the headlands of Stava Ness and Moul of Eswick, and the latter headland can become tricky if the tide is flooding south against a south-easterly wind. The trip can be done in either direction and the choice can be made according to whether the tide is flooding south or ebbing north.

Additional information

OS Explorer Map 467 and Admiralty Chart 3282 also cover this area.

Otters

The Shetland dialect name for otters is the 'draatsi', and they are thought to be genetically distinct from their mainland counterparts. Otters thrive along Shetland's coast, foraging amongst the kelp for fish, crabs and octopus and are particularly abundant on low rocky coastlines backed by peat. As Shetland's otters are active during the day, and Shetland has the highest density of otters in Europe, they are not uncommon to see while seakayaking. While they have successfully adapted to a marine environment, they need to return to the shore to rest and they need freshwater to groom and drink. Otters have relatively poor eyesight but a keen sense of smell, so if they are approached from a down wind direction, and kayakers remain still and quiet, they can be observed undisturbed fishing along the coast for some time. Historically otters were trapped for their skins, and the remains of 'otter hooses' or otter traps can still be found around the Shetland coast but with the doors now removed.

Otter catching a shore crab | Richard Shucksmith

© Symbister harbour, Whalsay | Mark Rainsley

Whalsay

No. 43	**Grade B**	**34km**	**8 hours**	**OS Sheet 2**	**Tidal Port Lerwick**
Start/Finish	△◯ Billister (537 624)
HW	HW Symbister is 15 minutes before HW Lerwick.
Tidal Times	In the S end of Lunning Sound and in Linga Sound the S going stream starts at approximately 4 hours 30 minutes before HW Lerwick, and the N going stream starts approximately 2 hours after HW Lerwick. At Skaw Taing the SW going stream starts approximately 30 minutes earlier.
Max Rate at Sp	In Lunning Sound and in Linga Sound is 6 knots. Off Skaw is 4 knots.
Coastguard	Shetland

Introduction

This prosperous little island off the east coast of the mainland is known as 'the bonny isle' in Shetland. The modern ferry terminal is at Laxo, but before the days of car ferries the Whalsay boats sailed from Billister in North Nesting. The trip round the island is described starting and finishing at Billister, but it can be easily shortened by taking the ferry to Symbister and starting from there.

229

Whalsay from Hamera Head | Tom Smith

Description

Billister is signposted off the B9075 Nesting road. Drive to the end of the road where there is a small turning area near the old pier. The 'vadill' here dries out at low tide. Leaving Billister the route takes us directly across Dury Voe, past the Green Isle to Hamera Head, then follows the coast north-east to Dragon Ness. Look out for ferries during the crossing of Dury Voe. A little north of Dragon Ness is the attractive deserted croft of Bonidale with a good landing at a traditional Shetland 'noost'. With no road access and a difficult path over the hill to the nearest village at Vidlin the croft house here is no longer occupied. Tides are strong in the south end of Lunning Sound, particularly around Hunder Holm, but there are many small islands further north giving shelter. The largest island, West Linga, is another possible stop. There are many possible routes through the islands to Whalsay but the most direct one crosses from the north end of Linga to Kirk Ness on Whalsay before following the coast past Challister Ness to Skaw. Tides are again strong around the Inner and Outer Holms of Skaw. These islands are home to a large seal population and the Inner Holm also has some interesting early Christian ruins. The headland a little further on at Skaw Taing has a well-concealed passage through it (not passable at low tide). Skaw is also the closest point to the Out Skerries.

The east side of Whalsay is not spectacular but continuously pleasant and interesting. There is a good landing here on a slipway below the houses at Isbister, which is the only settlement on the east side. The best way to return to Billister is to head west from the area of Haa Ness or Sandwick. The route then goes through the little group of rocks known as the Flaeshans of

Sandwick to Stava Ness on the mainland. You then follow the coast along the south shore of Dury Voe.

VARIATIONS

The trip can be shortened and the tides in Lunning Sound avoided by taking the ferry to Symbister and starting from there. The ferry normally leaves from Laxo on the north side of Dury Voe, but in strong easterlies it switches to the Vidlin terminal. It is unlikely you would plan to paddle round Whalsay when the ferry is running from Vidlin. Shetland ferry crews are generally helpful about carrying kayaks on to the car decks, and there is no need to take a vehicle across. At Symbister you will find a public slipway and a beach a short distance east from the ferry ramp.

Tide and weather

There are strong tides in both Lunning Sound and Linga Sound, and also around the headland at Skaw. The trip can be planned to take advantage of the last of the ebbing tide in the sounds. The best option is to aim to be at Skaw about 4 hours before HW Lerwick. The only problem with this is that the passage at Skaw Taing is likely to be impassable at low water. The tide is much less significant on the east side of the island, but easterly or southeasterly winds can create rough conditions.

Puffins, Noss (Route 44) | Rachel Shucksmith

Additional information

If you have taken the ferry option and have time before the return ferry crossing it is worth taking a short walk around the harbour to the Hanseatic Booth. This is a relic of the time when Shetland's principal trade partners were in Holland and northern Germany.

OS Explorer Map 468 and Admiralty Chart 3282 also cover this area.

Noss cliffs | Rachel Shucksmith

Bressay & Noss

No. 44 | Grade B | 18km | 5 hours | OS Sheet 4 | Tidal Port Lerwick

Start/Finish	△○ Voe of Cullingsburgh (517 419)
HW	Local HW is the same as HW Lerwick.
Tidal Times	The S going stream in Noss Sound starts about 4 hours 30 minutes before HW Lerwick, and the N going stream starts about 1 hour 30 minutes after HW Lerwick.
Max Rate at Sp	Generally about 2 knots.
Coastguard	Shetland

Introduction

Bressay is the large island to the east of Lerwick, which guards Lerwick harbour. Noss lies a little further off to the east, is a National Nature Reserve, and is uninhabited apart from a summer warden. Noss is home to almost 60,000 breeding seabirds from 13 different species, and the cliffs on its east side are a spectacular sight in June and early July. It is possible to paddle round both islands in a single day, starting from Lerwick, but this shorter trip takes us round Noss from a starting point on the east side of Bressay.

Noss Head | Richard Shucksmith

Description

To get to Noss take the short ferry trip across Lerwick harbour then drive across Bressay. If you are heading for Noss as a walker follow the signs to the car park then head down the steep path to the shore where a ferry, operated by the island's warden with an inflatable boat, will take you the short distance across to the visitor centre at Gungstie. However, if you are paddling and don't fancy a long carry up the hill at the end of the day, take a left fork (signposted 'Setter') as you leave the settled area on the west side of Bressay. Follow this road until you come to a gate and a parking area suitable for three or four cars. Vehicles must be left outside the gate. There follows a short carry down to the shore alongside a small stream, or a longer carry along the track to a small beach. After setting off from here the route first takes us north-east to Loder Head, where a right turn will bring the north side of Noss into view. Heading around to the east side the cliffs steadily increase in height and the birds become more numerous. Eventually the unmistakable outline of the Noup fills the view ahead and gannets fill the sky above. Just north of the Noup is an area of low-angle slabs at sea level. It is usually possible to land here and take in the scene.

Continuing round there are caves to explore, and the impressive Holm of Noss, better known as Cradle Holm. This is a tall stack which used to be linked to the island by a rope bridge. As the name suggests it was once an island but the gap has filled with fallen rocks and it is now only possible to paddle through at the top of a high tide.

Coming round to the south-west coast the cliffs gradually drop off. Continue round through Noss Sound and land on the beach just north of the visitor centre. This is well worth a visit for orientation, and if you have time you may want to walk the cliffs to see the sights from above as well as below. The trip finishes with a short paddle up the east side of Bressay to Loder Head, then back to the shore at Cullingsburgh.

BRESSAY

Bressay itself has much of interest, particularly on the south-east coast from Noss Sound down to the impressive headland of the Bard, which marks the south-east corner. At Bard head the seabed shallows considerably, which in wind or swell and opposing tide conditions can create larger and more confused seas. Most notable are the stack of Stoura Clett which has tunnels through it, and a fine natural arch, known as the Giant's Leg, on the west side of the Bard. Near here is a labyrinthine cave known as the Orkneyman's Cave, much visited by tour boats from Lerwick and well worth exploring. It is believed to get its name from an Orkney man who hid from the press gang inside it.

Score Head, on the north-east corner of Bressay, can be bypassed by a channel inside the Inner Score. The Inner and Outer Scores are separated by a narrow cleft called the Gloup of the

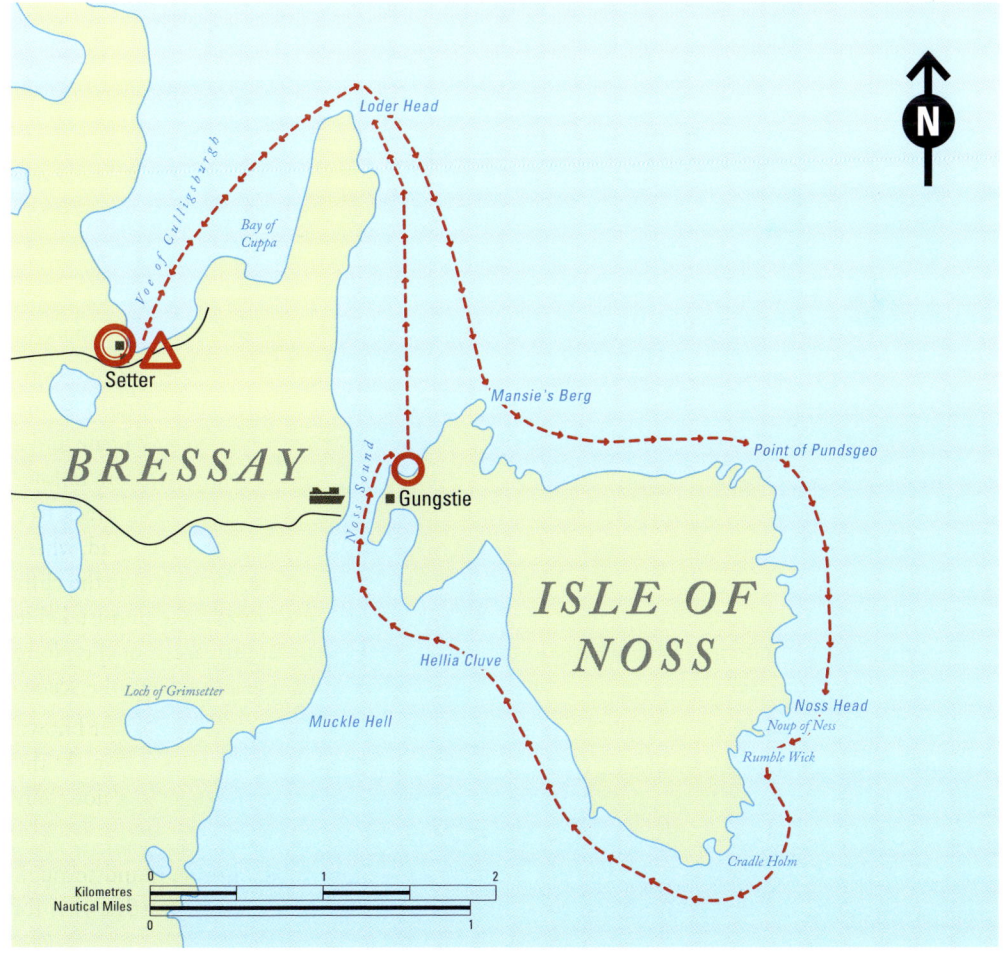

The slabs below the Noup | Tom Smith

Scores. The nearby Erne's Hill is home to a First World War coastal defense battery, guarding the northern approaches to Lerwick harbour, with the six-inch diameter gun still in place.

There are several possible launch points in Lerwick for a trip round Bressay. The easiest is probably the slipway at the Small Boat Harbour near the Market Cross in the centre of town. This is also the starting point for the daily tourist boat trips to Noss. Another good spot is on the left of the side road by the Tesco supermarket at the south end of the town (next to the Fjara cafe). If you are coming from the Northlink ferry terminal at Holmsgarth without a car the nearest access point to the sea is at Skippidock. Turn left as you leave the terminal and left again at the roundabout in front of the Co-op supermarket, and you will soon reach a shingle beach.

Tide and weather

Tides here are generally weak, with the exception of the narrows at the North Mouth of Lerwick Harbour, and in Noss Sound. The east side of Noss is exposed to easterly swell and especially to south-easterlies. Opposing tide, wind and swell can create larger sea conditions between Noss Head and Cradle Holm, and at Bard Head, Bressay.

Additional information

If you are paddling anywhere within the Lerwick harbour limits you should notify either the Port Authority or the Coastguard. Shetland Coastguard Station is on the headland of the Knab overlooking the harbour.

OS Explorer Map 466 and Admiralty Chart 3283 cover this area.

Coall Head | Tom Smith

Lerwick to Cunningsburgh

No. 45 | **Grade A** | **25km** | **5 hours** | **OS Sheet 4** | **Tidal Port Lerwick**

Start	△ Briewick Bay, Lerwick (468 405)
Finish	○ Aith Voe (438 285)
HW	Local HW is the same as HW Lerwick
Tidal Times	The S going stream at Helli Ness starts about 1 hour after HW Lerwick, and the N going stream starts 6 hours after HW Lerwick.
Max Rate at Sp	At Helli Ness is 1.5 knots.
Coastguard	Shetland

Introduction

This is an interesting paddle, close to Lerwick, and can be easily shortened or lengthened. The coastal features around Coall Head are quite distinctive. Along this coastline there are a number of caves, and seals and seabirds are common.

Description

This trip can either be started at Brei Wick bay, Lerwick or shortened slightly by starting at Gulberwick (or undertaken south to north if the wind is southerly). In Brei Wick bay launching and parking is easy at the slip to the east of the café Fjara. From here an interesting rocky coastline provides opportunities to rock hop.

The north coast of Gulberwick also provides good rock hopping opportunities. The tip of the wreck of a Russian herring factory ship, the klondyker the 'Pionersk' can be seen just above the surface, and care should be taken as the metal protruding from the water has the potential to damage a seakayak. Traveling south there is a goodsized and easily accessible cave immediately north of the Broch of Burland. Seals can almost always be seen between Longa Geo and the broch.

From Quarff, the first stretch of coast around Coall Head is worth taking time to explore. It has some remarkable rock formations, several caves, and at least one natural arch. This is a good area in which to see common seals. Just after Coall Head, in Leea Geo, are a number of caves, the first of which is very deep. There follow a number of stacks and skerries until you come into the Bay of Fladdabister, which is overlooked by a number of old croft houses. A landing is possible on the south side of the bay.

After Fladdabister there is another interesting but less dramatic section of cliffs with a couple of large stacks at Ockraquoy, before crossing Aith Wick to Helli Ness. This headland should be treated with respect as a combination of complex tidal streams can create difficult sea conditions, especially around the south-east point. A westerly or south-westerly wind with a south-going tide can cause a sharp break to extend some way to the south-east. This is also known as an area where there are magnetic anomalies, and compass readings cannot be relied on.

The trip finishes at the slipway on the west side of Aith Voe. Other possible landings are the pebble beach in front of the cemetery car park at South Voxter, or the sandy beach at Mail. All of these can be reached from the Voxter road through Cunningsburgh.

VARIATIONS

This trip can be shortened by alternatively starting at Gulberwick. To access the beach at Gulberwick there is a small track immediately opposite the community hall. It can also be lengthened by ending the trip at Leebitton, Sandwich.

Tide and weather

The only significant tidal problems here are those described above at Helli Ness.

Additional information

OS Explorer Map 466 and Admiralty Chart 3283 cover this area.

Common seal | Mark Rainsley

Seals

Seals, called 'selkies' in the Northern Isles, are common throughout Orkney and Shetland. Apart from the occasional harp seal or other Arctic vagrant they are all either common seals (also known as harbour seals) or Atlantic grey seals. Despite the names the grey seals are present in much larger numbers. There is a Shetland saying about the way to tell them apart – "the common seals are grey, while the grey seals are common". In practice the grey seals are larger, tend to be lighter in colour, though there are considerable variations, and have a much straighter 'nose to forehead' line in profile, with adult males having a distinctive 'Roman nose'. Common seals generally pup in June and the young are able to swim almost from birth. Grey seals pup later in the year, October or November, generally on remote pebble beaches. The young initially have a distinctive white coat and are unable to swim and are totally dependent on their mothers for three weeks or more, so it is particularly important not to disturb them.

© Mousa Broch | Richard Shucksmith

Mousa

| **No. 46** | **Grade A** | **12km** | **3 hours** | **OS Sheet 4** | **Tidal Port Lerwick** |

Start/Finish △○ Sandsayre (436 249)

HW Local HW is 10 minutes before HW Lerwick.

Tidal Times The S going stream in Mousa Sound starts 1 hour after HW Lerwick, and the N going stream starts 6 hours before HW Lerwick.

Max Rate at Sp In Mousa Sound is 1.5 knots.

Coastguard Shetland

Introduction

Mousa is a small uninhabited island off the east side of the south mainland of Shetland, near Sandwick. For most visitors the main point of interest on the island is the prominent broch, a 13m high Iron Age tower, easily seen from the mainland across Mousa Sound. However, for those interested in wildlife the island also offers large numbers of common and grey seals, otters, and in the summer is home to Europe's largest storm petrel colony, as well as being important for other iconic northerly seabirds such as Arctic and great skuas, Arctic terns and black guillemots.

West Ham, Mousa | Richard Shucksmith

Description

The paddle round Mousa is a relatively short one of about 12km if you start from the slipway at Sandsayre or the pebble beach alongside it. Coming from Lerwick take the first road into Sandwick and follow signs for Leebitten and the Mousa Ferry. Commercial boat trips to the island leave from here, and there are public toilets and a small visitor centre. Alternatively, if you have the time, you might choose to launch from the Mail Beach in Cunningsburgh and take in an interesting stretch of coastline between there and Sandwick. Mail Beach is close by the main road at the south end of the village.

Leaving from Sandsayre the route initially crosses Mousa Sound to the north end of the island. There is some tide in the sound, but not enough to cause problems unless the wind is against it. Look for a small natural arch here before rounding the headland onto the east side. The cliff scenery builds up to be quite interesting and there is often a fair amount of easterly swell even in calm weather. There are a few caves but none large. It is important not to land at East Ham during the spring and summer due to breeding birds, or East and West Pool during common or grey pupping seasons (summer and autumn respectively) and it is an offence to disturb the seals during these times. Landing is possible at the shingle beach at West Ham, adjacent to the ferry jetty.

The eastern extremity of Mousa features a lighthouse on a detached stack known as the Peerie Bard. There are a number of stacks and passages here, which are worth exploring if the swell allows. Next comes a large area of slabs backed by the brackish West Pool, where many of the seals congregate and landing should be avoided. Coming around the south end of the island there are a couple of reasonable sized caves to look for, then a small arch immediately in front of the broch. It is important not to attempt to land in this area as storm petrels nest in the boulder beach. Mousa Broch is the best-preserved Iron Age building in Europe. It is a double walled round tower standing well over 10m high, with an internal staircase by which it is possible to climb to the top.

The return to Sandwick is easiest done by continuing up the west side of the island past the pier at West Ham then crossing directly. Be aware of the large area of shallows just east of the Sandsayre pier.

A more interesting option is to cross directly to the mainland from the broch. You should make landfall close to the headland of Hoga where there is another broch, the Broch of Burraland. This broch is in full sight of its neighbour on Mousa, but is in poorer condition. It seems to have been quite common for brochs to be built facing each other across a stretch of water like this.

To explore the Broch of Burraland go round the headland to the south of it and land on the pebble beach at the head of the second geo in. From here it is an easy scramble up to the broch

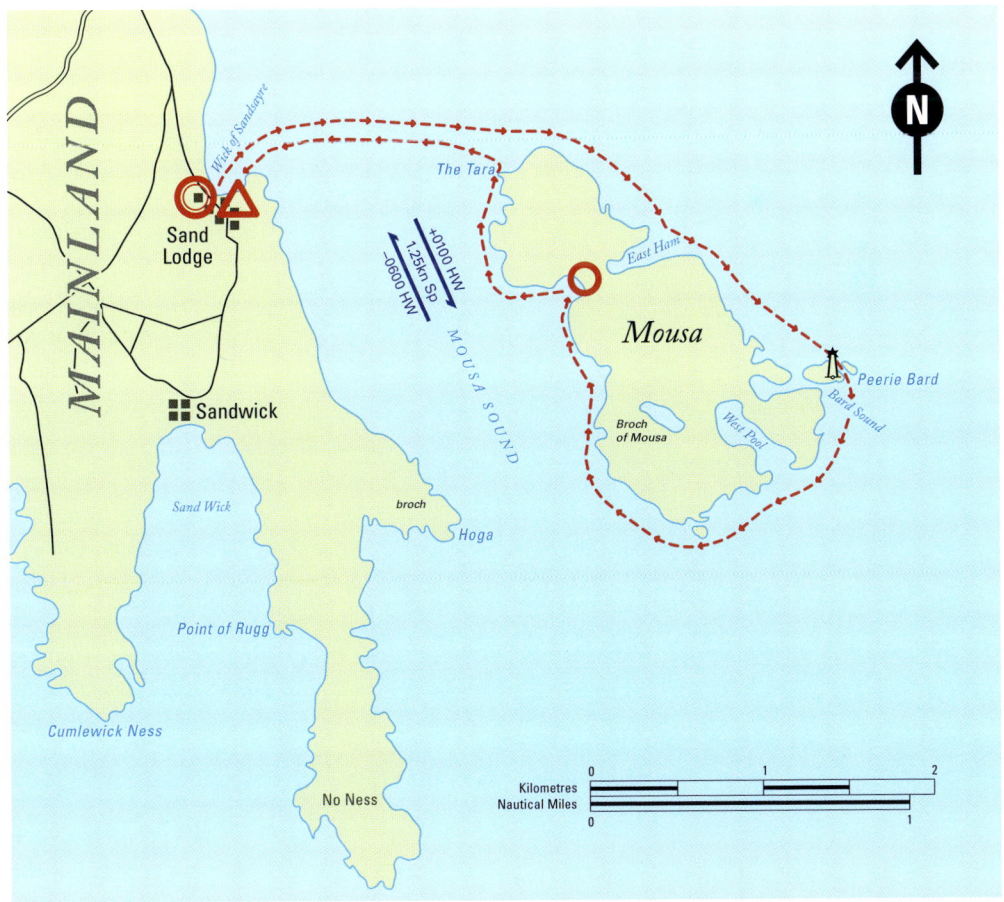

and the ruined croft nearby. It is highly likely that stones from this broch were incorporated in the building of the croft and other earlier buildings. This was common practice, and probably helps to explain why no other brochs have survived as well as Mousa, where good quality sandstone for building was abundant and used in numerous stone dykes and other later buildings as well as the broch. It is also clear that Mousa Broch was exceptionally well built and significantly smaller than its neighbours, which probably gave it greater structural strength. One cannot help but wonder how many buildings being constructed today are likely to be standing to their full height in 2,000 years' time. Brochs were commonplace throughout the western and northern highlands and islands of Scotland, but particularly common in the south mainland of Shetland.

VARIATIONS

The alternative starting point of Mail Beach in Cunningsburgh has already been mentioned. The coastline south from Hoga to the headland of Noness is also well worth exploring, if time permits. On offer are impressive bird cliffs, stacks and geos, culminating in a notably large cave called the Bannock Hole on the headland itself. From here the trip can be continued up the west side of Noness to land on the beach at Sandwick where there is good road access. Sandsayre is just over 1km due north of here.

Tide and weather

There is some tide in Mousa Sound, and the east side of the island is open to easterly swell.

Additional information

Sandwick, which just means 'sandy bay', is the name of the inlet immediately to the west of Noness, and of the small township at the head of this bay. However it is also the generic name for the whole area including the townships of Hoswick, Swinister, Cumlewick, Stove, Leebitten, and Setter.

OS Explorer Map 466 and Admiralty Chart 3283 cover this area.

Storm petrels

Mousa is home to Europe's largest colony of storm petrels (c.12,000 pairs). These ocean birds spend all winter far out to sea, but in summer they nest in the dykes and boulder beaches around the island, and even in the walls of the broch itself. By day one of the pair quietly guards the nest, while the other forages at sea. As dusk gathers the forager returns to its nest aided by the low throaty cries of its mate. If you can be there at dusk or camp on the island it is a truly memorable experience, but it is important not to walk unnecessarily on the boulder beaches between May and October.

Boddam coast | Geoff Burke

Grutness to Levenwick

No. 47 | Grade B | 14km | 5 hours | OS Sheet 4 | Tidal Port Lerwick

Start	Grutness (403 100)
Finish	Levenwick (414 214)
HW	Local HW is 15 minutes before HW Lerwick.
Tidal Times	The N going tidal stream along this coast starts 6 hours before HW Lerwick, and the S going stream starts about 1 hour after HW Lerwick.
Max Rate at Sp	Generally around 1 knot.
Coastguard	Shetland

Introduction

The south-east of mainland Shetland is often overlooked but this is a fine day trip when conditions are right. The main feature is the dramatic cliff scenery with some very large deep caves.

Cliffs near Troswick | Tom Smith

Description

If you are doing this trip from south to north the best starting point is the sandy beach at Grutness Voe near the airport. There is room to park just off the road at the junction where the road to the Grutness terminal for the Fair Isle ferry leaves the airport perimeter road. An alternative starting point is the beach alongside the Ness Boating Club, on the north side of the Pool of Virkie.

The trip starts by heading across the bay past the end of the airport runway to the Point of Tangpool, then following the cliffs north. There is much of interest to explore for the next 3 or 4km, until Boddam Voe opens up to the north-west. The voe itself is not particularly interesting so it is as well just to cross the outer end to the cliffs at Dalsetter. Here are to be found some really impressive caves, high and deep and relatively easy to explore in good conditions.

The first suitable landing is at Troswick. Care should be taken not to disturb any seals hauled out on the slabs. The name Troswick means 'Trow's Bay' and this is an area rich in stories of trows – Shetland's equivalent of 'little people' or fairies. From here to Levenwick the coast is continuously interesting, with some unusual and impressive cliff scenery, including the oddly (and aptly) named Drooping Point. Near the end the section from Gungstie to Levenwick Ness is littered with off lying rocks. There are no further landings until you round the last headland at Levenwick and turn sharp left to land on one of Shetland's best and most popular beaches. Again there is limited parking at the back of the beach, and good access through Levenwick village from the main Lerwick to Sumburgh road.

Cave at Boddam | Rachel Shucksmith

Tide and weather

There is some tide here, especially around the southern section. The tide flows north and ebbs south, and wind against tide can result in quite lumpy conditions. With a north-going or slack tide the trip is best done from south to north. It can readily be reversed if wind or tide conditions dictate.

Additional information

OS Explorer Map 466 and Admiralty Chart 3283 cover this area.

Fitfall Head | Doug Cooper

Sumburgh Head & Fitful Head

No. 48 | Grade C | 22km | 5 hours | OS Sheet 4 | Tidal Port Lerwick

Start	△ Grutness (403 100)
Finish	○ Spiggie (367 178)
HW	Local HW is 15 minutes before HW Lerwick.
Tidal Times	The E going stream at Sumburgh Head starts about 4 hours before HW Lerwick and ends about 30 minutes after HW Lerwick. There is then a half hour slack, known as 'the still' before the W going stream starts. There is no significant slack when the W going stream ends. Off Fitful Head the SE going stream starts about 4 hours 30 minutes before HW Lerwick, and the NW going stream about 2 hours after HW Lerwick.
Max Rate at Sp	At Sumburgh Head is 5 knots. At Fitful Head is 3 knots.
Coastguard	Shetland

Introduction

This is a committing paddle round the two major headlands in the south of the Shetland mainland. There are strong tides round both, with Fitful Head the more difficult of the two, in part as the rocky coast line of Sumburgh Head provides a near shore route which offers shelter from the tide. Back eddies can occur at both these headlands, more noticeably at spring tide.

Description

Launch from the beach at Grutness Voe, as for the Grutness to Levenwick trip. The best plan is to set off about an hour before HW Lerwick in order to be at Sumburgh Head just as the tide starts to run west. First paddle out past the ferry terminal and round the wonderfully named headland of Looss Laward. Look out for hidden dangers and unexpected breaks here if there is any swell. Then follows 2km of fairly dramatic cliffs covered with seabirds in summer, including large numbers of guillemots and puffins. At Sumburgh Head itself the most southerly point is actually a large stack with an easy passage inside, so it is quite possible to stay away from the tide race altogether, or to play in it if the conditions are favourable. In fact the infamous Sumburgh Roost sets up a little offshore and can be watched from a safe distance. However, note that on spring tides a back eddy can form in the opposite direction and at greater speed to the main flow; this can in the most part be avoided by paddling close to the cliffs of Sumburgh head.

The trip continues across the outer part of West Voe to the headland at Scatness and Horse Island. This island is difficult to land on, the best option being a north-west facing boulder beach. The tide runs strongly to the south of Horse Island and through the sound between it and Scatness. As you continue north towards the two small islands of Lady's Holm and Little Holm, the tide should by now be pushing you along towards the north-west. Beware of a strong eddy flowing out of the Bay of Quendale in this area. It tends to create sharp eddy lines and confused water around Lady's Holm.

Just over 1km north-west of Lady's Holm across Quendale Bay is Garths Ness, last resting place of the *Braer*, although there is no evidence of its passing now. Next comes the massive bulk of Siggar Ness. For the next 3km the cliffs of Fitful Head dominate, rising to 280m. Back eddies can also be encountered at Fitfull head, particularly during spring tides, running in the opposing direction to the main flow detailed in the tidal atlas. Eddy hopping is possible. There are numerous skerries and a few caves to explore if conditions allow. Rounding the headland of The Nev we come into the bay at Wick of Shunni. Here there is some shelter from the tide and any southerly winds allowing a more leisurely exploration. Finally we round Cloki Stack into Muckle Sound, which separates the mainland from the pretty island of Colsay, famous for its wild flowers, and land on the first small beach. This is Spiggie beach, with the road running close behind it. Around the next headland, Northern Ness, is a wide north facing beach which is correctly called Scousburgh, but often referred to as Spiggie.

VARIATIONS

If the trip was just to take in Sumburgh Head it is possible to follow the coast from there north, passing the famous Jarlshof historic site to land on the beach at West Voe in the shadow of the airport. From here it is a short walk back to Grutness. If there is southerly or south-westerly swell

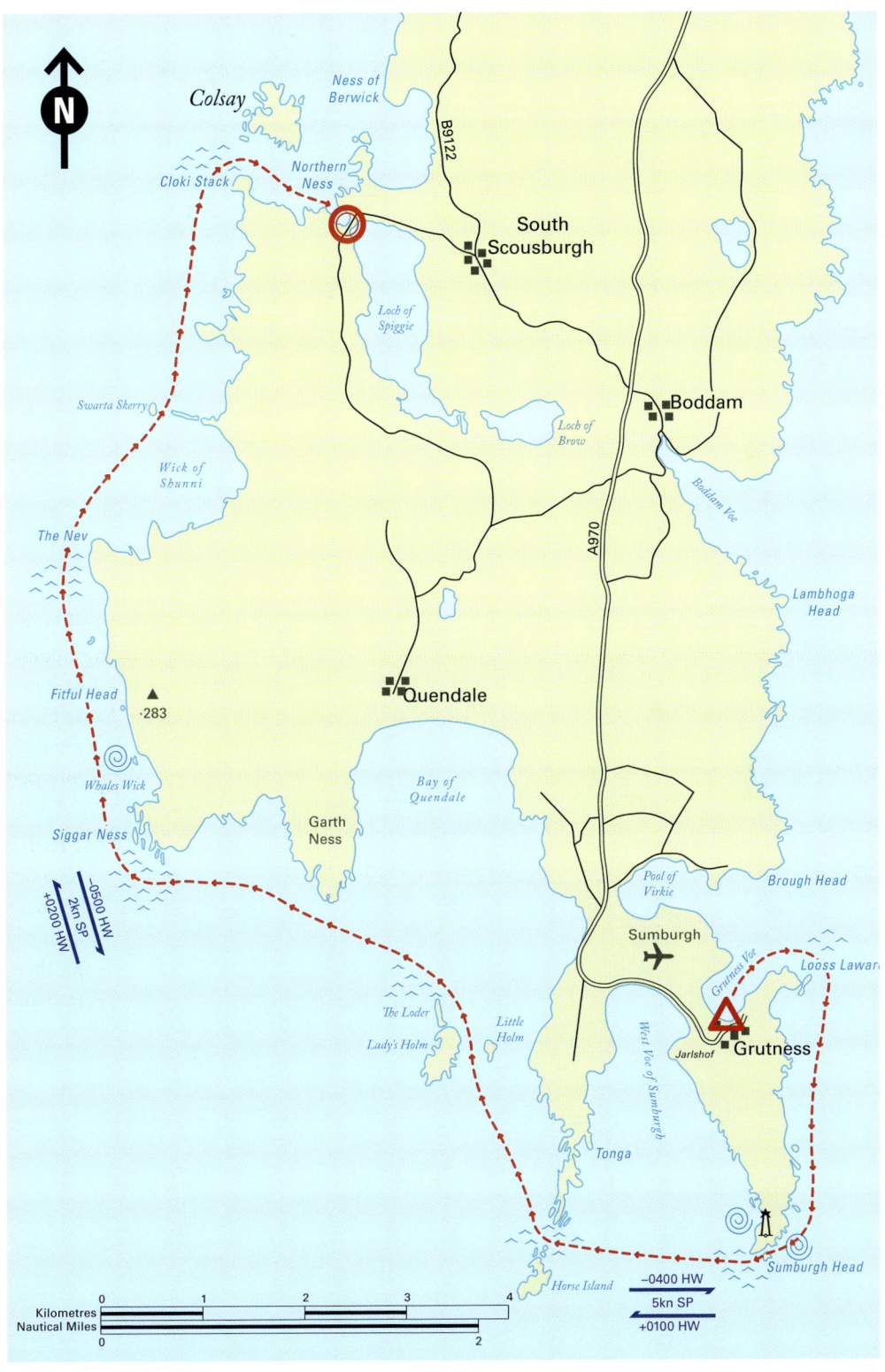

West Voe is one of the best surf beaches in Shetland, and probably the most accessible. Another alternative is to continue on to the wide sandy beach at the head of the Bay of Quendale. This is again an excellent surfing beach in a southerly swell.

Tide and weather

The major problem here is the Sumburgh Roost. The worst of this can be avoided by passing close to, or even inside the stack at the headland itself at High Water slack, then inside Horse Island, crossing Quendale Bay with the first of the ebb tide, which should then push you on round Fitful Head. Be aware that a westerly or north-westerly wind at Fitful Head will create wind over tide conditions, resulting in a very rough sea. There will also be a back eddy coming out of Quendale Bay in the region of Lady's Holm.

It should be noted that at both Sumburgh Head and Fitful Head powerful back eddies can form close to shore during spring tides. These eddies can form earlier and at greater speeds than the main flow further offshore. When rounding these headlands on spring tides it is advised to paddle in conditions which permit paddling close to the cliffs, out of both the main flow and back eddies.

Additional information

If you have time before or after the trip it is worth driving up to the car park just below the lighthouse at Sumburgh and walking up the last bit of the road. The lighthouse was built by Robert Stevenson in 1820 and like all Scottish lighthouses it is now unmanned. The lighthouse buildings have now been converted to a visitor centre and café, as well as being home to several environmental organizations and some self-catering holiday accommodation. The cliffs here offer the best vantage point in Shetland for whale watching and are among the most accessible for bird watching. Many of the major seabirds are here in numbers, with puffins nesting almost within touching distance.

OS Explorer Map 466 and Admiralty Chart 3283 cover this area.

The *Braer*

In the early hours of 5th January 1993 the oil tanker *Braer* was on route from Mongstad in Norway to the east coast of the United States, carrying 80,000 tonnes of North Sea crude. The tanker lost power in a Force 10 storm while passing through the Fair Isle channel, about 18km south of Sumburgh Head. She was eventually wrecked on Garths Ness, just east of Fitful Head and within sight of Sumburgh Airport. The crew was rescued by helicopter but the ship was a total loss. For the next month, as the world's media descended on Shetland, the wind seldom dropped below gale force. The dispersal teams sat helpless at Sumburgh while the weather did their job for them. By the time the gales eased the entire cargo had gone, though its legacy remained for some time in the fields and buildings, and particularly the shellfish beds, of the south of Shetland. As for the *Braer* itself, the bow section remained visible for a year or so before finally disappearing for good.

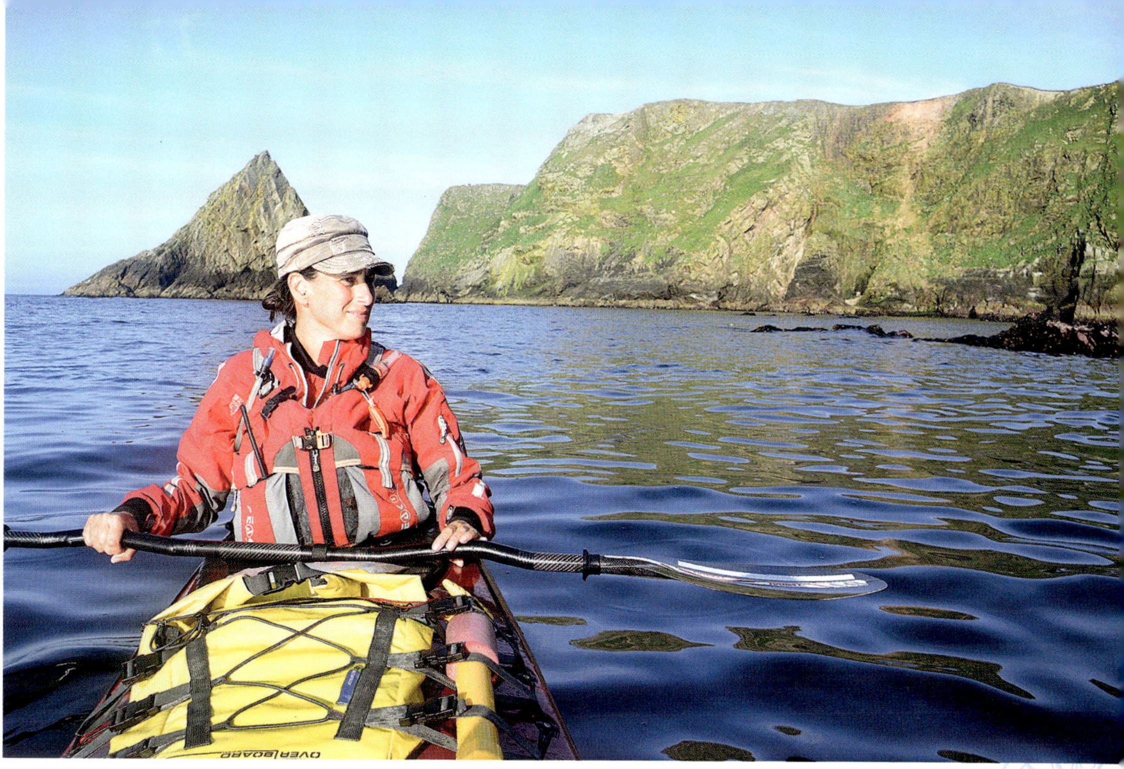

Fair Isle

No. 49 | **Grade C** | **63km** | **2 days** | **OS sheet 4** | **Tidal Port Lerwick**

Start	△ Grutness (403 100)
Finish	◯ North Haven (225 725)
HW	Local HW is 20 minutes before HW Lerwick.
Tidal Times	The E going stream at Sumburgh Head starts about 4 hours before HW Lerwick and ends about 30 minutes after HW Lerwick. There is then a half hour slack, known as 'the still' before the W going stream starts. There is no significant slack when the W going stream ends. Midway between Sumburgh Head and Fair Isle, and also south of Fair Isle, the E going stream starts about 3 hours before HW Lerwick and the W going stream starts about 3 hours after HW Lerwick.
Max Rate at Sp	At Sumburgh Head is 5 knots. In mid-channel and south of Fair Isle is typically 2.5 knots.
Coastguard	Shetland

Introduction

Fair Isle lies almost exactly halfway between Shetland and Orkney, but it is administratively part of Shetland and all its transport links are to the Shetland Mainland. It vies with Foula for the

Fair Isle in the mist | Mark Rainsley

49 Fair Isle

title of most remote community in the British Isles, but is nevertheless home to a remarkably diverse population of approximately 50 permanent residents. The island is famous for two things: its distinctive handmade knitwear, which first brought the island to the world's notice, and its status as one of the bird watching Meccas of Europe. The resident bird population is not notably different from the rest of Shetland, rather it is the island's popularity with migrant birds that brings large numbers of 'twitchers' in spring and autumn.

Description

The trip from the north of Scotland through Orkney and Fair Isle to Shetland is one of the great sea kayaking challenges in Britain. Here we will concentrate on the journey from Shetland to Fair Isle, and the circumnavigation of Fair Isle, a superb day trip in itself.

DAY 1 – CROSSING (45KM, 10 HOURS)

The starting point is the same as in Chapter 47 and 48, the Bay of Grutness, within sight of the airport and the Fair Isle ferry terminal. If you plan to set off a little before HW Dover you should be passing through the area of the Sumburgh Roost around HW slack. Fair Isle should be clearly visible to the SSW. For the first 5 hours or so the ebb tide will push you to the north-west, then the flood tide will reverse that effect. After nine or ten hours you should be approaching the north-east corner of Fair Isle, with the last of the flood continuing to push you to the east. Aim to pass east of the lighthouse and look for the recently constructed pier, which almost closes

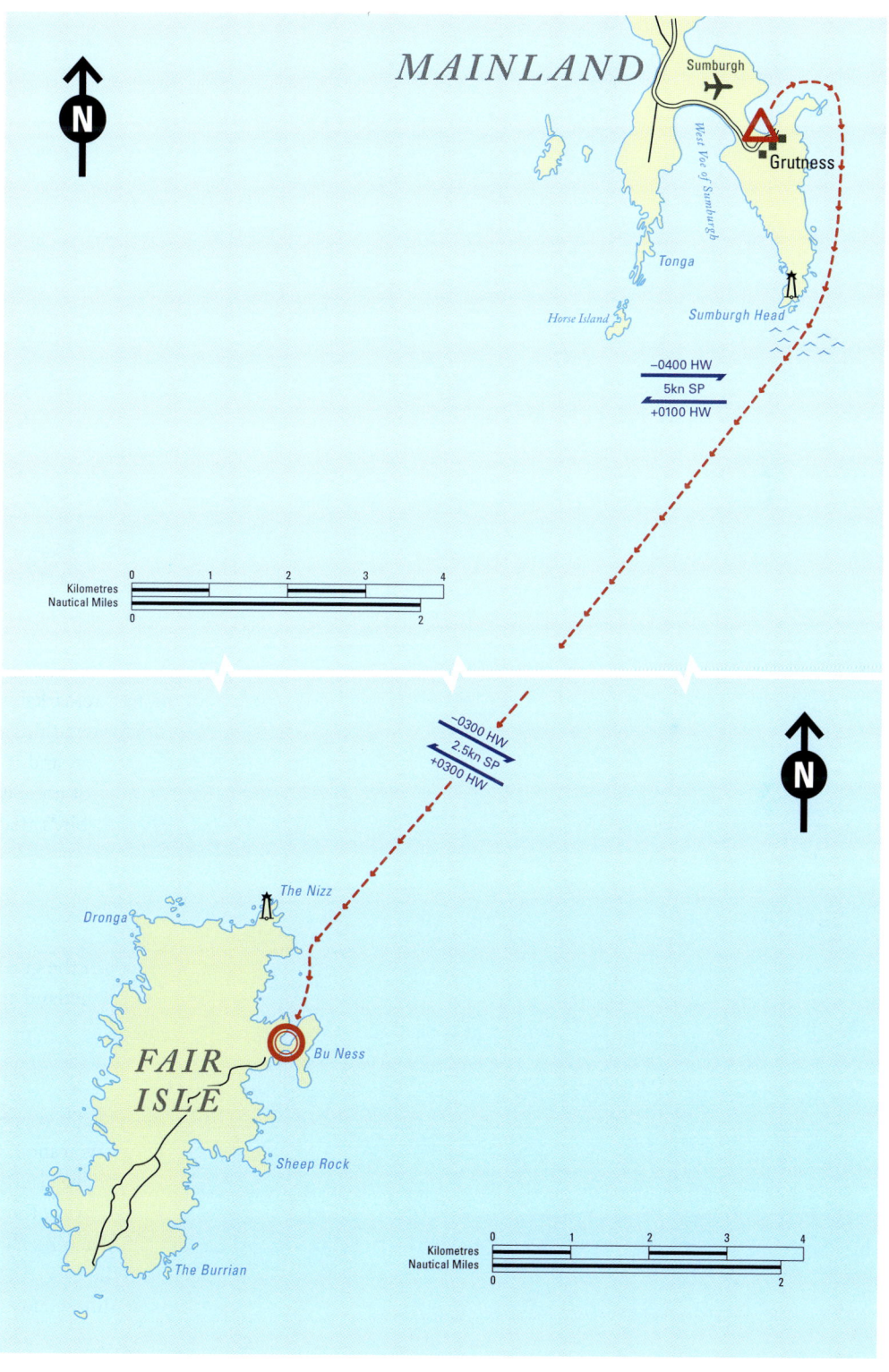

Fair Isle

Sheep Rock, Fair Isle | Mark Rainsley.

the entrance to North Haven. A northerly wind is helpful for the crossing, but this may cause difficult conditions at the entrance to North Haven, and it may then be easier to come around Bu Ness to the east and land on the other side of the headland in South Haven.

DAY 2 – CIRCUMNAVIGATION (18KM, 6 HOURS)

Set off again from the beach at North Haven and take a right turn around the hammerhead of Bu Ness. From here cross the bight of the South Haven to the headland of Goorn, where there are caves and a natural arch to investigate. From the headland it is a short distance to the distinctive shape of Sheep Rock. This is a large stack connected to the main island by a boulder causeway. It is over 130m high, vertical on the south west, grass-covered and sloping at around 45° to the east. Sheep are normally to be found grazing on this intimidating slope. There is a story that when islanders returned after the First World War they were allocated crofts, but one man was delayed and arrived later to find that all the land had been allocated except Sheep Rock, so that became his croft. Not much of a welcome home! For kayakers the main interest in Sheep Rock is that it has three parallel tunnels through it from north-east to south-west. These are narrow, slanted, and not very high, but they are straight and fairly unobstructed. In all but the calmest of conditions it is well worth sitting off and watching for a few minutes before attempting to go through, as there is little room for error in a swell.

Continuing on, the first inlet after Sheep Rock is Clavers Geo. This is a narrow slot between

90m cliffs with a natural arch at its head leading into the bay to the south-west. This arch features prominently in a near-legendary rescue tale. On 23rd May 1868 a German emigrant ship, the *Lessing*, with 465 people on board, was wrecked in Clavers Geo in thick fog. It proved impossible to effect a rescue via the near-vertical cliffs, so the islanders came with boats across the bay and managed to get everybody to safety through this small arch.

At the south-east corner of the island the large detached stack called the Burrian has an impressive double arch. Continuing round the south coast the South Harbour, despite its name, is a rather uninviting place for boats, littered as it is with rocks, and subject to strong tides across the entrance. The south-west corner of the island is an area of sloping slabs, much affected by westerly swell, and dominated by the impressive South Light, the last Scottish lighthouse to be automated.

The west side of Fair Isle is only about 4km on the map but this is an astonishing stretch of coast. The cliffs, which seldom fall below 100m, are deeply indented and full of caves, passages and arches, while the sea offshore is a maze of rocks, stacks, and skerries. In summer the skies are full of seabirds, especially gannets from the colony at Hoini. Landings on this coast can be discounted in all but the calmest of conditions. If you are lucky enough to be here without

North Haven, Fair Isle | Mark Rainsley

westerly swell take the time to explore as much as possible. Rounding the north coast there is little change except that the tide is again an important consideration. Look for some very large caves below the North Light, before heading back into North Haven.

Tide and weather

The Fair Isle Channel has a bad reputation and must be treated with respect. The main areas of concern are the tide races to the north and south of Fair Isle itself, and the Sumburgh Roost, but the whole area is subject to swell, and sea conditions can be difficult even in good weather.

Additional information

The Fair Isle Bird Observatory opened in spring 2025, after the previous observatory was lost to a fire in 2019.

The Shetland Islands Council ferry operates from North Haven to Grutness, normally three times a week. If the open crossing does not appeal it is well worth considering taking kayaks in on the ferry and doing the circumnavigation.

There are flights from Kirkwall to Fair Isle via North Ronaldsay on Thursdays and Sundays.

OS Explorer Map 465 and Admiralty Charts 3283 and 2622 cover this area.

St. Ninians Isle chapel | Mark Rainsley

St Ninian's Isle

No. 50 | Grade A | 8km | 3 hours | OS Sheet 4 | Tidal Port Lerwick

Start/Finish	Ireland (374 215)
HW	Local HW is 1 hour 10 minutes before HW Lerwick.
Tides	There are no significant tidal streams here.
Coastguard	Shetland

Introduction

St Ninian's Isle is not a true island, being joined to the mainland by a beautiful, and much photographed, tombolo beach. Depending on weather and swell either side of the tombolo might give respectable surf conditions. The island is small but full of interest, with a remarkable number of caves, stacks, and passages.

Cave on west side of St. Ninians Isle | Rachel Shucksmith

Description

It is possible to launch from the tombolo but this involves a bit of a carry from the car park. A better option is the pebble beach at Ireland Wick, which has a car turning area directly behind it. Follow signs for Ireland then keep turning left until the road runs directly down to the sea.

Setting off from Ireland, head directly across to the cliffs on the north-east side where there are several caves and a fine natural arch. St Ninian's Isle is said to have over thirty caves, some of which are quite small. Most of the bigger caves are on the west side, including one particularly large and easily accessible one near the north-west corner. Close by the west side is the 50m high stack of Hich Holm with a cave on its south-east side. A little further on Sweyn Holm on the south-west corner forms a narrow channel with the main part of the isle. On the south side there are a number of stacks with several caves and hidden beaches. This provides an ideal spot for pottering on a sunny day. The area is relatively sheltered from westerly swell, but look out for a possible change to the conditions if you head out onto the west side through the channel.

The trip finishes with a portage over the tombolo and a short paddle back to Ireland.

VARIATIONS

A longer trip is possible starting from Spiggie or Scousburgh and taking in the island of Colsay. The coastline between Scousburgh and St Ninian's Isle is not dramatic but pleasant and worth exploring. The broad sandy north-facing beach in Bay of Scousburgh is usually, but inaccurately, called Spiggie Beach. Access is by an unmarked turning off the road along the north shore of

Spiggie Loch, near the anglers' huts. In summer there will usually be caravans in the dunes behind the beach. The true Spiggie Beach is a little further west, where the outlet stream from Spiggie Loch runs to the sea. It is a much smaller beach with easier access but fewer parking spaces. Colsay is an attractive little island with deeply indented cliffs and a fine display of sea pinks and other wild flowers in spring. Porpoises ('neesiks' in Shetland) are often seen in the Muckle Sound between Colsay and the mainland.

The coastline north to Maywick is also worth exploring, with numerous stacks and caves. Parking is possible at Maywick or a circular trip back to Ireland is also possible, and avoids the need for a shuttle.

Tide and weather

There are no significant tidal considerations for St Ninian's Isle, but the west side of the Isle is exposed to westerly swell.

Additional information

OS Explorer Map 466 and Admiralty Chart 3283 cover this area.

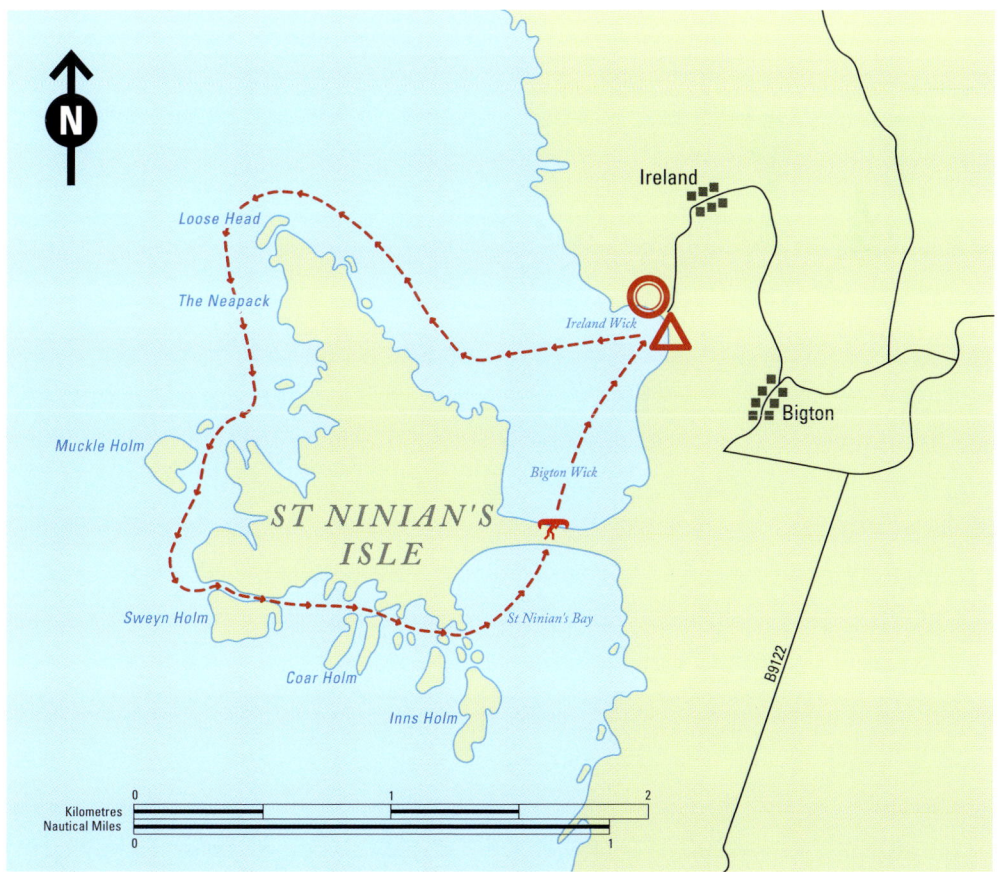

Brooch from St Ninian's Treasure | Shetland Museum Photographic Archive

The St Ninian's Isle Treasure

St Ninian's Isle, as the name suggests, is an important early Christian site. The ruins of a small chapel dating back to Viking times can be seen on the east side of the island, overlooking the tombolo beach a little to the north. This site was excavated by archaeologists in 1958 and a hoard of elaborately ornamented silver jewellery, bowls and other implements was discovered by Douglas Coutts, then a 15-year-old Lerwick schoolboy who was assisting the archaeologists during his school summer holiday. The hoard, known as the St Ninian's Isle Treasure, is in Edinburgh at the time of writing, with replicas in the Shetland Museum. Many people hope to see at least part of it returned to Shetland for the display in the Shetland Museum and Archives.

© The Gloup, Deerness, Orkney | Chris Jex

Appendix A – Planning

In order to avoid a potentially hazardous situation or emergency arising it is important to plan carefully and take into account the following areas of safety before getting onto the water:

1. Past, current and predicted weather
2. Planned Journey (distance, exposure, time, objective)
3. Group number/experience/ability
4. Equipment carried
5. Tidal information
6. Methods of emergency communication
7. Poor weather/escape routes
8. Self sufficiency
9. Overnight shelter/accommodation
10. Sensitive environmental areas (or breeding seasons)

An outline plan of the journey, including all relevant safety information, *should be completed as a matter of course.* This should be left with a friend or relative who will contact the emergency services should you not return on time or as planned.

Appendix B – Coastguard & Emergency Services

Prior to getting on to the water it would be prudent to contact the coastguard giving them relevant safety information about the group, the journey and estimated departure and arrival times. Journeys in and around the Pentland Firth and on the south side of Hoy (Orkney) may find a stronger VHF reception and you may prefer to communicate with Aberdeen Coastguard.

Shetland Coastguard
telephone 01595 692976 or use Channel 16 (VHF)
Aberdeen Coastguard
telephone 01224 529334 or use Channel 16 (VHF)

For emergency services telephone 999 or 112 and ask for the type of assistance required (Police, Ambulance, Fire Bridgade or Coastguard).

Route Planner Download

The A4 sized blank journey planner printout along with an explaination (as found in *Scottish Sea Kayaking* and *Welsh Sea Kayaking*) can be downloaded at pesdapress.com from the resources area. Combining up to date tidal information with the details in this guide on the Route Planner form will help you draw up all the information you need to take to sea.

Appendix C – Weather Information

For Met Office forecasts the whole of Shetland and Orkney is within sea area Fair Isle. The relevant Inshore Forecast area for both is announced as "Cape Wrath to Rattray Head including waters around the Northern Isles". Shetland Coastguard will give a local Inshore Waters forecast for Orkney and Shetland separately. The main sources of forecasts are:

NATIONAL RADIO

At the time of writing the BBC apppears to be discontinuing the LW service.

BBC Radio 4 (92-95 FM)		
0048	(FM)	Shipping and Inshore Waters
0534	(FM)	Shipping and Inshore Waters
1754	(FM)	Shipping Forecast, Sat/Sun only
BBC Radio Scotland (92-95 FM & 810 MW)		
1825	Mon-Fri	Outdoor Conditions, including Inshore Waters Forecast
0700	Sat & Sun	Outdoor Conditions, including Inshore Waters Forecast
1900	Sat & Sun	Outdoor Conditions, including Inshore Waters Forecast

LOCAL RADIO

BBC Radio Orkney broadcasts on the local BBC Scotland VHF frequencies – 93.7MHz in Orkney and 92.7MHz in Shetland. A detailed weather forecast for the Northern Isles follows the local news bulletin at 0730, Monday to Friday. BBC Radio Shetland broadcasts on the same frequencies and a detailed forecast follows their news bulletin at 1730, Monday to Friday.

The local newspapers also publish detailed weather forecasts and tide times. *The Orcadian* publish on Thursdays and *The Shetland Times* on Fridays.

VHF RADIO

Shetland Coastguard broadcasts Met Office weather information every three hours from 0110 UT. The initial call on Channel 16 will tell you which channel to select for the forecast. All broadcasts include Gale Warnings, plus relevant Strong Wind Warnings, Local Navigation Warnings, and the Inshore Forecast for Orkney or Shetland as appropriate. Broadcasts at 0710 and 1910 also include the full Shipping Forecast and the Three Day Northern North Sea Outlook. The actual forecast is updated twice a day at 0500 and 1700 UT.

Shetland Coastguard can be contacted either on VHF radio or by telephone, 01595 692976, for a repeat of the Inshore Forecast at other times.

INTERNET

There are numerous apps and websites to choose from. A particularly useful one is the Windy app.

Appendix D – Glossary

These are words which are still in common use or which give an insight into place names. There are many old words for weather, and names for birds and animals, which are still in regular use. Most of these words are common to both Orkney and Shetland. A few which are specific to one or the other are marked. For much more on dialect either John Graham's *Shetland Dictionary*, or *The Orkney Dictionary* by Margaret Flaws and Gregor Lamb, would be an excellent starting point.

alamootie the storm petrel
ayre a beach
baa a sunken rock
banks sea cliffs
banks-broo cliff edge
bard a steep headland
biggin a building, usually a house
bight A wide bay formed by a bend or curve in the shoreline
bister dwelling or farmstead
bonxie the great skua
böd a fisherman's hut or storehouse (Sh)
blashy heavy sleet and showers
broch Iron Age tower, fortification
bruck rubbish
cairn a pile of stones, usually deliberately built
calloo the long-tailed duck
crang carcase of a bird or animal
croft a small traditional rented farm
croo a sheepfold or enclosure
da the (the definite article) (Sh)
dim dusk, twilight (as in 'simmer dim')
draatsi the otter
drooie-lines a type of seaweed that forms in long lines on the surface
drush fine rain
dunter eider duck
ebb the foreshore, between high and low water
eela inshore fishing
ert direction (Sh)
fea / field a hill, high ground
flan gust of wind
fourareen a four-oared boat
foy a party or special occasion
gaet footpath (Sh)
garth dyke or enclosed area
geo a narrow cove or cleft in cliffs
gloup a deep chasm within the cliff line
grind a gate
grip cleft in the rock (Ork)
gutter mud
haa a large old house, normally a laird's house
haaf deep sea fishing ('da far haaf')
hairst harvest, autumn season
ham harbour

hamar rocky hill
hegri the heron
helly holiday, the weekend (Sh)
holm a small island
houb brackish lagoon at the head of an inlet (Sh)
kame a comb, a hill ridge
kelda water source, well or spring
kishie creel or straw basket
kist wooden chest, coffin
kletts / cletts large boulders on the seashore
knap to speak 'proper' English (the 'k' is pronounced) (Sh)
kokkaloorie daisy
kye cattle
laebrak surf
leerie the Manx shearwater
lodberrie a house with its foundations in the sea (Sh)
longie / lungie the guillemot
loons marshland (Ork)
maa general term for a gull
maalie the fulmar petrel
mareel phosphorescence on the sea
meid a transit bearing, generally used to locate fishing grounds
merry dancers the aurora borealis or northern lights
misanter an accident, mishap
möder dy underlying swell at sea (Sh)
mool / moul a headland
moor / moorie blinding snowstorm, blizzard
moorit brown, esp. sheep or wool
mootie very small
muckle large
neb a bird's beak
neesick porpoise
ness a headland
noost the place where a boat is drawn up on the shore
norn the old Norse language from which the dialect is derived
noup a steep headland
nyuggel a water-horse (in folklore)
olick the ling
oo wool
partan edible crab

peerie / peedie small
piltock the coalfish
plantiecrub / crub a small drystone enclosure for growing cabbage
pleep the call of a bird, especially the oystercatcher
pund animal enclosure
quoy a piece of cultivated land
raingoose the red-throated diver
reestit smoke-dried, usually mutton
rig a plot of land, a field
roog a heap or pile
roost a tide race
sandiloo the ringed plover
scarf the shag
scattald common grazings
scoot bird excrement
scooty-alan the Arctic skua
scord a cleft in the skyline of a hill
scorie the young herring gull
scran odds and ends, or to gather them, e.g. beachcombing
screed a swarm, a large number
sea craa the razorbill
seggies irises
selkie the seal
shaald shallow
shalder the oystercatcher
sharn cow dung
sheep's gaet a narrow path made by sheep (Sh)
shoormal the high water mark
sillock the young coalfish
simmer dim the time in midsummer when it is never fully dark
sixareen / sixern a six-oared boat, traditionally used for haaf fishing
skaadman's head sea urchin
skaill house or hall (Ork)
skerry a rock which is exposed at low tide, but covered at high tide
skyran very bright conditions
sneck latch, small inshore fishing ground
solan the gannet
sook dry conditions associated with a drying wind
sooth-moother an incomer (via the 'sooth mooth' of Lerwick harbour) (Sh)
spoot the razorshell

stanechakker the wheatear
steekit mist dense fog
strem spring tide
string strong current flowing through narrow water channel
sungaets the direction of the sun's movement, clockwise (Sh)
swaabie the great black-backed gull
swart black
swilkie whirlpool
tammy norie the puffin
taing a low-lying point of land
tang seaweed growing above the low water mark
tide-lumps steep breaking seas caused by tidal currents
tirrick the Arctic tern
toft ruined or abandoned house or dwelling
toog a small mound
toon / toonship a small group of crofts
trow a mischievous fairy in folklore
tystie the black guillemot
udal the old Norse system of land tenure
uncan foreign
Up-Helly-Aa winter fire festival (Sh)
vadil a pool at the head of an inlet which fills and dries with the tide (Sh)
voar the spring season
voe a sea inlet, usually long and narrow, a sea loch (Sh)
waar seaweed growing below low water, kelp
wart a lookout point on a hill
whaup the curlew
whitrit the stoat
widdergaets against the sun's direction, anti-clockwise (Sh)
yoag the horse-mussel
yoal a six-oared boat, smaller than a sixern and rowed by three men

Appendix E – Bibliography

Clyde Cruising Club Sailing Directions – Orkney and Shetland (Including North and Northeast Scotland) ISBN 9781786791610

Orkney

Dive Scapa Flow, Rod Macdonald, ISBN 9781851589838

Northern Highlands North (Climbers Guide), Scottish Mountaineering Club, ISBN 9780907521808

The Scottish Islands, Hamish Haswell-Smith, ISBN 9781782116783

This Great Harbour Scapa Flow, W.S. Hewison, ISBN 9781912476862

Shetland

Ancient Shetland, Val Turner ISBN 9780713480009

The Coastal Place Names of Papa Stour, George P.S. Peterson, ISBN 9781910997642

Otters in Shetland: The Tale of the 'Draatsi', Richard Shucksmith and Brydon Thomason ISBN 9781910997000

The Shetland Dictionary, John Graham, available online at https://www.shetlanddialect.org.uk/john-j-grahams-shetland-dictionary.php

Shetland Flowers, Paul Harvey and Jim Nicolson ISBN 9781910997376

The Shetland Guide Book, Charles Tait, ISBN 9781909036017

Walking the Coastline of Shetland, a series of guides by Peter Guy

Appendix F – Index

A
Aa Skerries 158
Aa Skerry 162
Aastack 206
accommodation 148, 156
Aesha Head 171
Aithbank 211
Aith Hope 35
Aith Voe 237, 238
Aith Wick 238
Altar, The 29
Arctic skua 37
Arctic tern 22, 63, 108, 121, 133, 152, 192
Aswick Skerries 226
Auskerry 103, 104, 105, 121
Auskerry Sound 105, 106
Ayre of Birrier 202
Ayre, The 35, 62

B
Back of the Breck 74
Balfour Castle 110
Baltasound 213, 218
Balti Isle, 218
Bannaminn 155
Bannock Hole 244
Bard 235
Barns of Ayre 58
Barrel of Butter 61, 63
Barswick 29
Barth Head 22, 29, 30
Bay of Backaland 129, 134
Bay of Brough 138
Bay of Carness 77
Bay of Deepdale 158, 166
Bay of Fladdabister 238
Bay of Franks 121
Bay of Furrowend 109
Bay of Greentoft 130
Bay of Holland 121
Bay of Houseby 120
Bay of Houton 32, 38, 62, 64, 82
Bay of Ireland 81, 84
Bay of Kirkwall 108
Bay of London 134
Bay of Lopness 136
Bay of Marwick 101
Bay of Moclett 143
Bay of Myre 83
Bay of Newark 136
Bay of Noup 142, 144
Bay of Otterwick 137
Bay of Pierowall 142, 144
Bay of Rackwick 36
Bay of Sandoyne 69
Bay of Sannick 20
Bay of Semolie 69
Bay of Skaill 96
Bay of Stove 136
Bay of Tafts 140
Bay of Westerwick 162
Belmont 220
Benelips 222
Benelip Sound 223
Berry Head 35
Berst Ness 141
Billister 225, 226, 229, 230
Birrier 206
Birsay 100, 102
Bis Geos 142
black backed gull 59, 60, 72, 121
Black Craig 92
black guillemot 210
Black Holm 58, 60
Blade, The 192, 194
Blaster Hole 59
blockships 47, 51, 52, 55
Bloie Geo 41
Blue Mull 206, 214
Bluemull Sound 205, 206, 208, 213, 214, 220
Bluthers Geo 119
Boardie 169, 171, 172, 174
Boats Geo 54
Boddam Voe 247
Bonidale 230
bonxie 37, 168
Booth, The 184
Bos Taurus 23
bothy 36
Bound Skerry 223, 224
Bousta 176
Bow Head 142, 144
Braer, oil tanker 252
Braewick 186
Brae Wick 184
Braewick Bay 185
Braga 92
Breck Ness 92
Breckness House 92
Breigeo Head 170
Breis Holm 172
Brei Wick 238
Bressay 233, 234, 235, 236
Bride's Ness 147
Bridge End Outdoor Centre 151, 152, 156
Bridge of Waithe 86, 90
Brims 31
Brims Ness 35
Brindister 175, 176
Brindister Voe 176
Bring Deeps 32, 38
Bring Head 126
broch 29, 46, 47, 54, 72, 89, 96, 98, 109, 114, 120, 124, 126, 127, 136, 140, 141, 238, 241, 243, 244
Broch of Gurness 97, 98, 123, 124
Brook, The 22
Brough 210
Brough Head 25, 97, 100, 102
Brough Lodge 212
Brough of Bigging 96
Brough of Birsay 98, 100
Brough of Deerness 72, 105
Bruddans 188
Bruray 221, 222
Bulta Skerry 159
Bu Ness 256
Burgh Head 105, 117, 119, 120
Burgi Geos 206
Burki Skerries 180
Burnhouse Settlement 88
Burn of Deepdale 167
Burn of Tingon 189
Burra 151, 152
Burrafirth 214, 216
Burraland 243
Burra Ness 204
Burra Sound 31, 38
Burrastow House 163, 167
Burravoe 197, 200, 201, 202, 204, 208
Burray 30, 45, 48, 49, 54
Burray Ness 25, 45, 46, 50, 51, 57, 65
Burwick 15, 17, 20, 21, 22, 25, 29

C
café 78, 121, 148, 186, 238
Cairn Head 143
Calders Geo 188
Calf of Eday 130, 133, 134, 137
Calf of Flotta 43
Calf Sound 43, 129, 133, 134
camping 24, 30, 36, 46, 50, 84, 126, 134, 138, 143, 144, 156, 157, 176, 186, 202, 211, 214, 216
Candle of the Sale 38
Cantick Head 31, 34, 38, 43
Cantick Sound 31, 34
Car Ness 111
Carness Bay 112
Carrick House 133
castle 160, 220
Castle O'Burrian 144
Castle of Yesnaby 95
Cata Sands 136
Cat Firth 226
Cava 31, 33, 61, 62, 64
cetaceans 224
Challister Ness 222, 230
Chalmers Hope 38
chambered cairn 23, 77, 86, 118, 120, 124, 136, 143, 176
chapel 100, 103, 109
Christie's Hole 170
church 46, 206
Churchill Barrier 25, 28, 45, 47, 49, 51, 52, 53, 55, 56, 69
Clavers Geo 256
clearances 125
Cleiver, The 192
Clestrain Sound 31, 79, 82, 84
Clett 162
Clettack Skerry 19
Clett of Crura 28
Cletts, The 41
click mills 180, 182
Clingri Geo 170
Cloki Stack 250
Clumpers 166
Coall Head 237, 238
Colgrave Sound 204, 209, 210, 212
Collaster 214
Colsay 250, 261
Colvadale 218
common tern 105
Copinsay 57, 58, 59, 60
Copinsay Pass 57, 58, 60
cormorant 28, 37, 52, 60, 108, 121, 133, 146
corncrake 36, 57
Corn Holm 60
Costa Head 97, 102
Covenanters Cave 126
Covenanters Memorial 72

Cow Head 176
Cradle Holm 234, 236
Cribba Sound 175, 176
croft 155, 159, 194, 218, 230, 238
Cuilags 38
Cullingsburgh 235
Cullivoe 205
Culswick 163
Cunningsburgh 237, 242

D
Dale of Walls 165, 166
Dalsetter 247
Dam of Hoxa 30
Deepdale 69, 158, 162, 163
Deerness 58, 71, 72, 104, 105
Deer Sound 71, 72, 78, 103
Dennis Head 145, 147, 148
Dennis Loch 147
Denwick Bay 72
Dingieshowe 65, 69, 70
Dingieshowe Bay 74
Dingieshowe Beach 71
Dog Geo 110
dolphin 173, 224
Dore Holm 187
Dovecot 114, 116
Dragon Ness 230
Drongs 183, 184, 185
Drooping Point 247
Duncansby Head 15, 16, 19
Dury Voe 226, 230, 231

E
Earl's Palace 100
East Burra 151, 152
Easter Skeld 157
East Ham 242
Echnaloch 48
Eday 121, 130, 133, 134, 138
Egilsay 123, 126, 128, 185
eider duck 52
Els Ness 136
Elwick Bay 111
Erne's Hill 236
Erne Stack 180
Eshaness 187
Eshaness peninsula 183
Eswick 226
Evie 97
Eynhallow 98, 102, 124, 128
Eynhallow Sound 97, 102, 123, 127

F
Fair Isle 253, 254, 257, 258
Fair Isle Bird Observatory 258
Fair Isle Channel 258
Faither 189
Falls of Warness 129, 130, 134
Fara 31, 33, 38
Faraclett Head 126
Faray 129, 130, 132, 134
feral cattle 23
ferry 20, 64, 106, 112, 118, 128, 134, 144, 148, 212, 231, 234, 247, 254, 258
Fers Ness 132
festivals in Orkney 88
Fethaland 197, 198, 200
Fethaland peninsula 198

Fetlar 204, 210, 212
Filla 222
fish farming 178
Fitful Head 162, 249, 250, 252
Fitty Hill 141
Fladda 198
Fladdabister 238
Flaeshans of Sandwick 230
Flotta 39, 40, 42, 44
Flotta oil terminal 42
Fogla Skerry 171
Footabrough 167
Foot, The 110
Forewick Holm 173
Forse 69
fort 109, 206
Foula 165, 166, 167
Fowl Crag 143
Framgord 218
Fugla Stack 155
fulmar 28, 37, 72, 114, 100
Funzie 211

G
Gaada Stacks 164
Gairsay 109, 113, 114, 115
Gallo Hill 141
Galti Stacks 170
Galt peninsula 109
gannet 59, 100, 217, 234
gannet colony 216, 257
Gardiesfauld 214, 220
Garmus Taing 198
Garthna Geo 95
Garths Ness 250, 252
Gentleman's Cave 142
Geo of Ockran 189
Geo of Vigon 206
Giant's Leg 235
Gills Bay 20
Giltarump 162
Gletness 226
Glimps Holm 51, 52, 56
Glimpsholm Skerry 54
Gloup Holm 206
Gloup of the Scores 235
Gloup, The 105
Gloup Voe 206
Golta 44
Goorn 256
Gorsendi Geo 189
Graemeshall 69
Graemsay 81
Grava Skerries 170
great auk 143
great skua 37, 168
Green Head 33
Green Holm 160
Green Isle 230
Green Skerry 146
Grey Head 133
greylag geese 108, 121
Grice Ness 118
Grim Ness 26, 28
Grimsetter 206
Grind of the Navir 188
Grobust 142
Grukalty Pier, 108
Gruna 176
Gruna Stacks 194
Grunay 221, 222, 223
Gruney 197, 198
Gruting 210

Grutness 245, 249, 250, 253, 254
Grutness Voe 247, 250
guillemot 28, 37, 60, 69, 100, 217
guillemots 241
Gulberwick 238
Gungstie 234, 247
Gunnister 183, 185
Gunnister Voe 185
guns 30, 32, 41, 46, 54, 69, 78, 109, 176
Gutcher 205, 206
Gutter Sound 31, 33

H
haaf fishing station 190, 198
Haaf Gruney 220
Haafs Hellia 98
Haa Ness 230
Hackness 33
Hacks Ness 136
Haco's Ness 110
Hagdale Ness 216
Halcro Head 26, 28, 29
Hall of Clestrain 81
Hall of Rendall 113
Hall of Tankerness 78
Ham 165, 166
Hamars Ness 211
Hamera Head 230
Ham Geo 29
Hamnavoe 156, 189
Hamna Voe 170, 174, 204
Hanseatic Booth 232
harbour porpoise 40, 41
Haroldswick 214, 216, 217, 218
Harrabrough Head 29
Hascosay 201, 209, 210, 212
Haven, The 22, 23
Hawick 35
Head of Work 77
Heads of Grocken 184
Heill Head 176, 177
Helliar Holm 77, 110, 111
Helliasour 126
Hellia Spur 126
Helli Ness 237, 238
Hell's Mouth 18
Hemp Stack 68
Hendry's Holes 37
Hen of Gairsay 113
Heoga Ness 202, 204
Heritage Walk' 124
Hermaness 213, 214, 216, 217
Herra, The 208
herring fishing 49, 80, 122
Heugg, The 155
Heylor 187, 191
Hich Holm 260
Highland Park distillery 66, 67, 83
Hildasay 158, 159
Hillswick 183, 185
Hillswick Ness 183, 184
HMS *Royal Oak* 68
Hobbister Nature Reserve 83
Hoe Skerries 146
Hoga 243, 244
Hogg of Papa 159
Hogg Sound 159
Hog Island 226
Hoini 257
Hole of Hellier 180
Hole of Roo 78

Hole of Row 41
Holes of Scraada 188
Holm 65
Holm of Boray 115
Holm of Copister 202
Holm of Elsness 136
Holm of Faray 132
Holm of Houss 152
Holm of Houton 38, 62, 82
Holm of Huip 121
Holm of Melby 173
Holm of Noss 234
Holm of Papa 143
Holm of Rendall 115
Holm of Scockness 126
Holm of Westsandwick 208
Holms of Burravoe 200
Holms of Uyeasound 176
Holm Sound 46, 50
Hol o' Boardie 169, 172
Hols Hellier 217
Hoo Stack 226
Horn o' Papa 171
Horse Island 250, 252
Horse of Burravoe 201, 202
Horse of Copinsay 59
Horse Sound 57, 59
hostel 121, 134, 138, 143, 144, 148, 214
Houbie 211
Housa Voe 172
Housa Wick 212
Housay 221, 222, 223
Houss Ness 156
Houton 31, 38, 61, 64, 84
Houton Bay 82
Houton Head 79, 81
Howan Lickan 72
Howequoy Head 69
Hoxa Head 30, 39, 41, 44
Hoxa Sound 40
Hoy 31, 32, 33
Hoy Sound 91, 92, 96
Huip Sound 121
Hunda 45, 48, 50
Hunder Holm 230
Huney 218

I
Icelanders 176
Iceland Skerry 76, 108
Inga Ness 95, 142, 144
Innan Neb 42
Inner Booth 200
Inner Holm 81, 230
Inner Holm of Skaw 217
Inner Score 235
Ireland 259, 260
Ireland Wick 260
Isbister 230
Isle of Westerhouse 184
Isles of Gletness 225, 226
Italian Chapel 56, 69

J
Jarlshof historic site 250
John Gow the pirate 133
John o' Groats 15, 18, 20
John Rae 81

K
Kame of Hoy 38
Kame of Isbister 200
Keen of Hamar 220

Ketligill 192
Ketligill Head 194, 195
Kettla Ness 155
Kettletoft 135, 136
killer whale 104
Kilns of Brin Novan 126
Kirk Ness 230
Kirk Rocks 92
Kirk Sound 53
Kirk Taing 140
Kirkwall 75, 76, 78, 79, 84, 107, 108
Kirkwall Bay 78, 104
Kirkwall Cathedral 83
Kitchener Memorial 101
kittiwake 37, 60, 154, 100
Knap of Howar 143
Knees, The 133

L
Lady's Holm 250, 252
Lairo Water 109
Lamb 51
Lamba Ness 172, 213, 220
Lamb Head 105, 117, 120
Lambhoga 210, 211, 212
Lamb Holm 52, 55, 56
Lang Ayre 191, 192, 195
Lang Clodie Wick 194
Lang Sound 156
Lash, The 83
Lashy Sound 129, 134, 135, 138
Lawrence's Piece 142
Laxo 229, 231
Leagarth 212
Leapers Geo 143
Leea Geo 238
Leebitton 238
Leif Erikson 206
Lera Voe 163, 167
Lerwick 233, 234, 236, 237, 238
Levenwick 245, 247
Levenwick Ness 247
Liddel Eddy 25
lighthouse 17, 18, 19, 30, 58, 62, 103, 104, 105, 110, 111, 136, 142, 146, 171, 43, 180, 184, 187, 213, 242
Linga 176, 230
Linga Holm 121
Linga Sound 121, 229, 231
Ling Holm 89
Linklet Bay 147
Linkshouse 202
Links of Burrafirth 216
Linton 109
Little Ayre 180
Little Havra 155
Little Holm 250
Little Linga 121
Little Ossa 189
Little Rackwick 36
Little Skerry 19
Lobust 126
Loch of Cliff 216
Loch of Harray 85, 89, 90
Loch of Stenness 85, 86, 90
Loder Head 234, 235
London Airport 134
Longa Geo 214, 238
Long Holm 89
Looss Laward 250
Lop Ness 143

Index

269

Loth 135, 136
Lothan Ness 180, 181
Lother Rock 25
Lowther Rocks 18, 29
Lunda Wick 214, 220
Lunning Head 222
Lunning Sound 221, 222, 229, 230, 231
Lurn, The 146
Lyness Bay 33
Lyness Naval Base 34
Lyra Skerry 171
Lyrawa Bay 33

M
Mae Sands 141
Maiden Stack 172, 173
Mail 238
Mail Beach 242
Mangaster Voe 185
Manse Bay 28
Manx shearwater 136
marina 79, 80, 160, 179, 204, 221, 222
martello tower 33, 43
Marwick 97
Marwick Bay 97
Marwick Head 100
Mavis Grind 185
Melby 166, 169
Melby House 173
Melby in Sandness 166, 170
Melsetter 35
memorial 206
Mermaid's Chair 118
Merry Holm 160
Mid Yell 201, 202, 204, 209, 210, 212
Mid Yell Voe 202
Migga Ness 206
Mill Bay 33, 106, 118, 134
Mill Loch 134
Mill Sand 75, 78
Mio Ness 223
Mires of Funzie 211
Mirkady Point 72
Mo Geo 170
monastery 73, 118, 200
Moness 38
Moo Stack 188
Moo Wick 211
Moul of Eswick 226, 228
Mousa 241, 242, 244
Mousa Broch 243
Mousa Ferry 242
Mousa Sound 241, 242, 244
Muckle Ayre 180
Muckle Bight 164
Muckle Castle 74
Muckle Flugga 213, 216, 217, 220
Muckle Green Holm 130
Muckle Head 38
Muckle Holm 208
Muckle Ossa 189
Muckle Roe 176, 179, 180, 181
Muckle Roe marina 179, 185
Muckle Skerry 16, 17, 18, 19, 20
Muckle Sound 250, 261
Muckle Ward 176
Mull Head 71, 72, 74, 103, 104, 106, 143
Muness 218
museum 160, 184, 186, 187, 202

N
National Nature Reserve 220, 233
National Scenic Area 179, 183, 198
Neap 216
Neban Point 95
Needle, The 35
Ness Boating Club 247
Ness of Brough 212
Ness of Cullivoe 205, 206, 208
Ness of Gairsay 115
Ness of Houlland 206
Ness of Ork 107, 109
Ness of Ramnageo 96
Ness of Snabrough 211
Ness of Sound 208
Ness, The 85, 86
Nesting 225, 230
Nevi Skerry 44
Nev, The 142, 250
Newark Bay 58, 60, 74
Nibon Isle 183, 185
Noltland Castle 144
Noness 244
North Bay 35, 58
Northern Ness 250
North Gaulton Castle 95
North Ham 180, 181
North Haven 256, 258
North Head 22, 115
North Hill 142
North Isles 106
North Light 258
North Lungi Geo 170
Northmavine 183
North Mouth 222, 236
North Nesting 225, 226, 229
North Nevi 60
Northquoy Point 74
Northra Voe 176
North Roe 198, 200, 208
North Ronaldsay 145, 148
North Ronaldsay Firth 135
North Sand 126
North Voe 159
North Yell 205
Norwick 218
Noss 233, 234, 236
Noss Head 236
Noss Sound 233, 234, 235, 236
Notster 69
Noup 234
Noup Head 142, 144
Noup Hill 133
Noust of Ayre 138
nousts 99
Nousty Sand 126

O
Oceanic 166
Ockraquoy 238
Oddsta 211
Odin Bay 119
Odin Ness 114
Odin's Stone 109
Odness 105, 117
Old Haa 202
Old Head 25
Old Man of Hoy, The 32, 37
orcas 224
Orfasay 204

Orkneyman's Cave 235
Orphir Bay 83
Ortie 137
otter 29, 48, 86, 89, 133, 212
Otterswick 202
Ouse, The 109
Outer Brough 211
Outer Holm 81, 230
Outer Scores 235
Out Skerries 221, 222, 224
Out Skerries Pier 221
Out Stack 214
Oxna 159, 160
Oyce 99

P
Pan Hope 44
Papa 159, 160
Papa Sound 106, 121, 143, 144, 173, 174
Papa Stour 169, 170
Papa Stronsay 118, 121
Papa Westray 139, 140, 143, 144
Papil Ness 206
Peerie Bard 242
Pegal Bay 33
Pentland Firth 16, 18, 21, 22, 23, 24, 29, 35, 38
Pentland Skerries 15, 16, 19, 20
Peter Skerry 81
Peter's Pool 72
Pierowall 139, 144
Point of Ayre 58, 74
Point of Burrian 147
Point of Huro 140, 144
Point of Lyregeo 95
Point of Sinsoss 146
Point of Tangpool 247
Point of Tuberry 63
Point of Ward 63
Pool of Cletts 28
Pool of Virkie 247
porpoise 29, 34, 40, 41, 104, 152, 158, 173, 224, 261
Pow, The 120
Primula scotica 143
puffin 22, 29, 37, 60, 100, 217, 250
Pund of Grevasand 184

Q
Quarff 238
Quendale Bay 250, 252
Quida Ness 192
Quoy Banks 138
Quoys Ness 136

R
Rackwick 38
Railsbrough 226
Rami Geo 18
Ramna Stacks 194, 197, 198, 200
Rapness 139, 140, 144
Rapness Sound 129, 140
razorbill 28, 37, 60, 100
Reawick 161, 162
Reawick peninsula 157, 158
Redayre 161
Red Head 133, 134, 137, 185
Red Holm 133
red-necked phalarope 211
red-throated diver 159
Reef Dyke 147
Reitta Ness 164

Rerwick Head 78
Rerwick Point 112
restaurant 111, 160
Ring of Brodgar 86, 87
Riv, The 137
Rivvalee 206
Roan Head 44
Roe Ness 158, 162, 163
Roe Sound 179, 181, 185
Ronas Voe 189, 191, 192, 194, 195
Roodrans 192
Roo Point 83
Rora Head 36
Rose Ness 65, 69, 70
Rothiesholm Head 117, 121
Round Point 55
Rousay 109, 124, 126, 128
Rousay Sound 126, 127
Row Head 96
Royal Oak 68, 84
RSPB reserve 57, 60, 100
Rullard Rost 126
Rumble, The 201, 202, 204
Rump 162
Rusk Holm 133
Russness Bay 115
Rysa Little 31, 33

S
Sacquoy Head 126
Saito 216
Samphrey 202, 204
Sandas 158
Sanda Stour 158
Sanday 121, 130, 134, 136, 137, 138
Sanday Sound 135
Sandi Sand 74
Sandness 166, 170
Sand of Rothiesholm 120
Sandsayre 241, 242, 243, 244
Sandside Bay 73, 74, 104, 105, 106
Sands of Breckon 206
Sands of Evie 97, 98, 124
Sands of Meal 156
Sands of Wright 30, 39, 41, 44
Sandvoe 191, 194, 197, 198
Sandwick 29, 184, 218, 230, 238, 241, 242, 243, 244
Sandy Voe 159
Saviskaill Bay 126, 128
Saviskaill Head 126
Saxa Vord 217, 218
Scaalie Point 152
Scabra Head 125
Scad Head 32
Scalloway 151, 157, 160
Scalloway Boating Club 157
Scalloway Islands 157, 158, 159
Scapa Bay 65, 66, 67, 79, 83, 84
Scapa Distillery 67, 83
Scapa Flow 32, 38, 40, 41, 44, 47, 50, 51, 53, 61, 62, 64, 69, 79, 81, 92
Scapa Flow Museum 33, 34
Scarf Skerry 30, 60, 184
Scarvi Taing 170
Scatness 250
Score Head 235
Scousburgh 250, 260
Scraada 188
Sea Geo 38, 46

270

seal 22, 29, 35, 38, 43, 48, 60, 61, 69, 86, 111, 115, 121, 137, 146, 158, 162, 192, 230, 237, 240, 241, 247
seal sanctuary 184
Seal Skerry 115, 130, 146
Selki Skerry 22
settlement 73, 100, 102, 109, 142, 143, 147
settlement (ruins) 206, 212
Shaabers Head 176
Shaalds 167
Shaalds o' Foula 166
shag 52, 152
Shapinsay 76, 107, 108, 111, 112
Shapinsay Sound 75, 77
Shapinsay village 111
Sheep Rock 256
Shetland Mainland 202
Sholma Wick 172
shop 121, 143, 148, 156, 211
Siggar Ness 250
Silwick 162, 163
Skaill 91
Skaill Bay 95
Skara Brae 95
Skaw 213, 220, 221, 222, 223, 231
Skaw, headland of 217
Skaw Roost 217
Skaw Taing 229, 230, 231
Skeld 157
Skelda Ness 162, 164
Skelda Voe 158, 162
Skeld Boating Club 157
Skerries lighthouse 224
Skerries of Clestrain 81
Skerry of Eshaness 188
Skipi Geo 99
Skippidock 236
skua 116, 217, 241
Small Boat Harbour 236
Smerry Geo 142
Smoogro Skerry 83
Snap 211, 212
Snarraness 176
Sneuk Head 36
Snolda 171
Sound of Faray 129
Sound of Hoxa 39, 41, 44
Sound of Orfasay 202, 204
Sound of Papa 169
South Bay 145, 146, 147
South Bay of Eswick 226
South Cara 28
South Geo 104
South Gill 189
South Ham 180, 181
South Haven 256
South Havra 151, 152, 154, 155, 156
South Holms 216
South Isle 226
South Links 46, 50
South Nesting 225, 226
South Nesting Bay 225, 226
South Nevi 60
South Ronaldsay 21, 22, 25, 26, 28
South Skerry 110
South Sound 204
South Voe 151
South Voxter 238

South Walls 34
South Yell 201
Spanish Armada 142
Spiggie 249, 250, 260, 261
Spiggie Loch 261
Spindle 180
Spur Ness 136
Spurness Sound 135
Stack of Birrier 211
Stack of Kame 28
Stacks of Duncansby 20
Stacks of Houssness 152
Standard Rock 97, 98, 102
Standing Stones of Stenness 86
Stanger Head 40, 41, 44, 144
Start Point 135, 136
Stava Ness 225, 228, 231
St Catherine's Bay 121
Steggies 159
Stenness 187, 188, 190
Stenness, Isle of 188
St John's Head 32, 37
St Kilda 167
St Magnus Bay 173, 175, 176, 177, 185
St Magnus Cathedral , 127
St Magnus Kirk , 127
St Margaret's Hope 20, 30
St Mary's 69
St Mary's Bay 69
St Ninian's Isle 259, 260, 261, 262
Stones of Stenness 89
storm petrel 23, 105, 241, 243
Stoura Clett 235
St Peter's Church 28
Strandburgh Ness 211
Stremness 166
Strem Ness 165
String, The 75, 76, 77, 78, 107, 108, 111, 112
Stromness 31, 61, 79, 80, 84, 91, 96
Strom Ness 164, 180
Stromness Marina 79
Stronsay 106, 117, 120, 121, 123, 129, 130, 135
Sullom Voe 200, 202, 204
Sumburgh Head 249, 250, 252, 253
Sumburgh Roost 250, 252, 254, 258
surf 156, 252, 259
Suthra Voe 176
Swannies Point 48
Swarbacks Head 176
Swarbacks Minn 176
Swarbacks Skerry 176, 177
Swarta Skerry 170
swell 196
Sweyn Holm 115, 260
Swin-Ber 72
Switha Sound 33, 34, 40, 41, 44
Swona 21, 22, 24, 26
Symbister 152, 229, 231

T

Tails of the Tarf, The 22
Taing of Tratland 127
Taing, The 114
Tammy Tiffy 74
Tangwick 183, 184, 187
Tankerness 75

Tarri Clett 52
tern 217, 241
Thieves Holm 76, 77, 78, 108, 111
Thorfinn Skullsplitter 30
Tingwall 128
Titanic 166
Tobacco Rock 137
Toft 201, 202
Tofts Ness 137
Tofts Voe 204
toilets 28, 41, 43, 46, 62, 69, 72, 76, 80, 83, 98, 108, 124, 127, 136, 140, 157, 162, 170, 184, 204, 214, 242
Tomb of the Eagles, The 28
tombolo beach 259
Tor Ness 31, 35, 38, 120
Toy Ness 83
Tres Ness 136
Tressa Ness 211
Trondra 151
Troswick 247
Turls Head 192
Twinyess 145

U

Ulsta 204, 208
Unst 205, 206, 213, 214, 218, 220
Unstan Chambered Cairn 86
Unst Boat Haven 218, 220
Ura Firth 185
Urie Ness 211
Uyea 191, 194, 195, 220
Uyeasound 213, 214, 220

V

Vaila 161, 163, 164
Vaila House 163
Vasa Loch 108
Vasa Skerry 107, 109
Vasa Sound 107
Vassa Voe 225, 226
Vat of Kirbuster 119
Veantrow Bay 109
Vementry 175, 176, 177
Vementry House 176
Ve Ness 83
Ve Skerries 171
Vidlin 222, 223, 230, 231
Vidlin marina 221
Viking burial boats 138
Voe of Clousta 176
Voe of Cullingsburgh 233
Voe of Dale 167

W

Walls 161, 163, 166
Walls Boating Club 161, 163
Ward Hill 38, 130
Ward Holm 60
Warebeth 92
Warie Gill 189
War Ness 130
Wart Holm 140
Wart, The 136
Watch Stone 86
Water Sound 30, 48
Watsness 167
Waulkmill Bay 83
Weather Ness 144
Weatherness Sound 144
Weddell Point 54
Weddell Sound 42, 43, 44, 47, 54

Weems Castle 29
Wells of Swona 22
West Burra 151, 155, 156
West Burrafirth 170
Wester Sound 167
Westerwick 161, 162, 163
West Ham 154, 242, 243
Westing 220
West Isle 155
West Linga 230
West Loch 158
Westness 124
West Pool 242
Westray 130, 139, 140, 142, 144
Westray Firth 123, 139
Westsandwick 205, 206, 208
West Voe 155, 222, 250
whale 104, 224, 252
Whale Firth 208
Whale Wick 155, 156
Whal Hor 192
Whallerie 206
Whalsay 221, 222, 223, 225, 226, 229, 230
Wha Taing 48
whimbrel 211
Whitaloo Point 99
Whitehall village 117, 118, 121, 122
Whitemill Point 137
White Wife 202
whooper swan 108
Wick of Aith 211
Wick of Gossabrough 202
Wick of Gruting 210
Wick of Shunni 250
Wick of Skaw 217
Wick of Tresta 211
Wick of Vatsetter 202
Widewall Bay 25, 30, 39, 41
Wife Geo 46
Willie's Taing 172
Windwick 28
Wing, The 22, 25
Wood Wick 214, 216
Wyre 128
Wyre Sound 128

Y

Yell 201, 202, 205, 209
Yell Sound 197, 198, 200, 201, 202, 204, 205, 206, 208
Yesnaby 95
Yettna Geo 96

Index

ULTRALIGHT

Boat Weight As Low as 14kg
Adventure Has Never Felt So Light

How will you customise yours?

www.phseakayaks.com   Designed and built in Britain, paddled Worldwide